PRAISE FOR DEVOTIONS ON F.I.R.E.

I read everything that Dr. Ken Burge writes! His F.I.R.E. series is simply amazing. He writes with the courage of a Daniel and with the compassion of a Barnabas. As a pastor, I find his material an excellent resource for sermon preparation and as a believer I am challenged and encouraged in my walk with King Jesus. I am thrilled that he has penned this daily devotional! Your heart will be thrilled too, as you make this a part of your daily journey with our Savior!

— Dr. Tony L. Wilson
White Oak Baptist Church
Chattanooga, Tennessee

The best time of day is when we get to spend time alone with God, reading His Word and meditating on what we've read. Sometimes it helps to have a little guidance on how to interpret the text and how to make use of it personally. In this book, *Devotions on F.I.R.E.*, Dr. Burge uses his F.I.R.E. methodology to guide us through daily devotions one question at a time. Asking a single, pointed question each day and using Scripture to answer that question helps us to become more familiar with the Word of God and apply it to our everyday lives. He even provides a one-year Bible reading plan "at no extra charge!" Whether you're well-disciplined in your daily devotions or just beginning, *Devotions on F.I.R.E.* will open your understanding and application of Scripture in a most profound way thereby allowing you to grow in your intimate relationship with the Father and with the Son.

— Maria J. Keyser
Principal Solutions Consultant, SAS Institute Inc.
Student at the Colmar Manor Bible Church Institute (CMBI)

Daily devotionals are normally light on content and do not provide sufficient biblical depth to support significant spiritual development. This is not the case with *Devotions on F.I.R.E.* Dr. Burge utilizes the F.I.R.E. methodology that provides a substantive devotional work that practically guides you through the chapters to be read daily. If you follow along each day you'll read through the Bible in one year. Within each chapter you will investigate and discover the key employment point. The key application point is given to provide you with the central thought for the day. This will allow you to personalize the text as you contemplate the daily application. I highly recommend *Devotions on F.I.R.E.* to everyone who desires to read through the Bible in one year and employ the practical daily application of the text.

— Joshua K. Burge
Senior Advisor—Treasury
Deacon, Youth Leader, and Pianist at the Colmar Manor Bible
Church

DEVOTIONS ON

Dr. Ken J. Burge, Sr.

Devotions on F.I.R.E.

Copyright @ 2018 by Ken J. Burge, Sr.
Published by Deep River Books
Sisters, Oregon
www.deepriverbooks.com

ISBN – 13: 9781632694898
Library of Congress: 2018946987

Printed in the USA

Cover design by Joe Bailen, Contajus Design

Dedication

I first met Kimberly Ann Hall in 1981. She lived just down the street from me, but I had never met her personally, although I was well aware of her presence. During our first encounter I quickly invited her to attend a Bible study at our church. Kimberly seemed quite shocked when I started teaching that night. After Bible study, I took her to a diner where my buddies and I often bought steak and eggs and drank coffee. That memorable night I popped the question to her: "Do you drink coffee?" My lovely date sheepishly said no. Yet I'm told by a reliable source that after I dropped her off at her house she asked her mom to fix her a strong cup of coffee.

Hence would be the start of a beautiful relationship! Kimberly Ann Hall became Kimberly Ann Burge on May 28, 1983. This virtuous woman has loyally been my best friend and confidant for more than three decades. It is because of her godly influence and encouragement that *Devotions on F.I.R.E.* is a reality. Thank you, sweetheart, for learning to love coffee and to share the Christian life with me! It is my honor to dedicate *Devotions on F.I.R.E.* to my lovely wife.

FOREWORD

BY CYNTHIA SIMMONS

I met Ken Burge and his wife Kimberly at the International Christian Retail Show when I interviewed him for Heart of the Matter Radio. What a gracious couple. He had just released his two-volume set *Revelation on F.I.R.E.* I felt immediate camaraderie with him and Kimberly, as we chatted about our families and our faith. Pastor Burge believes each Christian should study the Bible himself, and I heartily agree. However, Pastor Burge went a step further and developed a study tool he called F.I.R.E., which guides the student toward meticulous examination of the Scripture. The **F** stands for familiarity, which means asking questions leading to a complete understand the text. **I** represents interpreting or discerning the meaning God intended. **R** indicates relationship to other passages as well as the immediate context of the verses considered. **E** means employment—the student puts the Word into action.

The past few months, I have been reading *Devotions on F.I.R.E.*, Pastor Burge's daily devotional book, which makes use of his F. I.R.E. technique. I love this work. First, he chose a very balanced method of reading through the Bible. Second, his thoughtful commentary for the day pulled together Old and New Testament passages to demonstrate how God designed the Word as a whole, rather than sixty-six separate parts. Finally, he ends each daily lesson with a stirring challenge. I believe this book will encourage and bless those who read it.

— Cynthia L. Simmons
Author of *Pursuing Gold* and *Women Who Overcame*
Heart of the Matter Radio Host

INTRODUCTION TO
DEVOTIONS ON F.I.R.E.

God desires to walk with His children. Even after Adam and Eve disobeyed His explicit command (Genesis 2:17), He still seeks them out. When the Lord asks Adam the following question, it is not because He doesn't know the answer: "Then the LORD God called to Adam," writes Moses, "and said to him, 'Where are you?'" (Genesis 3:9). Perhaps your loving Father is seeking your company by calling out to you: Where are you?

Four decades have now passed since I started walking with the Lord. I've stumbled many times along the journey with Jesus, but have been sustained by His grace and a discipline that has kept me focused during the soul-nourishing relationship. It has been my yearly practice to read through the Bible one, two, even three times. Beginning each day communing with the Lord through His Word has promoted both spiritual health and an awareness of His presence.

Devotions on F.I.R.E. is designed to have you read through the assigned portion of the Old and New Testament daily to complete the Bible in one year. Each day you will also read my devotion based upon the F.I.R.E. method of Bible study.

F.I.R.E. is the acronym used for our study. This mnemonic (memory) device stands for familiarity, interpretation, relationship, and employment.

F represents familiarity. Although I've been privileged to study the Bible at both the undergraduate and graduate levels, the emphasis was always upon observation as the first step of Bible study. The origin of the word "familiarity" derives from the Latin *familiaritas* and means "familiar" or "intimate." Bible study should originate from a

9

deep-seated personal relationship with God. "Familiarity" roars out intimacy and relationship with the living God, while "observation" whimpers a frigid laboratory analysis of data.

Interpretation is the second stage of Bible study, represented here by the symbol **I**. Jesus has sent us a messenger to help us to understand the Scriptures—the eternal third member of the Godhead known as the Holy Spirit. Dependence upon Him is vital to enlighten our minds concerning God's truth. Jesus described the Holy Spirit as "the Spirit of truth" in John 16:13. He personally escorts us through the Bible, as the remainder of the verse says: "He will guide you into all truth."

Relationship becomes the third phase of our quest to understand the sacred text. The symbol **R** will stand for "relationship" throughout our travels. The Bible's value requires it to be treated with the utmost respect, "For the word of God is living and powerful, and sharper than any two-edged sword, piercing even to the division of soul and spirit, and of joints and marrow, and is a discerner of the thoughts and intents of the heart" (Hebrews 4:12). We will see how the life-giving parts ally with the whole.

The fourth and final part of this most excellent adventure is employment, represented by the symbol **E**. Employment, or application, began when those who originally received the living Word were given their authoritative marching orders. We too will transition together, in order to determine not only how those to whom the Bible first came responded, but also how we are called to respond today. God designed His Word to transform us into the image of Christ, and that cannot occur without us first personally employing the Bible to our lives.

Now that I've introduced *Devotions on F.I.R.E.* to you, I thought it would be beneficial to also have my wife Kimberly share some devotional insights. The concluding wisdom to the introduction comes from her:

> Unlike my husband, consistent Bible reading did not come
> as easily for me. I knew that God's Word was "sweeter

than honey," yet many days it seemed like I was digesting shredded wheat! I found it frustrating to read portions of Scripture that I didn't understand or that seemed irrelevant at this point in time. Sometimes after my devotions I couldn't even remember what I had read. I needed help!

Consistent Bible reading takes effort. I needed an uninterrupted *time* to meet with God daily, a *place* equipped with my Bible, paper, and pencil, and most importantly, a *plan*. Once those three things were established, I began to form the habit of Bible reading.

I found that as I read through my Bible, some books were more difficult than others. I could devour the narratives but struggled through the prophecies. I looked forward to the Psalms but would be a bit overwhelmed with the Proverbs. The detailed sections about the tabernacle, those endless genealogies or rules and regulations in the Law, seemed like drudgery. I was determined to enjoy my daily reading—like the honey I knew it should be—so I bought a set of colored pencils and decided to highlight key people or themes. I used my yellow pencil to highlight any attribute pertaining to God and His character. Looking for God in the various books became a delightful task. I decided to use my red pencil to mark references to Jesus—His character and especially His sacrifice. My pink pencil was used to mark references relating to women's issues, my green pencil for instructions in training up my children—I even had a blue pencil for those passages that I couldn't understand!

Now Bible reading becomes an exciting adventure. A time to meet with God, to see Him in every passage, to remind myself of the character and sacrifice Christ made for me, to read how to become a woman who pleases God, to find instructions in training my children, and to realize that I didn't need to understand everything at this point and time as I read through my Bible.

You may not use the same colors to mark your Bible, but work at creating the discipline to read and delight in your Bible—the entire Bible. Choose a *time*, a *place*, and a *plan* to read *Devotions on F.I.R.E.* Just like me, you will be able to say like David, "I will delight myself in Your commandments, which I love" (Psalm 119:47).

January 1

Genesis 1–2, with Matthew 1

━━◆━━

And she will bring forth a Son, and you shall call His name Jesus, for He will save His people from their sins (Matthew 1:21).

How important is the role of women in God's plan?

The Lord created a beautiful heavens and earth. In Genesis 1:31 He gives the following assessment: "Then God saw everything that He had made, and indeed *it was* very good." Yet in the next chapter "the LORD God said, 'It is not good that man should be alone; I will make him a helper comparable to him'" (Genesis 2:18). God graciously provided Eve for Adam as a helper in the same way that He helps His people (Exodus 18:4; Psalm 121:1–2). Similarly, the Lord chooses another woman, Mary, for a significant role. The virgin fulfills Scripture by giving birth to the Messiah (Genesis 3:15; Isaiah 7:14; Matthew 1:22–23).

Employment Point: *Imitate God, Eve, and Mary by becoming a godly helper to others.*

━━◆━━

9/12/14

JANUARY 2

GENESIS 3–5, WITH MATTHEW 2

And when they had opened their treasures, they presented gifts to Him: gold, frankincense, and myrrh (Matthew 2:11).

DO YOU OFFER GOD YOUR BEST?

Genesis 4 gives us a contrast between two brothers. Cain brings his offering "in the process of time" (Genesis 4:3), which means at the end of time. When the deadline arrives, Cain fulfills his obligation and nothing more. Yet by faith Abel presents to God a sacrificial gift. The writer of Hebrews says, "By faith Abel offered to God a more excellent sacrifice than Cain" (Hebrews 11:4). In a similar fashion the wise men travel as long as two years to bring their costly gifts to Jesus. They recognize who Jesus is and honor Him in a worthy manner. It should be noted that every time Jesus and Mary are mentioned together in Matthew 2, Jesus is named first (Matthew 2:11, 13, 14, 20, 21). Truly wise men still seek Him and offer Him their best gifts.

EMPLOYMENT POINT: *Offer worthy sacrifices to Jesus through faith.*

JANUARY 3

GENESIS 6–8, WITH MATTHEW 3

***

And did not spare the ancient world, but saved Noah, one of eight people, a preacher of righteousness, bringing in the flood on the world of the ungodly (2 Peter 2:5).

ARE YOU URGENTLY WITNESSING FOR JESUS KNOWING THAT JUDGMENT LOOMS?

God sees the widespread wickedness of mankind and says, "enough." He limits the duration of time until the worldwide flood at 120 years (Genesis 6:3). Yet Noah, who finds favor from God, not only builds an ark in obedience to the Lord, but also preaches to a sinful world for 120 years. No wonder he is placed next to Job and Daniel as a model saint (Ezekiel 14:14, 20). Another preacher, John the Baptist, comes with an urgent message. His words are penetrating; "Repent, for the kingdom of heaven is at hand!" (Matthew 3:2). Eternity is just around the corner. Let's heed Paul's words, "redeeming the time, because the days are evil" (Ephesians 5:16).

EMPLOYMENT POINT: *Proclaim Jesus to the lost, because judgment is coming.*

***

January 4

Genesis 9–11, with Matthew 4

———※———

Again, the devil took Him up on an exceedingly high mountain, and showed Him all the kingdoms of the world and their glory (Matthew 4:8).

Whose kingdom will you build?

Nimrod, whose name derives from the Hebrew that means *"rebel,"* builds for himself a kingdom. Moses records, "And the beginning of his kingdom was Babel, Erech, Accad, and Calneh, in the land of Shinar" (Genesis 10:10). Satan, who is called "the ruler of this world" (John 12:31), tries to divert Jesus from His calling by showing and then offering Him the kingdoms of this world. Our Lord isn't distracted, because He stays focused on the Word. "It is written" gives us the first recorded words of Jesus from the New Testament (Matthew 4:4). He preaches about a different kingdom than the one embraced by Nimrod and Satan. Jesus proclaims, "Repent, for the kingdom of heaven is at hand" (Matthew 4:17).

Employment Point: *Partner with Jesus to build His enduring kingdom.*

———※———

January 5

Genesis 12–14, with
Matthew 5:1–26

You are the light of the world. A city that is set on a hill cannot be hidden (Matthew 5:14).

Are you a bearer of God's light, like Sarah?

More space is dedicated to Sarah in the Bible than any other woman. An entire chapter covers her death and burial (Genesis 23). Sarah tenaciously stands by Abraham through thick and thin. Moreover, she is the only married woman cited along with her husband in Hebrews 11 concerning the heroes and heroines of faith. Faith can be defined as taking God at His word and acting upon it. The writer of Hebrews pens, "By faith Sarah herself also received strength to conceive seed, and she bore a child when she was past the age, because she judged Him faithful who had promised" (Hebrews 11:11). Peter cites Sarah as an example of modesty, faith, and of a loving wife (1 Peter 3:1–6).

Employment Point: *Imitate Sarah and let your faith bring God's light to the world.*

January 6

Genesis 15–17, with Matthew 5:27–48

Therefore you shall be perfect, just as your Father in heaven is perfect (Matthew 5:48).

Are you striving to live blamelessly before God?

God makes an unconditional covenant with Abraham, which is shown by only God's presence passing through the animal parts (Genesis 15:17). Yet the Lord has a standard He desires Abraham to uphold. The father of faith is ninety-nine years old, and God speaks to him: "I am Almighty God; walk before Me and be blameless" (Genesis 17:1). The adjective "blameless" is used of complete or healthy animals to be sacrificed to the Lord (Exodus 29:1; Leviticus 4:3). In both Exodus and Leviticus the term is translated "without blemish." We are to similarly live "blamelessly" and "without blemish." Paul writes, "just as He chose us in Him before the foundation of the world, that we should be holy and without blame ["without blemish"] before Him in love" (Ephesians 1:4).

Employment Point: *Live with integrity to match your heavenly calling.*

January 7

Genesis 18–19, with Matthew 6

The effective, fervent prayer of a righteous man avails much (James 5:16).

Are you a blessing to others?

God tells Abraham, "And you shall be a blessing" (Genesis 12:2). Literally the statement is an imperative; the Lord commands Abraham to be a blessing. Truly, Abraham turns out to be a blessing to Lot. His nephew had "pitched his tent even as far as Sodom" (Genesis 13:12), and later moves into the wicked city. His compromise led to moral failure demonstrated by offering his daughters to wicked men (Genesis 19:8). Thankfully the Lord honors the prayers of Abraham, which led to Lot's deliverance (Genesis 19:29). We should cultivate a vital relationship with the Lord also. Jesus says, "when you pray, go into your room, and when you have shut your door, pray to your Father who is in the secret place; and your Father who sees in secret will reward you openly" (Matthew 6:6).

Employment Point: *Intercede for others privately and watch God bless you openly.*

January 8

Genesis 20–22, with Matthew 7

Therefore whoever hears these sayings of Mine, and does them, I will liken him to a wise man who built his house on the rock (Matthew 7:24).

What is the basis of your foundation?

Abraham waits seemingly forever to bear a child through Sarah, and then God asks him to sacrifice Isaac. The elderly saint acts swiftly to obey the Lord, because he knows that God will honor His promise and make him a *father of a multitude*—the literal meaning of "Abraham." For this reason, Abraham tells his servants, "the lad and I will go yonder and worship, and we will come back to you" (Genesis 22:5). The writer of Hebrews documents Abraham's faith, "concluding that God was able to raise him up, even from the dead" (Hebrews 11:19). Let's imitate Abraham of whom it is written, "and being fully convinced that what He had promised He was also able to perform" (Romans 4:21).

EMPLOYMENT POINT: *Build your life upon the foundation of God's Word.*

January 9

Genesis 23–24, with Matthew 8

———◈———

Lord, I am not worthy that You should come under my roof. But only speak a word, and my servant will be healed (Matthew 8:8).

How will you cause Jesus to marvel?

Jesus visits His hometown of Nazareth. Although those in the synagogue "were astonished" at His teaching (Mark 6:2), they reject Him. Mark records Jesus' response: "And He marveled because of their unbelief" (Mark 6:6). By way of contrast our Lord enters Capernaum. A centurion who desires Jesus to heal a paralyzed servant who suffers greatly approaches Him. The centurion is a Gentile who commands one hundred soldiers. This man understands authority because he is both governing many troops and himself takes orders from a superior. He graciously turns down Jesus' offer to go to his home and demonstrates his profound faith by telling Jesus, "But only speak a word, and my servant will be healed."

Employment Point: *Cause Jesus to marvel by believing in His person and work.*

———◈———

January 10

Genesis 25–26, with Matthew 9:1–17

When Jesus saw their faith, He said to the paralytic, "Son, be of good cheer; your sins are forgiven you" (Matthew 9:2).

Are you living by sight or by faith?

Esau walks in from the field after hunting and smells the stew Jacob is making. Famished, Esau commands Jacob, "Please feed me with that same red stew, for I am weary" (Genesis 25:30). The Hebrew verb "feed" indicates *to gulp down greedily* or *to devour*. Esau is cited in the New Testament as follows: "who for one morsel of food sold his birthright" (Hebrews 12:16).

Unlike Esau, who could walk on his own power, a paralyzed man is brought to Jesus. His condition seems to be related to personal sin. Jesus says after observing the faith of his friends and the man, "Son, be of good cheer; your sins are forgiven you" (Matthew 9:2). Faith in Jesus led to the forgiveness of sin.

Employment Point: *Abstain from fleshly desires and live by faith to please Jesus.*

JANUARY 11

GENESIS 27–28, WITH MATTHEW 9:18–38

———◆———

But even if our gospel is veiled, it is veiled to those who are perishing (2 Corinthians 4:3).

DO YOU BELIEVE THAT JESUS CAN OPEN THE EYES OF THE SPIRITUALLY BLIND?

God requires believers to have faith that He is able to work miracles, whether that is through Ezekiel, who prophesied to dead bones to come alive (Ezekiel 37) or through us, who witness to the spiritually blind to be saved. Our Lord asks the blind men seeking to have sight a fascinating question in Matthew 9: "And Jesus said to them, 'Do you believe that I am able to do this?'" (Matthew 9:28). They respond in the affirmative and our Lord says, "According to your faith let it be to you" (Matthew 9:29). We must believe in Jesus' person (who He is) and His work (what He does) in order to please Him. The writer of Hebrews states it this way, "for he who comes to God must believe that He is" (Hebrews 11:6).

EMPLOYMENT POINT: *Believe that Jesus can open the eyes of the blind.*

———◆———

January 12

Genesis 29–30, with Matthew 10:1–23

Behold, the Lion of the tribe of Judah (Revelation 5:5).

Are you bringing praise to God by your life?

Leah has a share of physical and spiritual challenges. She lacks the beauty of her sister, Rachel. Moses reports, "Leah's eyes were delicate, but Rachel was beautiful of form and appearance" (Genesis 29:17). "Delicate" conveys either she has poor eyesight or doesn't possess dazzling eyes. Either way, she is no match physically compared to her sister. Moreover, she lacks the affection of her husband Jacob. After the birth of her third child, she says, "Now this time my husband will become attached to me" (Genesis 29:34). She gets the right focus with her fourth son. Leah says, "Now I will praise the LORD." Moses adds, "Therefore she called his name Judah," which means *praise* (Genesis 29:35). Our Lord Jesus would derive from this tribe and is worthy of eternal praise (Revelation 5:9–10).

EMPLOYMENT POINT: *Offer praises to the Lord, and live to bring Him the same.*

January 13

Genesis 31–32, with Matthew 10:24–42

———◦———

He who finds his life will lose it, and he who loses his life for My sake will find it (Matthew 10:39).

Have you lost your life to find life in Jesus?

God pursues Jacob, whose name means *supplanter*. He trips up his brother, snatching the birthright (Genesis 25) and the blessing (Genesis 27), and now fears for his life. Moses records, "Then Jacob was left alone; and a Man wrestled with him until the breaking of day" (Genesis 32:24). (Perhaps this is the only prayer meeting leaving the petitioner injured!) Hosea informs us that Jacob wrestles with the Angel of the Lord (Hosea 12:2–5), who is the preincarnate Jesus. Jacob finds his life by yielding to the Lord and subsequently is called a man of faith. The writer of Hebrews shares, "By faith Jacob, when he was dying, blessed each of the sons of Joseph, and worshiped, leaning on the top of his staff" (Hebrews 11:21).

Employment Point: *Submit to God's will to find your life.*

———◦———

January 14

Genesis 33–35, with Matthew 11

Now Dinah the daughter of Leah . . . went out to see the daughters of the land (Genesis 34:1).

HAVE YOU CONSIDERED THE DANGER OF MISPLACED CURIOSITY?

Jacob's daughter Dinah strays from home and becomes a victim of rape. Her brothers exacerbate the already bad situation by murdering the local male inhabitants. Poor Dinah is scarred for life, and the outcome of her unwise exploration among unbelievers culminates in mass murder. Sadly, Jacob and Leah didn't provide the protection and security Dinah needed. Jesus' generation also is not content with God's provision for them. He graciously sends them John the Baptist, and then later on He ministers to them. Instead of receiving the unified message of this dynamic duo, they complain that John is demon-possessed and leads an ascetic life (Matthew 11:18) while Jesus parties too much (Matthew 11:19). All generations need to receive Paul's following advice: "Now godliness with contentment is great gain" (1 Timothy 6:6).

EMPLOYMENT POINT: *Be content with Jesus, who alone gives rest to the soul.*

January 15

Genesis 36–37, with
Matthew 12:1–21

For even His [Jesus'] brothers did not believe in Him (John 7:5).

Do you worship and serve God, despite opposition?

Joseph and Jesus have something in common: They are subjected to persecution. Joseph is envied by his brothers since his father favors him and on account of his dreams. Yet he doesn't retaliate because he knows that God uses all things for good. Later he tells them, "But as for you, you meant evil against me, but God meant it for good" (Genesis 50:20). He worships and serves God regardless of the persecution. Similarly, Jesus is systematically attacked by the religious hierarchy and regularly accused of violating the Sabbath. He refuses to cave to the pressure upon Him and states the following: "Therefore it is lawful to do good on the Sabbath" (Matthew 12:12). In the very next verse, Matthew records Jesus again healing on the Sabbath.

Employment Point: *Worship and serve God, despite internal and external opposition.*

January 16

Genesis 38–40, with Matthew 12:22–50

———

Flee also youthful lusts (2 Timothy 2:22).

Do you run to, or from, temptation?

Judah and Joseph give us contrasting accounts (Genesis 38–39). Judah doesn't bring praise to God by his choices. He pursues an immoral relationship with a woman who portrays herself as a prostitute (Genesis 38:15–16). Unlike Judah, Joseph has to fight off the advances of a married woman. The Bible describes its characters' appearance when the story pertains to their looks. Moses writes, "Now Joseph was handsome in form and appearance" (Genesis 39:6). He desires to glorify God through holy living. Therefore he replies to Potiphar's wife, "How then can I do this great wickedness, and sin against God?" (Genesis 39:9). Centuries later Paul would write to his young associate Timothy, "Flee also youthful lusts; but pursue righteousness, faith, love, peace with those who call on the Lord out of a pure heart" (2 Timothy 2:22). Wise men still know when to run!

EMPLOYMENT POINT: *Run away from temptation to honor God with your body.*

———

January 17

Genesis 41, with Matthew 13:1–32

My times are in Your hand (Psalm 31:15).

Are you waiting upon God's perfect timing?

Joseph faithfully serves God whether in Potiphar's house or prison. He interprets the dreams of the butler and baker accurately. Yet he languishes in prison for another two years after the butler's restoration to his service (Genesis 41:1). Our responsibility is to wait upon God knowing that He will work according to His perfect timing. Isaiah writes about the Father, "Who acts for the one who waits for Him" (Isaiah 64:4). God's flawless punctuality also applies to the birth of Jesus Christ. Paul pens, "But when the fullness of the time had come, God sent forth His Son" (Galatians 4:4). Even the timing of Jesus' teaching on parables aligns with God's plan. Jesus transitions to regularly teaching parables "on the same day" (Matthew 13:1) that His miracles are being attributed to Satan's power by the religious hierarchy (Matthew 12:24).

Employment Point: *Wait upon the Lord, knowing that His timing is perfect.*

JANUARY 18

GENESIS 42–43, WITH MATTHEW 13:33–58

———◈———

I will cry out to God Most High, to God who performs all things for me (Psalm 57:2).

DO YOU LIVE AS IF GOD IS FOR YOU OR AGAINST YOU?

Jacob is experiencing hardship. For one, there exists a famine in Canaan. Then his sons return from Egypt having unknowingly met Joseph, and are told to bring Benjamin when they return. Jacob says, "All these things are against me" (Genesis 42:36). How well do you face the winds of adversity? Thankfully, Joseph views God as using difficult things for our good. After Jacob's death, Joseph tells his brothers, "But as for you, you meant evil against me; but God meant it for good" (Genesis 50:20). No circumstance defeats you when you embrace God's goodness. Let's internalize Romans 8:28: "And we know that all things work together for good to those who love God, to those who are the called according to His purpose."

EMPLOYMENT POINT: *Walk with God, knowing that He is for you.*

———◈———

JANUARY 19

GENESIS 44–45, WITH MATTHEW 14:1–21

And my God shall supply all your need according to His riches in glory by Christ Jesus (Philippians 4:19).

ARE YOU ACKNOWLEDGING THAT GOD ALONE IS THE GREAT PROVIDER OF NEEDS?

Joseph credits the Lord for His amazing provision. After he reveals himself to his brothers, he says, "So now it was not you who sent me here, but God" (Genesis 45:8). God's miraculous provision governed by Joseph would provide the needs of two nations: Egypt and Israel. Jesus, who is God, wants His disciples to learn the valuable lesson that Joseph grasped. "You give them something to eat" (Matthew 14:16), commands Jesus to His disciples after thousands gathered to hear Him teach. The wise Lord gives this directive to show His followers their inability to provide for the crowd, and also to then teach them that He uniquely has the capacity to care for the masses.

EMPLOYMENT POINT: *Trust in God alone to provide for all your needs, and acknowledge Him when He does.*

January 20

Genesis 46–48, with Matthew 14:22–36

Looking unto Jesus, the author and finisher of our faith (Hebrews 12:2).

Are you consistently looking to Jesus by faith?

The Lord's disciples participate in Jesus' feeding of the five thousand men by distributing the multiplied food. Subsequently Jesus puts them in a boat on the Sea of Galilee and heads to the mountain to pray. Perhaps He watches over them as He prays for them. Jesus then demonstrates His deity by walking on the water. Peter seeks to join Jesus and starts off fine, until he gets his eyes off the mark. At that moment "he is a double-minded man, unstable in all his ways" (James 1:8). By faith, let us finish strong and imitate the example of the heroes of faith (Hebrews 11), while keeping our focus upon the One who enlists us into His service and promises to be with us until the end.

Employment Point: *Focus your eyes of faith upon Jesus, who prays for you during stormy times.*

JANUARY 21

GENESIS 49–50, WITH MATTHEW 15:1–20

By faith Joseph, when he was dying, made mention of the departure of the children of Israel, and gave instructions concerning his bones (Hebrews 11:22).

WILL YOU LIVE AND DIE BY FAITH?

Joseph had a roller coaster of a life; however, by the grace of God knew that the Lord was with him whether he was going up or down. He becomes a model saint because he walks by faith throughout his life and trusts God with his final breath. The Lord promised to his great-grandfather Abraham, and then to his grandfather Isaac, and to his father Jacob that the land of Canaan would be given to them and their descendants. Joseph shows his enduring faith as recorded in Genesis 50:25. "Then Joseph took an oath from the children of Israel, saying, 'God will surely visit you, and you shall carry up my bones from here.'" Let's live by faith like Joseph!

EMPLOYMENT POINT: *Embrace God's promises by faith until your faith becomes sight.*

January 22

Exodus 1–3, with Matthew 15:21–39

———————

From the end of the earth I will cry to You, when my heart is overwhelmed; lead me to the rock that is higher than I (Psalm 61:2).

Where do you turn when everything seems to be against you?

Meet the individual who had multiple reasons to fold in the game of life being dealt a bad hand (Matthew 15:21–28). For one, she is a woman who comes to Jesus on account of her demon-possessed daughter. Rabbis didn't interact with women. Two, she is a double-dip Gentile. Mark records that she is "a Syro-Phoenician by birth" (Mark 7:26). Her geographical location and ethnicity could keep her from Jesus because He came to His own place and people (John 1:11). Moreover, she's a Canaanite, a people known as immoral pagans. Yet she acknowledges that Jesus is a rightful king, calling Him the "Son of David" (Matthew 15:22) and addressing Him as "Lord" (Matthew 15:27).

Employment Point: *By faith, approach King Jesus to overcome all adversity.*

———————

JANUARY 23

EXODUS 4–6, WITH MATTHEW 16

I will build My church, and the gates of hades shall not prevail against it (Matthew 16:18).

DO YOU BELIEVE THAT GOD IS LIMITED BECAUSE OF HUMAN FRAILTY?

The Lord calls Moses to an intimidating task. He needs to verbally inform Pharaoh that the Israelites are leaving Egypt. Moses tries twice to decline this assignment based upon his lack of eloquence. The sheepish leader says to God, "The children of Israel have not heeded me. How then shall Pharaoh heed me, for I am of uncircumcised lips?" (Exodus 6:12). Later he tries again, saying to God, "Behold, I am of uncircumcised lips, and how shall Pharaoh heed me?" (Exodus 6:30). God's earlier question to Moses should have steadied his nerves: "Who has made man's mouth?" (Exodus 4:11). Offer your service to God, knowing that He alone can free a nation from bondage or build His church.

EMPLOYMENT POINT: *Know that God will finish His work, despite our human frailty.*

JANUARY 24

EXODUS 7–8, WITH MATTHEW 17

———⋯———

However, this kind does not go out except by prayer and fasting (Matthew 17:21).

ARE YOU MAINTAINING YOUR SPIRITUAL DISCIPLINES?

Jesus chooses three disciples to display His glory before them. Do you think the other nine got jealous of Peter, James, and John who witness Jesus' transfiguration? Jesus previously empowered the twelve to expel demons (Matthew 10:1). Yet the nine couldn't cast out a demon from a boy (Matthew 17:16). Why did they lack the capacity to expel an unclean spirit, since they had previously been given that ability? Perhaps they become jealous of Peter, James, and John instead of being content with their designated service for Jesus; they temporarily lose their effectiveness since they are not walking with Jesus. I believe Jesus exposes their lack of spirituality by saying, "this kind does not go out except by prayer and fasting" (Matthew 17:21).

EMPLOYMENT POINT: *Maintain a close walk with Jesus, including fasting and prayer to effectively serve Him.*

———⋯———

January 25

Exodus 9–10, with Matthew 18:1–20

———— ◦ ————

Therefore whoever humbles himself as this little child is the greatest in the kingdom of heaven (Matthew 18:4).

How long will you refuse to humble yourself before Me? (Exodus 10:3).

The Pharaoh stands out as an arrogant man who refuses to bow before the eternal God. He exemplifies the following teaching from Proverbs 29:1: "He who is often rebuked, and hardens his neck, will suddenly be destroyed, and that without remedy." Today, when an adult acts like a child, we say, "Grow up." Yet Jesus tells His adult followers, "Become like a little child." Little children are totally dependent upon others for their needs. When Jesus gets tired of the disciples debating about their future greatness, He places a little child in their midst as an object lesson on humility (Matthew 18:1–2). Let's humble ourselves like little children, which shows the Lord that we rely upon Him for everything!

Employment Point: *Humble yourself before the Lord for future greatness.*

———— ◦ ————

January 26

Exodus 11–12, with Matthew 18:21–35

For indeed Christ, our Passover, was sacrificed for us (1 Corinthians 5:7).

Do you pass over the sins of others as Jesus has done for you?

The Israelites need deliverance from Egypt after 430 years of captivity; however, they need God's forgiveness more. He instructs them to apply lamb's blood to their doorposts and lintel, causing the angel of death not to kill their firstborn. He says, "I will pass over you; and the plague shall not be on you to destroy you when I strike the land of Egypt" (Exodus 12:13). Jesus is our Passover Lamb; His blood applied to our life should move us to forgive others. Paul writes, "forgiving one another, even as God in Christ forgave you" (Ephesians 4:32). We need to heed Jesus' parable on forgiveness (Matthew 18:21–35), showing that we must forgive others their trespasses against us because we've been forgiven so much more.

Employment Point: *Pass over the sins of others, because of God's Passover Lamb.*

JANUARY 27

EXODUS 13–15, WITH MATTHEW 19:1–15

———◦———

He has put a new song in my mouth—Praise to our God (Psalm 40:3).

WHY SHOULD WE SING TO GOD?

The Bible's first recorded song comes on the heels of the Lord giving the Egyptian soldiers a watery grave. Moses records, "I will sing to the LORD, For He has triumphed gloriously! The horse and its rider He has thrown into the sea!" (Exodus 15:1). Christians can also sing because Christ has conquered death. In Paul's extensive treatise on the resurrection, he pens, "But thanks be to God, who gives us the victory through our Lord Jesus Christ" (1 Corinthians 15:57). Moreover, we can sing to God because He graces little children with heaven who die prematurely. Jesus says, "Let the little children come to Me, and do not forbid them; for of such is the kingdom of heaven" (Matthew 19:14). Exuberantly, "Serve the LORD with gladness; come before His presence with singing" (Psalm 100:2).

EMPLOYMENT POINT: *Sing to God, who gives us the victory through Jesus.*

———◦———

JANUARY 28

EXODUS 16–18, WITH MATTHEW 19:16–30

Give us this day our daily bread (Matthew 6:11).

ARE YOU SELF-RELIANT OR GOD-RELIANT?

God says to the fallen Adam, "Cursed is the ground for your sake; In toil you shall eat of it" (Genesis 3:17). Yet the Lord later extends mercy to Israel showering them with food they didn't labor for. The psalmist shares that God "had rained down manna on them to eat, and given them of the bread of heaven. Men ate angels' food" (Psalm 78:24–25). Daily they are to retrieve breakfast and the day prior to the Sabbath take a double portion (Exodus 16:25–29). This object lesson is to teach the nation to depend upon God daily. Centuries later, a self-righteous rich man comes to Jesus asking how he could earn eternal life. Jesus exposes his covetousness by commanding him to sell his possession, give to the poor, and follow Him (Matthew 19:21). His departure reveals an independent spirit.

EMPLOYMENT POINT: *Rely daily upon Jesus for your spiritual and physical needs.*

JANUARY 29

EXODUS 19–21, WITH
MATTHEW 20:1–16

So the last will be first, and the first last (Matthew 20:16).

ARE YOU LIVING AS THE LAST MADE FIRST?

God chooses Israel for Himself not based upon her merits. Moses writes, "The LORD did not set His love on you nor choose you because you were more in number than any other people, for you were the least of all peoples" (Deuteronomy 7:7). He tells them as a result of His choice, "And you shall be to Me a kingdom of priests and a holy nation" (Exodus 19:6). God's favor toward Israel should produce a humble, loyal, and obedient people. Jesus' teaching on the landowner should likewise impact us (Luke 20:1–16). He paid the workers the same pay whether they labored all day or a short time. Moreover, He shocks all the workers by paying the laborers who came last, first (Matthew 20:8).

EMPLOYMENT POINT: *Choose the rearmost to be the foremost.*

January 30

Exodus 22–24, with Matthew 20:17–34

———————

I am the LORD, that is My name; and My glory I will not give to another (Isaiah 42:8).

To whom do you seek to ascribe glory?

Moses depicts God's glory, "The sight of the glory of the LORD was like a consuming fire on the top of the mountain in the eyes of the children of Israel" (Exodus 24:17). Jesus unveils His glory to Peter, James, and John, being transfigured before them (Matthew 17:1–2). Yet in conjunction with their mother, James and John seek their own future glory. They desire to sit at Jesus' right and left hand in His kingdom (Matthew 20:21). Jesus explains that He would be mocked, scourged, crucified, and resurrected (Matthew 20:19). Matthew immediately uses the adverb of time, "then," capturing the timing of their selfish request (Matthew 20:20). Our Lord reveals that His own future status is predicated upon His service by giving "His life a ransom for many" (Matthew 20:28).

EMPLOYMENT POINT: *Live for God's glory by becoming the servant of all.*

———————

January 31

Exodus 25–26, with Matthew 21:1–22

Then, behold, the veil of the temple was torn in two from top to bottom (Matthew 27:51).

Are you daily entering Jesus' presence through the veil?

God instructs Moses about the many details concerning the construction of the tabernacle in Exodus 25–31. He says, "You shall make a veil woven of blue, purple, and scarlet thread, and fine woven linen" (Exodus 26:31). The veil separates the Holy Place where the priest ministers daily from the Holy of Holies, which the High Priest only enters once a year. When Jesus dies the veil is ripped from top to bottom, signifying that all people have access to God's presence. The writer of Hebrews exhorts us with the following invitation: "Therefore, brethren, having boldness to enter the Holiest by the blood of Jesus, by a new and living way which He consecrated for us, through the veil, that is, His flesh" (Hebrew 10:19–20).

Employment Point: *Let's boldly enter into Jesus' presence daily through the veil.*

February 1

Exodus 27–28, with Matthew 21:23–46

Therefore submit to God. Resist the devil and he will flee from you (James 4:7).

What is the consequence of not honoring God's authority?

Jesus is asked by the religious leaders, "By what authority are You doing these things?" (Matthew 21:23). Jesus has just cleansed the Temple and is being asked by whose authorization did He act. In traditional Jewish form, Jesus answers a question with a question. He points the religious hypocrites back to John. The Lord's questions, "The baptism of John—where was it from? From heaven or from men?" (Matthew 21:25). Jesus imparts a profound truth: We need to direct rebels back to God's authority. Essentially, He shows that if they didn't listen to John who speaks for God, then He is not going to answer their question. We learn that if someone disregards God's authority, spiritual blindness follows.

Employment Point: *Get under God's authority and you'll receive further illumination.*

February 2

Exodus 29–30, with Matthew 22:1–22

———

But you are a chosen generation, a royal priesthood, a holy nation, His own special people (1 Peter 2:9).

Are you fulfilling your priestly role by holy living?

Moses receives directives from the Lord to sanctify Aaron and his sons for the priesthood. The Lord says to Moses, "And this is what you shall do to them to hallow them for ministering to Me as priests" (Exodus 29:1). Also, God previously chose Israel as a nation to serve Him in a priestly role. "And you shall be to Me a kingdom of priests and a holy nation" (Exodus 19:6). Whether Old Testament Israel, high priest, or a member of the church-age royal priesthood, God desires His people to separate from the moral contamination of this world's system. Peter proclaims, "but as He who called you is holy, you also be holy in all your conduct" (1 Peter 1:15).

Employment Point: *Live according to your holy calling as a royal priest.*

———

FEBRUARY 3

EXODUS 31–33, WITH MATTHEW 22:23–46

Now all these things happened to them as examples, and they were written for our admonition (1 Corinthians 10:11).

ARE YOU GUARDING YOUR HEART FROM IDOLATRY?

When the shepherd is away the sheep will play. Moses is receiving the Law from God upon the mountain. "And the LORD said to Moses, 'Go, get down! For your people whom you have brought out of the land of Egypt have corrupted themselves'" (Exodus 32:7). Paul quotes from Exodus 32:6 about the people's immorality: "Now these things became our examples, to the intent that we should not lust after evil things as they also lusted. And do not become idolaters as were some of them. As it is written, 'The people sat down to eat and drink, and rose up to play'" (1 Corinthians 10:6–7). Let's couple Paul's warning with John's: "Little children, keep yourselves from idols" (1 John 5:21).

EMPLOYMENT POINT: *Keep the Lord God as your only God.*

FEBRUARY 4

EXODUS 34–36, WITH
MATTHEW 23:1–22

Moses did not know that the skin of his face shone while he talked with Him (Exodus 34:29).

WHOSE GLORY ARE YOU REFLECTING?

Initially Moses doesn't know that his face carries a heavenly glow from meeting with the Lord. His shine is temporal. Paul informs us that today we carry a greater degree of God's glory because of the indwelling Spirit (2 Corinthians 3). He writes, "But we all, with unveiled face, beholding as in a mirror the glory of the Lord, are being transformed into the same image from glory to glory, just as by the Spirit of the Lord" (2 Corinthians 3:18). Sadly, the scribes and Pharisees pretend to display the Lord's presence in their lives by wearing large phylacteries (Matthew 23:5). Phylacteries are small boxes that house Bible verses, worn on the head or arm. We shouldn't imitate these hypocrites who aren't seeking to display God's glory, but their own.

EMPLOYMENT POINT: *Reflect God's glory by regularly basking in His glory.*

February 5

Exodus 37–38, with Matthew 23:23–39

How long, O Lord, holy and true, until You judge and avenge our blood on those who dwell on the earth? (Revelation 6:10).

Are you prayerfully awaiting God to enact vengeance?

Jesus verbally assaults the scribes and Pharisees for their ungodly living. He equates their bloodthirsty ways to those who murdered the prophets. Our Lord says, "that on you may come all the righteous blood shed on the earth, from the blood of righteous Abel to the blood of Zechariah" (Matthew 23:35). In one fell swoop, the Lord lays the murders of the first martyr Abel (Genesis 4) to the last Old Testament martyr Zechariah (2 Chronicles 24) at the feet of the religious hypocrites. (Second Chronicles is the last book in the Hebrew Bible.) They will not escape the Lord's wrath. Paul writes, "Beloved, do not avenge yourselves, but rather give place to wrath; for it is written, 'Vengeance is Mine, I will repay,' says the Lord" (Romans 12:19).

Employment Point: *Prayerfully wait upon the Lord to dispense justice.*

FEBRUARY 6

EXODUS 39–40, WITH MATTHEW 24:1–22

Assuredly, I say to you, not one stone shall be left here upon another, that shall not be thrown down (Matthew 24:2).

HAVE YOU CONSIDERED THE LESSON OF THE TEMPLE?

Moses is divinely instructed by God to build a transportable tabernacle, which is the precursor to the permanent Temple. God's presence hovers over the tabernacle by day as a cloud and by night as a pillar of fire (Exodus 40:38). Yet Israel doesn't revere the Lord as they are instructed, which brings God's judgment. The Babylonians destroy the Temple in 586 BC, which was subsequently rebuilt about seven decades later. Herod the Great added to the buildings of the Temple and the disciples are shocked when Jesus predicts its destruction, which is fulfilled in AD 70 after the nation rejects Him. Today, God's holy presence abides within each believer (Colossians 1:27). Let's dedicate our bodies, which house His Holy Spirit, to Him.

EMPLOYMENT POINT: *Honor God's holy presence in your life by living daily for Him.*

February 7

Leviticus 1–3, with Matthew 24:23–51

———◦———

Without shedding of blood there is no remission (Hebrews 9:22).

Have you personally applied the blood of Jesus?

The Book of Leviticus uses the term "blood" over eighty times. Moses writes, "For the life of the flesh is in the blood, and I have given it to you upon the altar to make atonement for your souls; for it is the blood that makes atonement for the soul" (Leviticus 17:11). Blood derived from an animal sacrifice provides a temporary covering for the sinner. The Day of Atonement specifies that on the tenth day of the seventh month the high priest would offer a sacrifice for his own sin, and then for the people (Leviticus 16). These repeated sacrifices point to "the Lamb of God who takes away the sin of the world" (John 1:29). As Paul states, "In Him we have redemption through His blood, the forgiveness of sins" (Ephesians 1:7).

EMPLOYMENT POINT: *Believe on Jesus' finished work to have His blood applied to your life.*

———◦———

FEBRUARY 8

LEVITICUS 4–6, WITH MATTHEW 25:1–30

Watch therefore, for you do not know what hour your Lord is coming (Matthew 24:42).

ARE YOU VIGILANTLY AWAITING JESUS' RETURN?

Jesus illustrates His teaching with a Jewish wedding. Parents would arrange their child's wedding. About one year later the bridegroom would retrieve his bride from her parents' house and they would observe certain religious ceremonies. Then he would take her to his home for the continuation of the festivities. The ten virgins are the bridesmaids; they would carry lamps to meet the bridegroom. Jesus declares that "five of them were wise, and five were foolish" (literally "morons," from the Greek) in Matthew 25:2. Jesus' story has a twist, because the groom is late (Matthew 25:5)! The lack of preparation by the five unmasks their unsaved condition (Matthew 25:11–12). This is why Jesus says, "Watch therefore, for you know neither the day nor the hour in which the Son of Man is coming" (Matthew 25:13).

EMPLOYMENT POINT: *Reveal your faith by watching for Jesus' return.*

FEBRUARY 9

LEVITICUS 7–9, WITH
MATTHEW 25:31–46

———◆———

Do not be deceived, God is not mocked; for whatever a man sows, that he will also reap (Galatians 6:7).

ARE YOU PROVIDING FOR THOSE WHO CARE FOR YOUR SOUL?

God's primary means of meeting His shepherds' needs consist of the saints' offerings. Concerning the wave offering, Moses writes, "And the priest shall burn the fat on the altar, but the breast shall be Aaron's and his sons'" (Leviticus 7:31). The people provide for the priests in the Old Testament. Paul states six reasons why pastors should similarly be cared for from the flock in 1 Corinthians 9:1–14. Furthermore, Paul gives the following command in Galatians 6:6: "Let him who is taught the word share in all good things with him who teaches." The very next verse shows the danger of ignoring this teaching (review Galatians 6:7). As the Old Testament saints were to give, so the New Testament believers are likewise commanded (1 Corinthians 16:1–2).

EMPLOYMENT POINT: *Honor God by faithfully caring for His shepherds.*

———◆———

February 10

Leviticus 10–12, with Matthew 26:1–19

For where your treasure is, there your heart will be also (Matthew 6:21).

What value have you placed upon Jesus?

Jesus earlier commands His disciples, "Do not lay up for yourselves treasures on earth" (Matthew 6:19). Then He gives His followers the right focus, "but lay up for yourselves treasures in heaven" (Matthew 6:20). Mary, the sister of Martha and Lazarus, is practicing the latter; she lays up treasures in heaven by anointing the body of Jesus with a perfume that would cost a year's pay for the average day laborer (John 12:5). By way of contrast, Judas sells out his Lord, friend, and provider for thirty pieces of silver (Matthew 26:15). This is the value of a male or female slave gored to death by an ox (Exodus 21:32). Mary's sacrificial act stands in stark contrast to the selfish betrayal of Judas. Whose example will you choose to follow?

Employment Point: *Value Jesus highly, by offering sacrifices worthy of heaven's recognition and reward.*

FEBRUARY 11

LEVITICUS 13, WITH MATTHEW 26:20–54

Behold, I stand at the door and knock. If anyone hears My voice and opens the door, I will come in to him and dine with him, and he with Me (Revelation 3:20).

HOW ARE YOU RESPONDING TO JESUS' HOSPITALITY, AS AN HONORED GUEST?

The triclinium is used for the Passover meal. It consists of three couches. Guests would recline with their left hand supporting their head while feeding themselves with their right hand. Traditionally the two most honored guests at the feast would recline on the right and left hand of the host. John, who reclines on the Lord's breast, sits at Jesus' right (John 13:23) and Judas on His left. When Jesus identifies His betrayer, no one hears but Judas, who is sitting next to Him (Matthew 26:25). John repays Jesus' invitation for eternal life and intimacy by a lifetime of service; Judas betrays Him for thirty pieces of silver.

EMPLOYMENT POINT: *Fellowship with Jesus daily and serve Him faithfully, to honor His invitation.*

FEBRUARY 12

LEVITICUS 14, WITH MATTHEW 26:55–75

Simon, son of Jonah, do you love Me more than these? (John 21:15).

HOW MUCH DO YOU LOVE JESUS?

Peter tells Jesus, "Even if all are made to stumble because of You, I will never be made to stumble" (Matthew 26:33). The implication from the proud fisherman's statement is that he loves Jesus more than the other disciples do. What means did God use to humble self-confident Peter? To begin with, "a servant girl came to him, saying, 'You also were with Jesus of Galilee'" (Matthew 26:69). Peter strikes out after three swings by denying Jesus each time, and then remembers His prediction when the rooster crows. Matthew records, "So he went out and wept bitterly" (Matthew 26:75). Perhaps Peter has this in mind, writing, "and be clothed with humility, for 'God resists the proud, but gives grace to the humble'" (1 Peter 5:5).

EMPLOYMENT POINT: *Dress for Christian success by adorning God's recommended garment of humility.*

FEBRUARY 13

LEVITICUS 15–17, WITH MATTHEW 27:1–31

———◈———

For He made Him who knew no sin to be sin for us, that we might become the righteousness of God in Him (2 Corinthians 5:21).

HAVE YOU THOUGHT ABOUT THE TWO GOATS AND ONE SAVIOR?

The Day of Atonement occurs on the tenth day of the seventh month (Leviticus 16). God's high priest would offer a sacrifice for his sin, and then cast lots on two goats (Leviticus 16:3–10). The one goat upon which the Lord's lot fell then became a sin offering for the people. The second goat, designated as the scapegoat, is sent away into the wilderness. Jesus takes on the role of the first goat because the sin of the world is placed upon Him (John 1:29). Likewise, He fulfills the obligation of the second goat, since "as far as the east is from the west, so far has He removed our transgressions from us" (Psalm 103:12).

EMPLOYMENT POINT: *Celebrate Jesus as He who both bore and carried away your sins.*

———◈———

February 14

Leviticus 18–19, with Matthew 27:32–66

You shall love your neighbor as yourself (Leviticus 19:18).

Do you love your neighbor as Jesus loved you?

Jesus sums up the Law in Luke 10: "You shall love the LORD your God with all your heart, with all your soul, with all your strength, and with all your mind, and your neighbor as yourself" (Luke 10:27). The lawyer to whom He speaks then asks, "And who is my neighbor?" (Luke 10:29). The Lord answers with the story about the Samaritan who demonstrates his love for God by loving the injured man in need; that is his neighbor. Jesus knows the need of the entire world and takes upon Himself the sin of all people. Matthew writes, "Then two robbers were crucified with Him, one on the right and another on the left" (Matthew 27:38). They are also His neighbors for whom He dies.

Employment Point: *Demonstrate your love for God by meeting your neighbor's needs.*

FEBRUARY 15

LEVITICUS 20–21, WITH MATTHEW 28

Do not be afraid, for I know that you seek Jesus who was crucified. He is not here; for He is risen (Matthew 28:5–6).

HOW DO YOU CALM THE FEARS OF OTHERS?

A few loyal women followed Jesus while He lived, watched Him be crucified, and now go to the tomb expecting to find His body. Their natural fears are calmed by a supernatural response from an angel: "Do not be afraid" (Matthew 28:5). He then proceeds to calm them through the life of Jesus. In essence the angel could be paraphrased: "Stop being alarmed, because Jesus is alive." Since Jesus conquered death and promises to be with us always, there is nothing to fear. God expels our fears through His presence in our lives. Paul reminds Timothy, "For God has not given us a spirit of fear, but of power and of love and of a sound mind" (2 Timothy 1:7).

EMPLOYMENT POINT: *Live fearlessly through the power and presence of Jesus.*

FEBRUARY 16

LEVITICUS 22–23, WITH MARK 1:1–22

He who has an ear, let him hear what the Spirit says to the churches (Revelation 2:7).

DO YOU PRIZE THE PREACHING OF GOD'S WORD?

Mark captures the commencement of Jesus' ministry with the following words: "Jesus came to Galilee, preaching the gospel of the kingdom of God" (Mark 1:14). The author of the second gospel writes to a Roman audience. This gospel is action-oriented, and so is the Son of God. Matthew shows the urgency of Jesus' message: "Repent," says Jesus, "for the kingdom of heaven is at hand" (Matthew 4:17). Preaching was a primary function of Jesus' forerunner, John the Baptist, as it is for the Messiah. Paul, noted for preaching the gospel everywhere he goes, tells Timothy, "Preach the word! Be ready in season and out of season" (2 Timothy 4:2). Are you ready to hear God's Word preached in season and out of season?

EMPLOYMENT POINT: *Be faithful to hear and obey the preaching of the Bible.*

February 17

Leviticus 24–25, with Mark 1:23–45

———

Now faith is the substance of things hoped for, the evidence of things not seen (Hebrews 11:1).

Do your actions reflect faith in the power of God's Word?

The Israelites were to work their fields for six years, "but in the seventh year there shall be a Sabbath of solemn rest for the land" (Leviticus 25:4). God anticipates the following question, so He asks it: "What shall we eat in the seventh year, since we shall not sow nor gather in our produce?" (Leviticus 25:20). He answers the question, "Then I will command My blessing on you in the sixth year, and it will bring forth produce enough for three years" (Leviticus 25:21). Similarly, we are to trust God with our finances today. Paul writes in the context of giving, "He who sows sparingly will also reap sparingly, and he who sows bountifully will also reap bountifully" (2 Corinthians 9:6).

Employment Point: *Honor God's Word, trusting Him to supply your needs as you give.*

———

FEBRUARY 18

LEVITICUS 26–27, WITH MARK 2

———※———

He is a rewarder of those who diligently seek Him (Hebrews 11:6).

HOW MUCH EFFORT DO YOU EXERT TO BE CLOSE TO JESUS?

Jesus would not be deterred from His mission to preach (Mark 1:38), so He continues proclaiming God's Word from a crowed home (Mark 2:2). The four friends of a paralyzed man are determined to reach Jesus to the extent that they peel back the roof of the owner's house and let the man down to Jesus. Jesus forgives the man's sins and miraculously heals him. The four friends live out Hebrews 11:6: "But without faith it is impossible to please Him, for he who comes to God must believe that He is, and that He is a rewarder of those who diligently seek Him." The verb "diligently" derives from the root meaning *to seek* and also has an intensifier. That is how these men approach Jesus!

EMPLOYMENT POINT: *Diligently seek Jesus by faith, and you'll be rewarded for your effort.*

———※———

FEBRUARY 19

NUMBERS 1–2, WITH MARK 3:1–21

—————

Then He appointed twelve, that they might be with Him and that He might send them out to preach (Mark 3:14).

ARE YOU CLOSE TO GOD?

God desires intimacy with His people. He arranges the encampment around the tabernacle, which makes Him central to Israel. Moses writes, "Everyone of the children of Israel shall camp by his own standard" (Numbers 2:2). The Lord chooses Israel to fellowship with Him and as a light to the nations. Jesus also calls His apostles to Himself. Mark pens, "And He went up on the mountain and called to Him those He Himself wanted" (Mark 3:13). The verb "called" occurs in the middle voice and shows Jesus picking them for His purpose. We should pursue an intimate relationship with Jesus, since He calls us to Himself. Like Paul, let's say, "that I may know Him and the power of His resurrection" (Philippians 3:10).

EMPLOYMENT POINT: *Stay close to God and faithfully proclaim His Word.*

—————

FEBRUARY 20

NUMBERS 3–4, WITH MARK 3:22–35

———◦———

But they shall not touch any holy thing, lest they die (Numbers 4:15).

HAVE YOU CONSIDERED THE CONSEQUENCES OF DISOBEDIENCE?

God delineates right from wrong. Moses records, "And the LORD God commanded the man, saying, 'Of every tree of the garden you may freely eat; but of the tree of the knowledge of good and evil you shall not eat, for in the day that you eat of it you shall surely die'" (Genesis 2:16–17). Adam's disobedience brings sin, suffering, and death for mankind.

Uzzah is a Kohathite. We are informed from Numbers 4 that he was strictly trained never to touch the ark of God, lest he die. Moreover, we learn from 2 Samuel 6:7, "Then the anger of the LORD was aroused against Uzzah, and God struck him there for his error; and he died there by the ark of God" (2 Samuel 6:7). Uzzah's disobedience by touching the ark brought his swift demise.

EMPLOYMENT POINT: *Avoid the path of death by honoring God's Word.*

———◦———

February 21

Numbers 5–6, with Mark 4:1–20

———

He who continually goes forth weeping, bearing seed for sowing, shall doubtless come again with rejoicing, bringing his sheaves with him (Psalm 126:6).

Are you by faith generously spreading the seed of God's Word?

Jesus gives us the parable of the sower. The Greek term "parable" literally means *to cast along side of.* Parables give a story derived from life that conveys a simple truth. Parables can be used to make a comparison or give a contrast. Our Lord begins, "Listen! Behold, a sower went out to sow" (Mark 4:3). Jesus' apostles desperately need to grasp the meaning of this parable, since they are the ones called upon to fulfill the Great Commission (Matthew 28:18–20). We have also been called to bring the gospel to the lost. Jesus says, "But you shall receive power when the Holy Spirit has come upon you; and you shall be witnesses to Me" (Acts 1:8).

Employment Point: *Scatter the seed of God's Word, leaving the results to Him.*

———

February 22

Numbers 7, with Mark 4:21–41

Let us cross over to the other side (Mark 4:35).

How confident are you in Jesus' promises?

Mark introduces the account of Jesus' disciples going through a storm with the words, "On the same day" (Mark 4:35). Jesus teaches His followers all day and then decides to test their knowledge. Just the statement, "Let us cross over to the other side" should have assured the Twelve that they are going to reach the shore. A great windstorm arises on the Sea of Galilee, which is approximately 690 feet below sea level and surrounded by mountains. The Twelve panic as their boat is rapidly filling with water. And where do we find Jesus? "But He was in the stern, asleep on a pillow" (Mark 4:38). After He is awakened, Jesus rebukes the storm and chides His disciples for lacking faith. Why is Jesus going to the other side? He will free a demon-possessed man (Mark 5).

EMPLOYMENT POINT: *Embrace the promises of Jesus.*

FEBRUARY 23

NUMBERS 8–10, WITH MARK 5:1–20

———※———

I wait for the LORD, my soul waits, and in His word I do hope (Psalm 130:5).

DO YOU PATIENTLY WAIT UPON GOD'S PERFECT TIMING?

The Lord clearly leads His people. Moses writes about God's presence above the tabernacle, "Whether it was two days, a month, or a year that the cloud remained above the tabernacle, the children of Israel would remain encamped and not journey; but when it was taken up, they would journey" (Numbers 9:22).

By nature, we are impatient. The Bible is replete with examples of those who didn't wait upon God and paid a hefty price. For instance, King Saul didn't wait upon God's set timing by Samuel and took on a priestly role, which cost him the kingdom (1 Samuel 13:1–14). David's following words should be heeded: "Wait on the LORD; be of good courage, and He shall strengthen your heart; wait, I say, on the LORD" (Psalm 27:14).

EMPLOYMENT POINT: *Wait upon God's leading in all matters.*

———※———

February 24

Numbers 11–13, with Mark 5:21–43

For we walk by faith, not by sight (2 Corinthians 5:7).

WHAT OBSTACLE DO YOU NEED TO OVERCOME BY FAITH?

Sight can get you into trouble when you magnify the object of your sight above God. Ten of the twelve spies give the following report after their inspection of Canaan, "There we saw the giants and we were like grasshoppers in our own sight, and so we were in their sight" (Numbers 13:33). How quickly Israel forgets the display of God's power in Egypt.

Moreover, Jairus seeks out Jesus to heal his daughter. Yet word comes while Jesus is going to Jairus' home that the child died. Jesus responds to the distraught father, "Do not be afraid; only believe" (Mark 5:36). Our Lord then restores her life. Like Jairus, we cannot please God without faith (Hebrews 11:6). Our great God is more powerful that any barrier we may encounter.

EMPLOYMENT POINT: *Don't let sight become your obstacle, but exhibit faith in the Almighty.*

FEBRUARY 25

NUMBERS 14–15, WITH MARK 6:1–32

———⊗———

And He marveled because of their unbelief (Mark 6:6).

HOW DO YOU CAUSE JESUS TO MARVEL?

Jesus returns to His hometown of Nazareth. This visit displays the mercy and grace of God because one year earlier His former community rejected and sought to kill Him (Luke 4:16–29). Jesus' teaching "astonished" its hearers (Mark 6:2). The verb "astonished" means *to strike*, and has an intensifier affixed to it. Although being *strongly struck* by His teaching, they stumble over His lineage. Jesus responds, "A prophet is not without honor except in his own country, among his own relatives, and in his own house" (Mark 6:4). Jesus brings the twin virtues of grace and truth to Nazareth, but "He could do no mighty work there" (Mark 6:5). Why? Mark answers, "And He marveled because of their unbelief" (Mark 6:6). Even though they were struck by Jesus' words, He could only be astonished at their unbelief.

EMPLOYMENT POINT: *Cause Jesus to marvel because of your faith, and not unbelief.*

———⊗———

FEBRUARY 26

NUMBERS 16–17, WITH MARK 6:33–56

Submitting to one another in the fear of God (Ephesians 5:21).

ARE YOU CONTENT WITH YOUR GOD-GIVEN STATUS?

God expresses His unique relationship with Moses after Miriam and Aaron verbally assault their brother. The Lord communicates with him "face to face" (Numbers 12:8). Then God asks them in the same verse, "Why then were you not afraid to speak against My servant Moses?" Similarly, Korah is jealous of Moses and leads an uprising to usurp his authority. Moses perceives that Korah and his followers have an authority issue. He exposes them with the following words: "You take too much upon yourselves, you sons of Levi!" (Numbers 16:7). They should have been satisfied with their divine placement.

Furthermore, Paul advises Timothy to be aware of those who would corrupt the church with the teaching that gain equals godliness. He adds, "Now godliness with contentment is great gain" (1 Timothy 6:6). That's application for all generations!

EMPLOYMENT POINT: *Support God's authorities, and be content with your own.*

February 27

Numbers 18–20, with Mark 7:1–13

———

Therefore let him who thinks he stands take heed lest he fall (1 Corinthians 10:12).

Do you understand your own weaknesses?

Moses is physically and emotionally fatigued. Once again the people lack water, and they complain bitterly (Numbers 20:1–3). The Israelites are like verbal hit men; they aim their lethal questions at Moses' heart. They ask, "Why have you brought up the assembly of the LORD into the wilderness, that we and our animals should die here? And why have you made us come up out of Egypt, to bring us to this evil place?" (Numbers 20:4–5). No wonder Moses is exasperated, especially when you couple these questions with Miriam's recent death. Kindly, the Lord instructs Moses to speak to the rock and the people's thirst will be quenched (Numbers 20:7–8). Moses makes two costly mistakes: He takes credit for the water coming from the rock, and twice strikes the rock instead of speaking to it.

EMPLOYMENT POINT: *Draw continually upon God's strength, while honoring His person and work.*

———

FEBRUARY 28

NUMBERS 21–23, WITH MARK 7:14–37

And as Moses lifted up the serpent in the wilderness, even so must the Son of Man be lifted up (John 3:14).

DO YOU HAVE THE LOOK OF FAITH?

The murmurings of the children of Israel become more intense. They complain that God erred rescuing them from Egypt. Moreover, they bellyache about not having food and water. "So the LORD sent fiery serpents among the people, and they bit the people; and many of the people of Israel died" (Numbers 21:6). God didn't simply honor the cries of the people to take the snakes away, but instructs Moses to make a bronze serpent and affix it to a pole. Any bitten Israelites are then to look up by faith to the serpent and be made well. Similarly, we need to look to Jesus by faith for salvation "that whoever believes in Him should not perish but have eternal life" (John 3:15).

EMPLOYMENT POINT: *Look up to Jesus, by faith, to meet all your spiritual needs.*

March 1

Numbers 24–27, with Mark 8

———⊰◉⊱———

Do you not yet perceive nor understand? Is your heart still hardened? (Mark 8:17).

IS YOUR HEART STILL HARDENED?

Jesus is grieved after displaying His vast power and hearts are unmoved. There is a man in the synagogue on the Sabbath who has a withered hand. Is he there to entrap Jesus? Our Lord displays His emotion because the religious hierarchy is more interested in finding fault with Him than helping people. Before Jesus heals the man, Mark records, "And when He had looked around at them with anger, being grieved by the hardness of their hearts" (Mark 3:5).

Jesus again shows His deity; this time He walks on the water. His disciples still don't grasp His person and work. Mark writes, "For they had not understood about the loaves, because their heart was hardened" (Mark 6:52). Following the incident in Mark 8, Jesus heals a blind man as an object lesson, revealing the disciples' obtuseness (Mark 8:22–25).

EMPLOYMENT POINT: *Ponder Jesus' person and work, lest your heart becomes hard.*

———⊰◉⊱———

MARCH 2

NUMBERS 28–29, WITH MARK 9:1–29

This is My beloved Son. Hear Him! (Mark 9:7).

DO YOU VALUE JESUS ABOVE ALL PEOPLE?

Jesus displays His glory before Peter, James, and John giving them a glimpse of God's majestic kingdom. Mark describes Jesus' glory. "His clothes became shining, exceedingly white, like snow, such as no launderer on earth can whiten them" (Mark 9:3). Mark informs us that Elijah and Moses also appear. Is this Moses' first trip into the Promised Land? Peter, expecting God's kingdom to appear immediately says, "Let us make three tabernacles: one for You, one for Moses, and one for Elijah" (Mark 9:5). The Father allows no one to be equated with Jesus. For this reason He says, "This is My beloved Son. Hear Him!" (Mark 9:7). In other words, don't categorize Jesus with Elijah and Moses. It is true that Elijah and Moses are both men of God; however, only Jesus is the Son of God.

EMPLOYMENT POINT: *Honor God's glorious Son above all men.*

MARCH 3

NUMBERS 30–31, WITH MARK 9:30–50

Whoever desires to come after Me, let him deny himself, and take up his cross, and follow Me (Mark 8:34).

ARE YOU IGNORING THE MESSAGE OF THE CROSS?

Jesus clearly tells His disciples, "The Son of Man is being betrayed into the hands of men, and they will kill Him. And after He is killed, He will rise the third day" (Mark 9:31). Shortly thereafter Jesus asks His followers what they were discussing on the road. Mark records, "But they kept silent, for on the road they had disputed among themselves who would be the greatest" (Mark 9:34). They will once again show their gross insensitivity (Mark 10:32–45). Jesus doesn't correct the disciples for desiring to be great, but does strive to change their selfish worldview on *how* to become great: "If anyone desires to be first, he shall be last of all and servant of all" (Mark 9:35).

EMPLOYMENT POINT: *Don't ignore the message of the cross and become self-centered.*

MARCH 4

NUMBERS 32–33, WITH
MARK 10:1–31

———◦◦◦———

Caleb the son of Jephunneh, the Kenizzite, and Joshua the son of
Nun, for they have wholly followed the LORD (Numbers 32:12).

HOW COMMITTED ARE YOU TO FOLLOWING JESUS?

The rich young ruler comes to Jesus seeking eternal life. He asks,
"Good Teacher, what shall I do that I may inherit eternal life?" (Mark
10:17). Erroneously he claims to have kept all the commandments.
Jesus exposes his violation of the tenth commandment (covetousness)
by telling him to sell everything and follow Him (Mark 10:21). His
departure shows his unsaved condition. Similarly, God calls Israel to
exhibit faith in Him by entering Canaan. Moses records, "Surely none
of the men who came up from Egypt, from twenty years old and
above, shall see the land of which I swore to Abraham, Isaac, and
Jacob, because they have not wholly followed Me" (Numbers 32:11).
God is looking for people of faith like Caleb and Joshua.

EMPLOYMENT POINT: *Completely follow Jesus to experience His
promises to you.*

———◦◦◦———

MARCH 5

NUMBERS 34–36, WITH MARK 10:32–52

And whoever of you desires to be first shall be slave of all (Mark 10:44).

IS JESUS TRYING TO TEACH YOU THE SAME OLD LESSON?

Earlier we observed how Jesus clearly laid out to His disciples His path of suffering, death, and resurrection (Mark 9:31). His followers miss the message because they are too consumed debating about their future greatness (Mark 9:34). Jesus repeats to His disciples about His suffering and resurrection, but with greater detail (Mark 10:33–34). What is their response? "Then James and John, the sons of Zebedee, came to Him, saying, 'Teacher, we want You to do for us whatever we ask'" (Mark 10:35). After Jesus had explained all that He will endure, they insensitively ask for a blank check from Him to be written out with their future greatness. The Lord expresses that our future greatness will come if we identify with His sufferings and become slaves of all.

EMPLOYMENT POINT: *Willingly suffer for Jesus and serve everyone, for future greatness.*

MARCH 6

DEUTERONOMY 1–2, WITH MARK 11:1–19

For You are my rock and my fortress; therefore, for Your name's sake, lead me and guide me (Psalm 31:3).

ARE YOU WANDERING AIMLESSLY?

Moses informs us, "It is eleven days' journey from Horeb by way of Mount Seir to Kadesh Barnea" (Deuteronomy 1:2). What should have been an eleven-day trek for the nation of Israel turned into a forty-year wilderness wandering, with only two of the original wanderers (Joshua and Caleb) ever entering the Promised Land.

The writer of Hebrews elaborates about those twenty years old and above who wouldn't be permitted to enter Canaan: "Do not harden your hearts as in the rebellion, in the day of trial in the wilderness, where your fathers tested Me, tried Me, and saw My works forty years" (Hebrews 3:8–9). What kept them out of Canaan? The author of Hebrews concludes, "So we see that they could not enter in because of unbelief" (Hebrews 3:19).

EMPLOYMENT POINT: *Walk by faith, obeying God's Word to avoid aimless living.*

MARCH 7

DEUTERONOMY 3–4, WITH MARK 11:20–33

———

As far as the east is from the west, so far has He removed our transgressions from us (Psalm 103:12).

ARE YOU IMITATING GOD IN THE AREA OF FORGIVENESS?

Jesus explains that we can have a roadblock inhibiting our prayers. He states, "And whenever you stand praying, if you have anything against anyone, forgive him, that your Father in heaven may also forgive you your trespasses" (Mark 11:25). Our Lord took upon Himself the sin of the world (John 1:29). Since He has made a provision for all people to have forgiveness of sin, we should forgive others their trespasses. What is the consequence for not forgiving others? Jesus teaches, "But if you do not forgive, neither will your Father in heaven forgive your trespasses" (Mark 11:26). Paul sums up this teaching beautifully. "And be kind to one another, tenderhearted, forgiving one another, even as God in Christ forgave you" (Ephesians 4:32).

EMPLOYMENT POINT: *Forgive others their trespasses, and have an open pathway to God.*

———

MARCH 8

DEUTERONOMY 5–7, WITH MARK 12:1–27

———◈———

Little children, keep yourselves from idols (1 John 5:21).

ARE YOU FREE FROM IDOLATRY?

God desires to protect His people from idolatry; therefore, He specifies His uniqueness. Moses gives us the passage traditionally called the Shema, which means *hear,* from Deuteronomy 6:4–5: "Hear, O Israel: The LORD our God, the LORD is one! You shall love the LORD your God with all your heart, with all your soul, and with all your strength." The Hebrew term for "one" refers to *a one of unity.*

This word also appears in Genesis 2:24. Moses records about Adam and Eve, "Therefore a man shall leave his father and mother and be joined to his wife, and they shall become one flesh." As the two (Adam and Eve) become one flesh, there is one God in three persons: Father, Son, and Holy Spirit. Interestingly, the model for unity given to the Ephesian saints consists of the Trinity (Ephesians 4:4–6).

EMPLOYMENT POINT: *Fully love the Triune God.*

———◈———

MARCH 9

DEUTERONOMY 8–10, WITH MARK 12:28–44

———◦———

And the second, like it, is this: You shall love your neighbor as yourself. There is no other commandment greater than these (Mark 12:31).

HOW DO YOU DEMONSTRATE THAT YOU FULLY LOVE GOD?

Jesus is asked to give "the first commandment of all" (Mark 12:28). He quotes from Deuteronomy 6:4–5 and gives the Shema (literally, "hear"). The Lord says, "The first of all the commandments is: 'Hear, O Israel, the LORD our God, the LORD is one. And you shall love the LORD your God with all your heart, with all your soul, with all your mind, and with all your strength'" (Mark 12:29–30). Then Jesus adds, "And the second, like it, is this: 'You shall love your neighbor as yourself'" (Mark 12:31). The adjective "like" means *one and the same*. In essence, to demonstrate that you love the invisible God completely, you must equally love your visible neighbor.

EMPLOYMENT POINT: *Love your neighbor as yourself to demonstrate that you love God.*

———◦———

March 10

Deuteronomy 11–13, with Mark 13:1–13

Therefore you shall lay up these words of mine in your heart and in your soul, and bind them as a sign on your hand, and they shall be as frontlets between your eyes (Deuteronomy 11:18).

Are you a carrier and distributor of God's Word?

The instruction given to the Israelites to bind the Scripture on their hands and before their eyes is probably given metaphorically, but later the Jews took this literally. They would copy Bible verses on a parchment and put them in a small container called a "frontlet." Similarly they took a small leather pouch called a phylactery, and wore it around the head and around the left arm, which would be close to the heart. God desires us to communicate His Word to our children, "when you sit in your house, when you walk by the way, when you lie down, and when you rise up" (Deuteronomy 6:7).

Employment Point: *Treasure God's Word internally while sharing it externally.*

MARCH 11

DEUTERONOMY 14–16, WITH
MARK 13:14–37

———◦———

But take heed; see, I have told you all things beforehand (Mark 13:23).

ARE YOU AWARE OF FUTURE EVENTS FROM STUDYING BIBLICAL PROPHECY?

Jesus predicts the future. He warns those who are saved during the Tribulation, "So when you see the 'abomination of desolation,' spoken of by Daniel the prophet, standing where it ought not, then let those who are in Judea flee to the mountains" (Mark 13:14). Normally safety is found behind the city walls; however, that will not be the case when the prophecy about the abomination of desolation, which Daniel writes about (Daniel 9:27; 12:11), is fulfilled. John writes about the false prophet, "He was granted power to give breath to the image of the beast [the image is the abomination of desolation], that the image of the beast [the beast is the Antichrist] should both speak and cause as many as would not worship the image of the beast to be killed" (Revelation 13:15).

EMPLOYMENT POINT: *Study biblical prophecy to remain vigilant.*

———◦———

MARCH 12

DEUTERONOMY 17–19, WITH MARK 14:1–25

———※———

Gather the people to Me, and I will let them hear My words, that they may learn to fear Me all the days they live on the earth, and that they may teach their children (Deuteronomy 4:10).

ARE YOU PERSONALLY GROWING IN THE FEAR OF THE LORD?

The Lord knows that Israel will ask for a king. For this reason, He gives the following instruction: "And it shall be with him, and he shall read it [the Law] all the days of his life, that he may learn to fear the LORD his God" (Deuteronomy 17:19). The application of the Word would then produce longevity for the king and his children (Deuteronomy 17:20). Whether king or pauper, we all need to be maturing in the fear of the Lord through reading the Bible and teaching its message to the next generation.

EMPLOYMENT POINT: *Learn to fear the Lord through personal Bible study, and then teach that lesson to the next generation.*

———※———

MARCH 13

DEUTERONOMY 20–22, WITH MARK 14:26–50

The fear of man brings a snare, but whoever trusts in the LORD shall be safe (Proverbs 29:25).

DO YOU FEAR MAN OR THE LORD?

Moses writes the principles of warfare for Israel. His officers are to inquire, "What man is there who is fearful and fainthearted? Let him go and return to his house, lest the heart of the brethren faint like his heart" (Deuteronomy 20:8). Jesus chooses twelve apostles and one betrays Him and the others run away at His arrest. The Lord predicts this. He says, "All of you will be made to stumble because of Me this night" (Mark 14:27). The apostles deny it. Yet Mark records, "Then they all forsook Him and fled" (Mark 14:50). Their plight is caused because they ignored Jesus' message that a man must "deny himself, and take up his cross, and follow Me" (Mark 8:34).

EMPLOYMENT POINT: *Fear God and not man through heeding the message of the cross.*

MARCH 14

DEUTERONOMY 23–25, WITH MARK 14:51–72

———

Jesus Christ is the same yesterday, today, and forever (Hebrews 13:8).

CAN YOU TRUST JESUS WITH YOUR PAST, PRESENT, AND FUTURE?

The Lord Jesus knows Peter's past perfectly since He created him. When He meets Peter, He says to him, "You are Simon the Son of Jonah. You shall be called Cephas" (John 1:42). Later Peter and his associates struggle one night to catch fish and their nets were barren, Jesus says to him, "Launch out into the deep and let down your nets for a catch" (Luke 5:4). Jesus shows Peter by the enormous haul of fish that he can trust the Lord with his present. Finally, Jesus predicts Peter's three denials. Mark records what happens after Peter's third denial, "A second time the rooster crowed" (Mark 14:72). Jesus' prediction and fulfillment show that He knows the future perfectly. Since "Jesus Christ is the same yesterday, today, and forever," we can trust Him.

EMPLOYMENT POINT: *Commit to perpetually trusting Jesus.*

———

MARCH 15

DEUTERONOMY 26–27, WITH MARK 15:1–26

And when they crucified Him, they divided His garments, casting lots for them to determine what every man should take (Mark 15:24).

DO YOU APPRECIATE THE FACT THAT NOTHING TAKES JESUS BY SURPRISE?

Our Lord predicted what He would experience. Mark quotes Jesus, "The Son of Man is being betrayed into the hands of men, and they will kill Him. And after He is killed, He will rise the third day" (Mark 9:31). Moreover, the Scripture predicted one thousand years earlier that Jesus' garments would be divided through casting lots. David writes about Jesus, "They divide My garments among them, and for My clothing they cast lots" (Psalm 22:18). Going beyond Jesus' prediction and that of Psalm 22, we are told about His crucifixion, "He indeed was foreordained before the foundation of the world" (1 Peter 1:20). Take heart, because Jesus knows all and endured much for you!

EMPLOYMENT POINT: *Honor the omniscient Jesus by trusting Him with your life.*

MARCH 16

DEUTERONOMY 28, WITH MARK 15:27–47

———◈———

The LORD bless you and keep you; the LORD make His face shine upon you, and be gracious to you; the LORD lift up His countenance upon you, and give you peace (Numbers 6:24–26).

WOULD GOD PREFER TO BLESS OR CURSE YOU?

God says to Abram, "I will bless those who bless you, and I will curse him who curses you" (Genesis 12:3). The Lord reveals His desire to bless many by using the plural term "those," and shows His lack of desire to curse by the singular word "him." God longed to bless Israel as a nation and have them bless others. In Deuteronomy 28, God displays His longing to bless His people for their obedience, but discourages them from disobedience through the many curses. Furthermore, the Sermon on the Mount conveys the heart of God. The beatitudes (blessings) in Matthew 5:1–11 each begin with the word "blessed," which means marked by God's favor.

EMPLOYMENT POINT: *Walk with God, who desires to daily bless you.*

———◈———

MARCH 17

DEUTERONOMY 29–30, WITH MARK 16

The secret things belong to the LORD our God, but those things which are revealed belong to us and to our children forever, that we may do all the words of this law (Deuteronomy 29:29).

DO WE KNOW ENOUGH TO WALK WITH GOD?

God is praised by the following words in Revelation 4:8: "Holy, holy, holy, Lord God Almighty, who was and is and is to come!" The Almighty has always existed, continues to exist, and lives forever. For this reason only He can know all things; however, God has imparted to us through His Word everything that we need to become mature Christians. As the ladies went to anoint the body of Jesus at the tomb, the angel said, "Do not be alarmed. You seek Jesus of Nazareth, who was crucified. He is risen!" (Mark 16:6). We shouldn't fear anything knowing that Jesus was born of a virgin, died for our sin, and conquered death.

EMPLOYMENT POINT: *Knowing and applying God's Word are sufficient to walk with God.*

March 18

Deuteronomy 31–32, with Luke 1:1–23

For I proclaim the name of the LORD: Ascribe greatness to our God (Deuteronomy 32:3).

Do your lips and life testify to God's greatness?

Jesus bears witness to the life of John the Baptist. He says, "Assuredly, I say to you, among those born of women there has not risen one greater than John the Baptist" (Matthew 11:11). This great man of God had a godly upbringing by Zacharias and Elizabeth. Luke describes their lives as follows: "And they were both righteous before God, walking in all the commandments and ordinances of the Lord blameless" (Luke 1:6). "They were" derives from the imperfect tense, which displays continuous action in past time. In other words, Zacharias and Elizabeth regularly walked with God. That is the greatest model parents can display for their children. Teach your children about the attributes of God, exalt Him greatly, and live daily for His glory!

EMPLOYMENT POINT: *Magnify God's awesomeness with your life and lips.*

MARCH 19

DEUTERONOMY 33–34, WITH LUKE 1:24–56

And He buried him in a valley in the land of Moab (Deuteronomy 34:6).

WILL GOD HONOR YOU AT DEATH?

God buries Moses. This is the only place recorded in Scripture when God honored one of His servants by personally burying him. A special relationship existed between God and Moses. The Lord spoke to Moses directly at the burning bush and called him into ministry (Exodus 3). Then God defended Moses when Miriam and Aaron sought to usurp his leadership. "I speak with him face to face," says the Lord, who then asks, "Why then were you not afraid to speak against My servant Moses?" (Numbers 12:8). Moses honored the Lord in life and God honored him in death. Stephen also glorified God in life, and Jesus stands to greet him in heaven at his death (Acts 7:55–56). We should live for the Lord now, to be honored by Him later.

EMPLOYMENT POINT: *Honor God in life and He'll honor you in death.*

MARCH 20

JOSHUA 1–3, WITH
LUKE 1:57–80

—————◦◦◦—————

The LORD is on my side; I will not fear. What can man do to me?
(Psalm 118:6).

ARE YOU COURAGEOUS IN CHRIST?

The Lord plainly reminds Joshua, "Moses My servant is dead" (Joshua
1:2). Joshua must now lead the children of Israel into Canaan. He
knows that there are giants in the land (Numbers 13:33). Four times
the Lord commands Joshua, using the same word to "be strong," in
chapter one (Joshua 1:6, 7, 9, 18). The verb also means *to overpower*
and *to be courageous.* Joshua walks by faith and not by sight, and on
one unique day witnessed the sun stand still, so that God would give
more light to his army to defeat the enemy (Joshua 10). After the
victory Joshua tells his captains, "Do not be afraid, nor be dismayed;
be strong and of good courage, for thus the LORD will do to all your
enemies against whom you fight" (Joshua 10:25).

EMPLOYMENT POINT: *Be courageous through walking by faith.*

—————◦◦◦—————

MARCH 21

JOSHUA 4–6, WITH
LUKE 2:1–24

I bring you good tidings of great joy which will be to all people (Luke 2:10).

ARE YOU HERALDING THE MOST IMPORTANT ANNOUNCEMENT EVER?

God dispatches the angels who are members from His advertising agency for their infomercial to His chosen audience: the shepherds. These lowly men are ceremonially unclean because their occupation keeps them in the fields and away from the Temple. The angels give the following advertisement: "For there is born to you this day in the city a David a Savior, who is Christ the Lord" (Luke 2:11). The term advertisement is defined as a notice or announcement in a public medium promoting a product, service, or event. We have the greatest event to proclaim to mankind. Let's not forget the simplicity of that message. John writes, "For God so loved the world that He gave His only begotten Son, that whoever believes in Him should not perish but have everlasting life" (John 3:16).

EMPLOYMENT POINT: *Proclaim the good news about Jesus to all people.*

MARCH 22

JOSHUA 7–8, WITH LUKE 2:25–52

———

Do you not know that a little leaven leavens the whole lump? (1 Corinthians 5:6).

HAVE YOU CONSIDERED HOW YOUR CHOICES IMPACT OTHERS?

Jericho is conquered, and comparatively small Ai is next. Joshua doesn't know that Achan violated God's directive concerning Jericho. Joshua informs us, "Now the city shall be doomed by the LORD to destruction" (Joshua 6:17). One man's disobedience impacted all of Israel. "And the men of Ai struck down about thirty-six men" (Joshua 7:5). The consequences from this one man's sin not only cost innocent lives, but also devastated the people. Joshua continues, "Therefore the hearts of the people melted and became like water" (Joshua 7:5). Just as the unnamed Corinthian man committing incest needed to be removed (1 Corinthians 5:7), so also must Achan. Leaven is used as a symbol of sin in the 1 Corinthians 5 passage. The man in sin is identified with leaven and must be evicted.

EMPLOYMENT POINT: *Obey God's Word, so that you don't contaminate other lives.*

———

MARCH 23

JOSHUA 9–10, WITH LUKE 3

———◦◦———

But One mightier than I is coming, whose sandal strap I am not worthy to loose (Luke 3:16).

DO YOU PRACTICE TRUE HUMILITY?

I've heard it said that humility is the state that when you know you have it, you've lost it. Slaves were to loosen or fasten their master's sandal straps. John the Baptist considers himself unworthy of even this role for Jesus. He models sincere humility. First, he directs people away from himself and to Jesus. John exclaims to his disciples, "Behold! The Lamb of God who takes away the sin of the world!" (John 1:29). John grasps that only Jesus can remove sin. Moreover, he practices the words of the psalmist, "Oh, magnify the LORD with me, and let us exalt His name together" (Psalm 34:3). Let us say and do the following, like John did about Jesus: "He must increase, but I must decrease" (John 3:30).

EMPLOYMENT POINT: *Embrace John's mindset and magnify the greatness of Jesus.*

———◦◦———

MARCH 24

JOSHUA 11–13, WITH
LUKE 4:1–32

For as many as are led by the Spirit of God, these are sons of God (Romans 8:14).

ARE YOU OVERCOMING TEMPTATIONS THROUGH THE SPIRIT'S LEADING?

Every New Testament passage referring to the leading of the Holy Spirit appears in the context of struggling with sin. Jesus is "led by the Spirit into the wilderness" (Luke 4:1) and overcomes Satan's three temptations using Scripture (Luke 4:1–13). Paul writes the following in Romans 8:13: "For if you live according to the flesh you will die; but if by the Spirit you put to death the deeds of the body, you will live." Then Paul gives the reason for the victory, "For as many as are led by the Spirit of God, these are sons of God" (Romans 8:14). Similarly Paul writes, "But if you are led by the Spirit, you are not under the law" (Galatians 5:18). He makes this statement after showing the battle between the flesh and Spirit (Galatians 5:17).

EMPLOYMENT POINT: *Follow the Spirit of God for victorious living.*

MARCH 25

JOSHUA 14–15, WITH
LUKE 4:33–44

———※———

And Caleb said, "He who attacks Kirjath Sepher and takes it, to him I will give Achsah my daughter as wife" (Joshua 15:16).

WHAT MERITS YOUR STAMP OF APPROVAL TO OTHERS?

Caleb is an exceptional man. His peers die in the wilderness while he and Joshua enter Canaan. What makes the difference? The writer of Hebrews speaking about the former group reveals, "So we see that they could not enter in because of unbelief" (Hebrews 3:19). Caleb recounts God's blessing on his life. He says, "So Moses swore on that day, saying, 'Surely the land where your foot has trodden shall be your inheritance and your children's forever, because you have wholly followed the Lord my God'" (Joshua 14:9). Caleb applies God's same standard for his daughter's marriage. He desires a man of faith, which will be shown by that man's actions to claim the Promised Land.

EMPLOYMENT POINT: *Apply God's standard of faith to give your stamp of approval.*

———※———

MARCH 26

JOSHUA 16–18, WITH LUKE 5:1–16

Do not be afraid. From now on you will catch men (Luke 5:10).

HOW HAS THE LORD'S INTERVENTION IN YOUR LIFE CHANGED YOU?

Peter and associates have fished all night and caught nothing. After Jesus teaches He tells the tired fisherman, "Launch out into the deep and let down your nets for a catch" (Luke 5:4). The hesitant apostle takes Jesus at His word and has a huge catch of fish (Luke 5:6). Jesus assures the broken fisherman, "Do not be afraid. From now on you will catch men" (Luke 5:10). The expression "from now on" is a favorite of Luke, which shows that God's intervention in one's life changes things forever. Luke first uses this expression in Luke 1:48. Mary says, "henceforth [from now on] all generations will call me blessed." She, like Peter, responds to the Lord's working by faith (Luke 1:38), and that is why they are forever different.

EMPLOYMENT POINT: *Respond by faith to the Lord's intervention to be forever changed.*

MARCH 27

JOSHUA 19–20, WITH
LUKE 5:17–39

So he left all, rose up, and followed Him (Luke 5:28).

ARE YOU WILLING TO SACRIFICE EVERYTHING FOR JESUS?

Levi, also called Matthew, is rich. He is a tax collector. The Jewish people hate Matthew because he collects taxes for the occupiers, the Romans; however, he is wealthy. Jesus intervenes in Matthew's life and forever changes him with the following two words: "Follow Me" (Luke 5:27). Luke reports, "So he left all, rose up, and followed Him" (Luke 5:28). The term "all" literally means *all together* and conveys *the universal whole.* Matthew understands Jesus' axiom, "For whoever desires to save his life will lose it, but whoever loses his life for My sake and the gospel's will save it" (Mark 8:35). Moreover, Matthew shows his commitment to Jesus by inviting his unsaved friends to a banquet to meet Jesus (Luke 5:29). The follower of Jesus leaves all, and uses what he has to reach the lost.

EMPLOYMENT POINT: *Follow Jesus and abandon the old for the new.*

MARCH 28

JOSHUA 21–22, WITH
LUKE 6:1–26

———◆———

And the Scripture cannot be broken (John 10:35).

HOW CONFIDENT ARE YOU IN THE POWER OF GOD'S WORD?

God promises the Jews the land of Canaan. Joshua takes God at His word and begins to conquer the Promised Land. The Book of Joshua records, "Not a word failed of any good thing which the LORD had spoken to the house of Israel. All came to pass" (Joshua 21:45). Godly Joshua prepares to pass the baton to the next generation; he rehearses God's faithfulness and promises to his people. The aging warrior says, "Behold, this day I am going the way of all the earth. And you know in all your hearts and in all your souls that not one thing has failed of all the good things which the LORD your God spoke concerning you. All have come to pass for you; not one word of them has failed" (Joshua 23:14).

EMPLOYMENT POINT: *Have confidence in the power and promises from God's Word.*

———◆———

MARCH 29

JOSHUA 23–24, WITH
LUKE 6:27–49

———◦———

But you shall hold fast to the LORD your God (Joshua 23:8).

ARE YOU CLINGING TENACIOUSLY TO GOD?

Joshua brings the nation of Israel to a fork in the road and says, "Choose for yourselves this day whom you will serve, whether the gods which your fathers served that were on the other side of the River, or the gods of the Amorites" (Joshua 24:15). He completes the verse with his decision, "But as for me and my house, we will serve the LORD." He desires Israel to "hold fast to the LORD your God" (Joshua 23:8). The verb "hold fast" means *to cling to, join together,* or *stay with.* It appears in Genesis 2:24 that a man should separate from his parents "and be joined to his wife." Moreover, it is used of the Leviathan's scales that "are joined one to another" (Job 41:17). In like fashion, we should cleave to God.

EMPLOYMENT POINT: *Cling to the Lord and forsake idolatry.*

———◦———

MARCH 30

JUDGES 1–2, WITH LUKE 7:1–30

Blessed are the merciful, for they shall obtain mercy (Matthew 5:7).

DOES YOUR COMPASSION LEAD TO ACTION?

Perhaps you've heard about individuals crashing a wedding. How about a funeral? Jesus interrupts a funeral procession because His heart was touched. Luke writes about the Son of Man, "When the Lord saw her, He had compassion on her and said to her, 'Do not weep'" (Luke 7:13). Our Lord extends mercy to a widow whose only son has died (Luke 7:12). Most likely she would have no means of support, not having a husband or son to care for her. Jesus makes Himself ceremonially unclean by choosing to come in contact with the dead. Yet He "touched the open coffin, and those who carried him stood still. And He said, 'Young man, I say to you, arise'" (Luke 7:14). Similarly, we ought to grant compassion to the needy who come upon our path.

EMPLOYMENT POINT: *Turn your compassion into action by extending mercy to the needy.*

MARCH 31

JUDGES 3–5, WITH LUKE 7:31–50

When leaders lead in Israel, when the people willingly offer themselves, bless the LORD! (Judges 5:2).

DO YOU MOTIVATE OTHERS TO SERVE THE LORD?

Deborah is raised up by God to stir the people to action. After Ehud dies, "the children of Israel again did evil in the sight of the LORD. So the LORD sold them into the hand of Jabin king of Canaan" (Judges 4:1–2). Deborah is an exceptional leader. Being a prophetess, she hears and proclaims the Word of the Lord (Judges 4:4). Not only that, Deborah knows how to motivate people. The prophetess desires a hesitant Barak to lead the troops. He finally agrees, because she is willing to go with him (Judges 4:9). The courageous Deborah risks her life for the work of the Lord. God's victory moves Deborah to praise the Lord through song. What a great leader!

EMPLOYMENT POINT: *Willingly offer yourself to do the work of the Lord, and motivate others to join you.*

APRIL 1

JUDGES 6–7, WITH LUKE 8:1–21

———◦———

And what more shall I say? For the time would fail me to tell of Gideon (Hebrews 11:32).

WILL YOU OBEY GOD'S MISSION FOR YOU?

Gideon is a reluctant judge. He is threshing wheat in a cave hoping to evade the Midianites from stealing his crop. Yet "the Angel of the LORD appeared to him, and said to him, 'The LORD is with you, you mighty man of valor!'" (Judges 6:12). God reveals to Gideon who he will become with His help. There are two reasons given why Gideon should trust the Lord. First, God asks, "Have I not sent you?" (Judges 6:14). Shortly thereafter He promises, "Surely I will be with you" (Judges 6:16).

Similarly, Jesus sends us to make disciples and also promises to be with us, in the passage on the Great Commission (Matthew 28:18–20). God has been faithful to those who obey His mission and embrace His presence.

EMPLOYMENT POINT: *Finish the mission that you've been given, knowing God is with you.*

———◦———

April 2

Judges 8–9, with Luke 8:22–56

———※———

Somebody touched Me, for I perceived power going out from Me (Luke 8:46).

Are you in touch with Jesus?

Jesus is making His way to Jairus' house when someone in the vast crowd touched Him. Dr. Luke begins the account, "Now a woman, having a flow of blood for twelve years, who had spent all her livelihood on physicians and could not be healed by any" (Luke 8:43). She reaches out and touches Jesus' "border of His garment" (Luke 8:44). Jesus subsequently asks, "Who touched Me?" (Luke 8:45). He doesn't ask the question because He lacks the answer—Jesus desires the lady to come forward. Luke continues, "and falling down before Him, she declared to Him in the presence of all the people the reason she had touched Him and how she was healed immediately" (Luke 8:47). Her declaration let all the people know that she is no longer ceremonially unclean, and that she could now worship at the Temple.

Employment Point: *Reach out to Jesus with all your needs.*

———※———

April 3

Judges 10–11, with
Luke 9:1–36

———※———

For with God nothing will be impossible (Luke 1:37).

HAVE YOU LIMITED GOD IN YOUR THINKING?

An elderly Sarah is asked the following question that all of us should ponder: "Is anything too hard for the LORD?" (Genesis 18:14). Jesus seeks to expand the faith of the apostles. There is a crowd consisting of five thousand men alone who gathered before Him. The hour is late and Jesus says to His disciples, "You give them something to eat" (Luke 9:13). Our Lord's directive is given to show the impossibility of the apostles feeding this hungry large multitude. Did the disciples forget a lesson that they perhaps learned in the synagogue about the Lord supernaturally feeding the Israelites quail for one month? God then probed Moses, "Has the LORD's arm been shortened?" (Number 11:23). As the Lord gave Isaac to Sarah, quail to the Israelites, bread and fish to the five thousand, He can still do the impossible today.

EMPLOYMENT POINT: *Trust God for the impossible.*

———※———

April 4

Judges 12–14, with Luke 9:37–62

I have made a covenant with my eyes; why then should I look upon a young woman? (Job 31:1).

Have you dedicated your body to God?

The Angel of the Lord informs the unnamed wife of Manoah that her child "shall be a Nazarite to God from the womb" (Judges 13:5). He is to abstain from wine, having contact with a dead body, and is not to cut his hair (Numbers 6:1–6). Sadly, he defiles himself with the carcass of a lion (Judges 14:8–9), most likely drinks wine at the feast he gives (Judges 14:10), and subsequently has his hair cut (Judges 16:19). With his third act of disobedience comes the following statement when the Philistines attack him: "But he did not know that the LORD had departed from him" (Judges 16:20). Samson is set apart for God from birth; we are set apart from eternity to "be holy and without blame before Him" (Ephesians 1:4).

EMPLOYMENT POINT: *Present your bodily members as instruments of righteousness to God.*

APRIL 5

JUDGES 15–17, WITH
LUKE 10:1–24

———◉———

Nevertheless do not rejoice in this, that the spirits are subject to you, but rather rejoice because your names are written in heaven (Luke 10:20).

WHAT BRINGS YOU ENDLESS JOY?

Jesus dispatches seventy disciples on a mission. He teaches these followers about faith, saying, "Carry neither money bag, knapsack, nor sandals" (Luke 10:4). Jesus provides for all their needs. Once they return and give their praise report, He gives two commands: One is stated negatively and the other positively (Luke 10:20). Although our Lord "saw Satan fall like lightning from heaven" (Luke 10:18), He doesn't want them focusing upon the expulsion of demons. Rather, Jesus uses the present tense verb guiding them habitually to "rejoice because your names are written in heaven" (Luke 10:20). Conversely, many throughout the ages reject Jesus; they will be eternally separated from His presence. John writes, "And anyone not found written in the Book of Life was cast into the lake of fire" (Revelation 20:15).

EMPLOYMENT POINT: *Continually rejoice in your salvation.*

———◉———

APRIL 6

JUDGES 18–19, WITH
LUKE 10:25–42

But you shall love your neighbor as yourself (Leviticus 19:18).

DO YOU PRACTICE THE OLD TESTAMENT BIBLE VERSE THAT IS QUOTED MOST OFTEN IN THE NEW TESTAMENT?

Jesus, the Master Storyteller, shares a story to express that loving God is displayed through loving your neighbor just as you would care for yourself. He powerfully makes His point through the life of the Samaritan (Luke 10:33–37). Technically speaking from the Jewish mindset, there is no such thing as a Samaritan who is good. They were half Jewish and half Assyrian; therefore, the Jews despised them—these fellow Israelites had married into an ethnicity that had captured the northern kingdom of Israel (722 BC). Yet the bad guy (the Samaritan) becomes the good guy by demonstrating God's love through sacrificially meeting the needs of his neighbor. Likewise, we show our love for the invisible Father by caring for those that He brings upon our path.

EMPLOYMENT POINT: *Love your neighbor even as you would care for yourself.*

April 7

Judges 20–21, with Luke 11:1–28

———◆———

In those days there was no king in Israel; everyone did what was right in his own eyes (Judges 21:25).

How are you representing King Jesus in a darkened world?

Israel didn't obey their heavenly King and the last verse in Judges sums up that period of time. The Book of Judges stands in stark contrast to the previous Book of Joshua. God is looking for men and women of faith to display His light during spiritual blackouts. Allow the following examples of faith to inspire you to action: "For the time would fail me to tell of Gideon and Barak and Samson and Jephthah, also of David and Samuel and the prophets: who through faith subdued kingdoms, worked righteousness, obtained promises, stopped the mouths of lions . . . out of weakness were made strong, became valiant in battle, turned to flight the armies of the aliens" (Hebrews 11:32–34).

Employment Point: *Live by faith and display God's light to a dark world.*

———◆———

APRIL 8

RUTH 1–4, WITH LUKE 11:29–54

Who can find a virtuous wife? For her worth is far above rubies (Proverbs 31:10).

ARE YOU CLINGING TO GOD AND HIS PEOPLE?

Ruth lives during the period of the judges (Ruth 1:1). She is like a diamond placed on a jet-black cloth; Ruth stands out because of her strength of character. Her mother-in-law, Naomi, had modeled to this woman brought up in a pagan land (Moab) the ways of God. While Orpah returns to her people (Ruth 1:14), "Ruth clung to her" [Naomi]. The term "clung" is translated "stay close" in Ruth 2:8, 21 when Boaz advises the young maiden to "stay close" to his people working in the fields. Moses applies the word to the marriage relationship (Genesis 2:24). Moreover, the Israelites are exhorted to serve the Lord, "and to Him you shall hold fast" (Deuteronomy 10:20). We should also "hold fast" or "cling" to the Lord and godly people.

EMPLOYMENT POINT: *Embrace God and godly people for a virtuous existence.*

April 9

1 Samuel 1–3, with
Luke 12:1–34

The fear of man brings a snare, but whoever trusts in the LORD shall be safe (Proverbs 29:25).

Are you more afraid of man or God?

Christianity has always been hazardous to the believer's health. Jesus, therefore, gives the following admonition: "My friends, do not be afraid of those who kill the body, and after that have no more that they can do" (Luke 12:4). Conversely, He commands His disciples, "Fear Him who, after He has killed, has power to cast into hell; yes, I say to you, fear Him! (Luke 12:5). Our Lord Jesus builds His case using sparrows. These birds are a food source for the poor and ceremonially clean, which means Jews could eat them. The sovereign Lord cares for these seemingly insignificant creatures; therefore, He will watch over His disciples. Jesus adds, "Do not fear therefore; you are of more value than many sparrows" (Luke 12:7).

EMPLOYMENT POINT: *Fear only the Almighty God, who cares deeply for you.*

APRIL 10

1 SAMUEL 4–6, WITH LUKE 12:35–59

And that servant who knew his master's will, and did not prepare himself or do according to his will, shall be beaten with many stripes (Luke 12:47).

ARE YOU PRACTICING THE KNOWN WILL OF GOD?

First Samuel gives a stark contrast between godly Samuel and the two wicked sons of Eli, Hophni and Phinehas. Eli is confronted because he honors his sons more than the Lord. A man of God asks the priest, "Why do you kick at My sacrifice and My offering which I have commanded in My dwelling place, and honor your sons more than Me" (1 Samuel 2:29)? Eli, Hophni, and Phinehas know what God expects of them; however, they disobey the Lord, which costs their lives (1 Samuel 4:11, 18). Eli and his sons exemplify the principle written by James centuries later. "Therefore, to him who knows to do good and does not do it, to him it is sin" (James 4:17).

EMPLOYMENT POINT: *Practice the known will of God to please your Master.*

APRIL 11

1 SAMUEL 7–9, WITH
LUKE 13:1–21

Far be it from me that I should sin against the LORD in ceasing to pray for you (1 Samuel 12:23).

ARE YOU A PERSON OF PRAYER?

It has been said that the apple doesn't fall far from the tree. This is the case with Samuel, who had a praying mother. Hannah overcomes difficult circumstances through prayer (1 Samuel 1:10–12), and offers another prayer after God honors her petition (1 Samuel 2:1–10). Samuel is grieved that the nation of Israel wants a king to become like the other nations. He shares his disappointment with the Lord and receives the Lord's assessment on the situation (1 Samuel 8:6–9). As a result of God's response, Samuel knows how to address the people (1 Samuel 8:10–18). The nation still persists for a king (1 Samuel 8:19–20), which leads Samuel to report back to the Lord through prayer (1 Samuel 8:21–22). Both Hannah and Samuel's lives instruct us how to "pray without ceasing" (1 Thessalonians 5:17).

EMPLOYMENT POINT: *Converse regularly with God for His strength and guidance.*

APRIL 12

1 SAMUEL 10–12, WITH
LUKE 13:22–35

I am Almighty God; walk before Me and be blameless (Genesis 17:1).

ARE YOU A GODLY EXAMPLE TO OTHERS?

Samuel serves Israel as priest, prophet, and judge. He models integrity to those he serves. After publicly asking the people about his integrity, they reply, "You have not cheated us or oppressed us, nor have you taken anything from any man's hand" (1 Samuel 12:4). Next, he imparts a history lesson to the people on their disobedience to the Lord. Then he adds, "but I will teach you the good and the right way. Only fear the LORD, and serve Him in truth with all your heart; for consider what great things He has done for you" (1 Samuel 12:23–24).

Fallen creatures need to witness Christians walking with God showcasing integrity. "Enoch walked with God" (Genesis 5:24). Likewise, "Noah was a just man, perfect in his generations. Noah walked with God" (Genesis 6:9). It is now your turn.

EMPLOYMENT POINT: *Model godliness by blamelessly walking with God.*

APRIL 13

1 SAMUEL 13–14, WITH LUKE 14:1–24

For whoever exalts himself will be humbled, and he who humbles himself will be exalted (Luke 14:11).

ARE YOU A PROUD OR HUMBLE SERVANT OF THE LORD?

We are introduced to a humble Saul. He doesn't boast to his uncle that he is chosen king when his uncle inquires about his time with Samuel (1 Samuel 10:16). Next, he is found hiding when the Lord reveals to the people that he is Israel's king (1 Samuel 10:21–23). The humility quickly turns to hubris. Saul disobeys the command of Samuel and offers a sacrifice which he is not qualified to give (1 Samuel 13:9). Samuel rebukes him, saying, "You have done foolishly. You have not kept the commandment of the LORD your God" (1 Samuel 13:13). Later he disobeys again by not obliterating the Amalekites (1 Samuel 15). Subsequently, the wise Samuel exposes Saul's fatal flaw by pointing out to the king "when you were little in your own eyes" (1 Samuel 15:17).

EMPLOYMENT POINT: *Serve God humbly now for future exaltation.*

APRIL 14

1 SAMUEL 15–16, WITH LUKE 14:25–35

The LORD has sought for Himself a man after His own heart (1 Samuel 13:14).

HOW DO YOU BECOME AN INDIVIDUAL AFTER GOD'S OWN HEART?

Godly Samuel is sent to anoint a king from Jesse's house. Israel wants a king who looks like kings of other nations. It seems that Samuel believes that Eliab is the Lord's choice, based upon his height. Yet the Lord points out to Samuel, "Do not look at his appearance or at his physical stature, because I have refused him. For the LORD does not see as man sees; for man looks at the outward appearance, but the LORD looks at the heart" (1 Samuel 16:7). Unlike Saul, David is committed to obeying God; that is what establishes him as an exemplary king. The Lord chooses David, says Paul, "a man after My own heart, who will do all My will" (Acts 13:22).

EMPLOYMENT POINT: *Become an individual after God's own heart by doing all His will.*

April 15

1 Samuel 17–18, with Luke 15:1–10

For we walk by faith, not by sight (2 Corinthians 5:7).

How big is too big for God?

There are conceivably more details about Goliath's physical appearance than any other biblical character, to show the behemoth's invincibility. The man's head almost reaches an NBA rim of ten feet. Not only is he tall as a modern skyscraper, but he is also strong. The coat of armor he dons weighs about 125 pounds. Even his iron spearhead, which is shaped like a flame, weighs fifteen pounds. The giant's challenge becomes Saul's worst nightmare, because he and the nation walk by sight. They earlier wanted a visible king to lead them (1 Samuel 8:19–20). David marches to the beat of a different drum; he walks by faith. The shepherd tells Goliath, "I come to you in the name of the LORD of hosts, the God of the armies of Israel" (1 Samuel 17:45). Let's choose David's path of faith.

EMPLOYMENT POINT: *Trust the invisible Lord Almighty when visibly challenged.*

APRIL 16

1 SAMUEL 19–21, WITH LUKE 15:11–32

———◦———

There is joy in the presence of the angels of God over one sinner who repents (Luke 15:10).

WHAT CAUSES YOU TO CELEBRATE?

The father in our parable has two sons. A devastating request comes from the younger, "Father, give me the portion of goods that falls to me" (Luke 15:12). In essence, the son is saying, "Dad, I wish you were dead; give me my inheritance." This loving father doesn't argue with his adult son, but complies with his request. How does the loving father respond when the chastened son returns home? "But when he was still a great way off, his father saw him and had compassion, and ran and fell on his neck and kissed him" (Luke 15:20). The father reveals the heart of God. Jesus says, "for the Son of Man has come to seek and to save that which was lost" (Luke 19:10).

EMPLOYMENT POINT: *Celebrate when the lost are found and the dead come to life.*

———◦———

April 17

1 Samuel 22–24, with Luke 16:1–18

For You are my rock and my fortress; therefore, for Your name's sake, lead me and guide me (Psalm 31:3).

Where do you receive direction when under attack?

What principles will govern David as Saul seeks his demise? First, he follows godly counsel. "Now the prophet Gad said to David, 'Do not stay in the stronghold; depart, and go to the land of Judah'" (1 Samuel 22:5). David acts upon this guidance. He also checks with God before advancing. First Samuel 23:2 reports, "Therefore David inquired of the LORD" about attacking the Philistines. Finally, Saul comes to a cave unaware that David and his men are present. David secretly cuts off a part of Saul's robe, but the text shares "that David's heart troubled him" (1 Samuel 24:5). David let his conscience be his guide, and doesn't kill Saul. King David receives direction from godly people, prayer, and conscience. Go and do likewise!

Employment Point: *Seek God's guidance through godly counsel, prayer, and your conscience.*

APRIL 18

1 SAMUEL 25–26, WITH
LUKE 16:19–31

A gracious woman retains honor (Proverbs 11:16).

ARE YOU A PERSON OF WISDOM AND GOOD TASTE?

An attractive but tasteless woman is described in Proverbs 11:22: "As a ring of gold in a swine's snout, so is a lovely woman who lacks discretion." The Hebrew term for "discretion" conveys the idea of *taste*. Abigail stands in contrast to the Proverbs 11:22 woman. She is described as "a woman of good understanding and beautiful appearance" (1 Samuel 25:3). In a day when marriages were arranged, Abigail was betrothed to Nabal. His name literally means *a fool*, and it matches him (1 Samuel 25:25). Abigail's prudent actions save her moronic husband's life from an enraged David. Subsequently he gives a triple blessing (1 Samuel 25:32–33). After David blesses God, he pronounces to Abigail, "And blessed is your advice and blessed are you, because you have kept me this day from coming to bloodshed and from avenging myself with my own hand" (1 Samuel 25:33). No wonder Abigail's story is biblically recorded.

EMPLOYMENT POINT: *Display the twin virtues of wisdom and discretion.*

APRIL 19

1 SAMUEL 27–29, WITH LUKE 17:1–19

He who trusts in his own heart is a fool (Proverbs 28:26).

SHOULD GODLY PEOPLE FOLLOW THEIR OWN HEART?

David is a man after God's own heart; however, he is discouraged and listens to his heart. "And David said in his heart, 'Now I shall perish someday by the hand of Saul'" (1 Samuel 27:1). His heart deceives this man of God. The Lord had David ordained king (1 Samuel 16) and confirmed to him repeatedly that he would succeed Saul. Yet he focuses upon the wrong voice. Five centuries after David comes Jeremiah. He exposes the danger of the heart with a profound question. He inquires, "The heart is deceitful above all things, and desperately wicked; who can know it?" (Jeremiah 17:9). The Hebrew term translated "desperately wicked" (also in Jeremiah 15:18; 30:12) carries the basic meaning *to be sick* and usually refers to an incurable wound or pain. Scripture shows the folly of following one's heart.

EMPLOYMENT POINT: *Trust in God's Word, and avoid following your heart.*

April 20

1 Samuel 30–31, with Luke 17:20–37

Remember Lot's wife (Luke 17:32).

Why remember Lot's wife?

The Bible records information about Lot concerning his ancestry and background. Yet we don't know the same details about his wife. We are not even given her name. Sadly, the nameless woman didn't have to die. The Lord gives her ample reasons to choose abandoning Sodom. She would have been among those kidnapped that Abraham rescues (Genesis 14:11–16). It would be at this time that she may have been exposed to Abraham's dealings with Melchizedek (Genesis 14:18–24). Moreover, Lot's wife had the privilege to have Abraham in the family. Abraham is dubbed as "the father of faith," and Lot's wife likely saw and heard about his trust in the living God. Nonetheless, this world's system consisting of the lust of the flesh, the lust of the eyes, and the pride of life captivates Lot's wife, and its allurements kill her!

Employment Point: *Don't attach yourself to this world's system, but the one to come.*

April 21

2 Samuel 1–3, with
Luke 18:1–17

———◈———

How long will my enemy be exalted over me? (Psalm 13:2).

Are you prayerfully waiting for God's justice?

Jesus gives a parable about praying for justice. He chooses a widow as the primary character because she lacks influence with no husband to defend her or financial means for support. Her weapon of choice to fight this battle seems rather unorthodox; she uses shameless persistence. Our Lord describes the scenario as follows: "Now there was a widow in that city; and she came to him, saying, 'Get justice for me from my adversary'" (Luke 18:3). The verb translated "she came" refers to a continual coming in past time. In other words, she pestered the judge daily. He relents, saying, "because this widow troubles me I will avenge her, lest by her continual coming she weary me" (Luke 18:5). Jesus then compares the widow's persistence to God's elect who petition Him consistently for justice (Luke 18:7).

Employment Point: *Boldly and persistently seek God's justice when wronged.*

———◈———

APRIL 22

2 SAMUEL 4–6, WITH
LUKE 18:18–43

The things which are impossible with men are possible with God (Luke 18:27).

WHERE IS YOUR HOPE FOR THE SALVATION OF SINNERS?

First-century Jews often equated riches with God's favor; therefore, the rich young ruler must be going to heaven. Jesus shocks His audience after the affluent ruler walks away from Him with the following statement: "For it is easier for a camel to go through the eye of a needle than for a rich man to enter the kingdom of God" (Luke 18:25). The Lord picks the largest animal (the camel) and smallest object (a needle) familiar to the people to illustrate His lesson. "And those who heard it said, 'Who then can be saved?'" (Luke 18:26). Jesus has already pulled the rug out from under them by exposing their erroneous worldview on salvation. Then He exclaims, "The things which are impossible with men are possible with God" (Luke 18:27).

EMPLOYMENT POINT: *Rely upon God and the gospel's saving power to reach all people.*

APRIL 23

2 SAMUEL 7–9, WITH
LUKE 19:1–28

He has delivered us from the power of darkness and conveyed us into the kingdom of the Son of His love (Colossians 1:13).

WHOSE KINGDOM ARE YOU BUILDING?

David reigns over a united Israel and desires to build a house for the "ark of God" (2 Samuel 7:2). The king's idea will be brought to fruition, but under the reign of Solomon. Nathan relays the following shocking message to David: "Also the LORD tells you that He will make you a house" (2 Samuel 7:11). Subsequently the surprised king is informed that God will give him an eternal house, throne, and kingdom (2 Samuel 7:12–16). Approximately one thousand years later, Gabriel tells Mary the virgin that her Son will fulfill the promise shared with David (Luke 1:30–33). As the Lord honors David for his desire to build the Temple to house the ark of the covenant, so God honors those who live for Him.

EMPLOYMENT POINT: *Build upon Christ's eternal kingdom, and your reward will last.*

April 24

2 Samuel 10–12, with Luke 19:29–48

Your word I have hidden in my heart, that I might not sin against You (Psalm 119:11).

Where should you go when temptation knocks at your door?

King David is a powerbroker. Repeatedly the word "sent" is used in 2 Samuel 11 showing that David carries great authority and dispatches people at will. After observing Bathsheba bathing he "sent and inquired about the woman" (2 Samuel 11:3). Then, after learning that she was married, "David sent messengers, and took her" (2 Samuel 11:4). Even after trying to cover up the scandal, "David wrote a letter to Joab and sent it by the hand of Uriah" (2 Samuel 11:14). This letter, carried by a loyal subject of the king, is Uriah's death sentence. Subsequent to David committing adultery and having Uriah murdered, "the LORD sent Nathan to David" (2 Samuel 12:1). David should have turned to the Lord and the man of God before he entered into temptation.

Employment Point: *Turn to God and godly people for strength in time of need.*

APRIL 25

2 SAMUEL 13–14, WITH LUKE 20:1–26

Render therefore to Caesar the things that are Caesar's, and to God the things that are God's (Luke 20:25).

DO GOD AND GOVERNMENT HAVE TO BE IN CONFLICT?

The religious hierarchy seeks to entrap Jesus. They ask, "Is it lawful for us to pay taxes to Caesar or not?" (Luke 20:22). An affirmative reply by Jesus would stir ill will with the Jews, because the Romans controlled both land and taxes. Conversely, if He answered in the negative, then the Roman government would seek retribution. Our Lord wisely points to the image on the denarius, which was Caesar's. Referring to the term "image" would cause the Jews to think about man being made in God's image (as shown in Genesis 1:26). Those hearing Jesus understand that they are to pay the government the tax money due to them, and similarly render what belongs to God.

EMPLOYMENT POINT: *Render government their due, and to God who created you.*

APRIL 26

2 SAMUEL 15–16, WITH LUKE 20:27–47

The LORD said to my Lord, "Sit at My right hand, till I make Your enemies Your footstool" (Psalm 110:1).

DO YOU HONOR JESUS AS FULLY MAN AND FULLY GOD?

Jesus asks the following question: "How can they say that the Christ is the Son of David?" (Luke 20:41). His question leads them beyond His humanity to His deity. Jesus quotes from Psalm 110:1, which refers to the Father (LORD) speaking to His Son (Lord). Although Jesus is the Son of David (emphasizing His humanity), He is also the Son of God (pointing to His deity). Moreover, the Psalm Jesus quotes from shows that He's a King. The Father speaking to the Son says, "Rule in the midst of Your enemies!" (Psalm 110:2). Furthermore, Jesus is an eternal High Priest "according to the order of Melchizedek" (Psalm 110:4). Finally, the Lord is depicted as a Judge. "He shall judge among the nations" (Psalm 110:6).

EMPLOYMENT POINT: *Honor Jesus, who is fully man and fully God.*

APRIL 27

2 SAMUEL 17–18, WITH LUKE 21:1–19

And David said, "O LORD, I pray, turn the counsel of Ahithophel into foolishness! (2 Samuel 15:31).

DO YOU TURN TO PRAYER WHEN YOU ARE OVERMATCHED?

Ahithophel's council is renowned. "Now the advice of Ahithophel, which he gave in those days, was as if one had inquired at the oracle of God. So was all the advice of Ahithophel both with David and with Absalom" (2 Samuel 16:23). This is why David petitions the Lord to "turn the counsel of Ahithophel into foolishness." Why does Ahithophel betray David? It seems that Ahithophel is Bathsheba's grandfather. "Eliam [is] the son of Ahithophel the Gilonite" (2 Samuel 23:34). Connect this with 2 Samuel 11:3, "Is this not Bathsheba, the daughter of Eliam, the wife of Uriah the Hittite?" Nonetheless God honors David's prayer and the counsel of Ahithophel is rejected for the advice of Hushai (2 Samuel 17:1–14) that spares David's life from Absalom and his conspirators. Sadly, Ahithophel kills himself (2 Samuel 17:23).

EMPLOYMENT POINT: *Pray for God's intervention when you are overwhelmed.*

April 28

2 Samuel 19–20, with
Luke 21:20–38

———◆———

Pray for the peace of Jerusalem: May they prosper who love you (Psalm 122:6).

Are you praying for the peace of Jerusalem?

The name Jerusalem means *city of peace*. Jesus rides into Jerusalem on Palm Sunday; however, the people miss the significance of the Lord being their Savior (Luke 19:28, 42). John writes, "He came to His own, and His own did not receive Him" (John 1:11). Both people and place experience judgment as a consequence for not believing on the Messiah.

Because the Jews didn't receive the One who fulfilled prophecy on Palm Sunday (Daniel 9:24–25; Zechariah 9:1–9), they are the recipients of another prophecy (Luke 21:20–24). Titus, son of Emperor Vespasian, surrounded Jerusalem on April 9 in AD 70 as Jesus predicted (Luke 21:20) and several months later devastated the city. Our Lord says, "For these are the days of vengeance, that all things which are written may be fulfilled" (Luke 21:22). We should pray for Jerusalem's peace, which will ultimately be established at Jesus' Second Coming.

Employment Point: *Pray for the peace of Jerusalem.*

———◆———

APRIL 29

2 SAMUEL 21–22, WITH LUKE 22:1–30

And I bestow upon you a kingdom, just as My Father bestowed one upon Me (Luke 22:29).

WHAT'S THE CONNECTION BETWEEN SUFFERING AND GLORY?

Jesus promises His apostles, "when the Son of Man sits on the throne of His glory, you who have followed Me will also sit on twelve thrones, judging the twelve tribes of Israel" (Matthew 19:28). Why is this specific promise given? Previously Jesus shared with them, "But you are those who have continued with Me in My trials" (Luke 22:28). Before the crown comes the suffering. Observe the following association Paul makes with the saints present suffering and future glory in Romans 8:17: "and if children, then heirs—heirs of God and joint heirs with Christ, if indeed we suffer with Him, that we may also be glorified together." Similarly, our Lord Jesus suffered and "God also has highly exalted Him and given Him the name which is above every name" (Philippians 2:9).

EMPLOYMENT POINT: *Endure present suffering for future glory.*

April 30

2 Samuel 23–24, with Luke 22:31–53

For by You I can run against a troop (2 Samuel 22:30).

Are you willing to stand alone for the Lord?

David knows how to stand alone against the opposition. He volunteers to fight against the behemoth Goliath when no one dared. The aging king praises his loyal soldiers and lists a number of their mighty feats. Adino the Eznite leads the list of these mighty warriors "because he had killed eight hundred men at one time" (2 Samuel 23:8). Next, Eleazar makes a stand when his fellow soldiers retreated (2 Samuel 23:9). The following is said about his prowess during the battle: "He arose and attacked the Philistines until his hand was weary, and his hand stuck to the sword. The LORD brought about a great victory that day; and the people returned after him only to plunder" (2 Samuel 23:10). God honors those who boldly fight His battles.

EMPLOYMENT POINT: *Be willing to stand alone, if necessary, for the Lord.*

May 1

1 Kings 1–2, with
Luke 22:54–71

I tell you, Peter, the rooster shall not crow this day before you will deny three times that you know Me (Luke 22:34).

What do we know that is surer than death and taxes?

Peter is abounding with self-confidence. Earlier that day he had told Jesus, "Even if I have to die with You, I will not deny You!" (Matthew 26:35). The self-assured fisherman should have recalled Jesus' following statement before he made his bold proclamation: "Heaven and earth will pass away," declares Jesus, "but My words will by no means pass away" (Matthew 24:35). Jesus' prediction about Peter comes to pass because He cannot lie (Luke 22:60–61). His promises are wrapped up in His perfect nature. Because He not only speaks truth, but also is truth, we can rest assured knowing that "the entirety of Your word is truth, and every one of Your righteous judgments endures forever" (Psalm 119:160).

Employment Point: *Submit to God's Word because it is true.*

May 2

1 Kings 3–5, with
Luke 23:1–26

———◆———

Therefore give to Your servant an understanding heart to judge Your people, that I may discern between good and evil (1 Kings 3:9).

What would you ask God for if He granted you one request?

The verb for "understanding" literally means *to hear*. At times it carries the idea of understanding, as it does in 1 Kings 3:9. Solomon desires to govern the children of Israel by discerning good and evil. James informs us that God grants wisdom to all those who asks (James 1:5). Then he continues, "But let him ask in faith, with no doubting, for he who doubts is like a wave of the sea driven and tossed by the wind" (James 1:6). Clearly the Lord of all wisdom gives Solomon a "hearing heart," as is demonstrated by his wise decision between the two prostitutes and two babies—one alive and one dead (1 Kings 3:16–28). Let's seek the wisdom from above by faith.

Employment Point: *Ask God for an understanding heart, to serve Him wisely.*

———◆———

MAY 3

1 KINGS 6–7, WITH
LUKE 23:27–38

And when they had come to the place called Calvary, there they cruci-fied Him, and the criminals, one on the right hand and the other on the left (Luke 23:33).

HOW DID JESUS ASSOCIATE WITH SINNERS?

Jesus begins His ministry by identifying with sinners. Luke records, "When all the people were baptized, it came to pass that Jesus also was baptized" (Luke 3:21). Similarly, He ends His ministry on earth between two thieves. Why? For one, He fulfills prophecy. Isaiah writes, "And He was numbered with the transgressors, and He bore the sin of many" (Isaiah 53:12). Paul captures the essence of why Jesus is bap-tized with sinners and dies between two sinners. "For He [God] made Him [Jesus] who knew no sin to be sin for us, that we might become the righteousness of God in Him" (2 Corinthians 5:21). Although Jesus never sinned, He becomes the substitute for sinners and will-ingly identified with them.

EMPLOYMENT POINT: *Believe on Jesus, who died among sinners to save sinners.*

MAY 4

1 KINGS 8–9, WITH
LUKE 23:39–56

For there is one God and one Mediator between God and men, the Man Christ Jesus (1 Timothy 2:5).

ARE YOU REGULARLY PRAYING TO OVERCOME SUBMITTING TO TEMPTATION?

Jesus tells Peter, James, and John, "Pray that you may not enter into temptation" (Luke 22:40). Our Lord understands temptation experientially. Satan hurled hellish enticements at Him (Luke 4:1–13). He never bows to the wishes of Satan and temporal pleasures. The writer of Hebrews shares, "For we do not have a High Priest who cannot sympathize with our weaknesses, but was in all points tempted as we are, yet without sin" (Hebrews 4:15). Jesus prays and then submits to partaking of the cup, which means He will endure suffering and the wrath of God (since the sin of the world will be placed upon Him). Today our Mediator and High Priest according to Hebrews 7:25 "always lives to make intercession for them."

EMPLOYMENT POINT: *Follow Jesus' example and pray, lest you submit to temptation.*

May 5

1 Kings 10–11, with
Luke 24:1–35

And they said to one another, "Did not our heart burn within us while He talked with us on the road, and while He opened the Scriptures to us?" (Luke 24:32).

Do you systematically experience biblical heartburn?

Jesus conceals His identity as He treks seven miles with Cleopas and an unnamed follower. They tell the sad tale about Jesus' death and don't anticipate His resurrection. Our Lord then says to them: "O foolish ones, and slow of heart to believe in all that the prophets have spoken! Ought not the Christ to have suffered these things and to enter into His glory?" (Luke 24:25–26). Subsequently, Dr. Luke gives the prescription for biblical heartburn using two imperfect tense verbs, which show continual action in past time—"He talked" and "He opened" (Luke 24:32). As we open the Bible and allow the Word to speak to us, we can also enjoy biblical heartburn!

Employment Point: *Regularly open the Scriptures to experience biblical heartburn.*

MAY 6

1 KINGS 12–13, WITH
LUKE 24:36–53

God is Spirit, and those who worship Him must worship in spirit and truth (John 4:24).

ARE YOU WORSHIPING GOD IN SPIRIT AND TRUTH?

God instructed Solomon to erect the Temple in Jerusalem where Jewish males are annually required to attend the Feasts of Passover, Pentecost, and Tabernacles (Deuteronomy 16:16). Jeroboam exudes ungodliness by establishing an idolatrous system of worship to encourage the residents of the Northern Kingdom not to depart for Judah in the south, which might lead to their permanent relocation. For this reason he designs two golden calves. "And he set up one in Bethel, and the other he put in Dan" (1 Kings 12:29). The Lord dispatches a man of God from Judah (the southern region) to confront the wicked king (1 Kings 13:1). He not only condemns Jeroboam's activity, but also predicts the zeal of godly king Josiah, who wouldn't be born for nearly three hundred years (1 Kings 13:2). Sadly, Jeroboam persists in wickedness.

EMPLOYMENT POINT: *Worship God in spirit and truth to please Him.*

MAY 7

1 KINGS 14–15, WITH JOHN 1:1–28

And the Word became flesh and dwelt among us, and we beheld His glory, the glory as of the only begotten of the Father, full of grace and truth (John 1:14).

DO YOU STILL MARVEL THAT GOD BECAME LIKE US, SO THAT WE COULD BECOME LIKE HIM?

Jesus took on flesh in order that He could become "the Lamb of God who takes away the sin of the world!" (John 1:29). Paul marvels and calls this a mystery, which biblically means a sacred secret that was once unknown but now has been revealed. He writes, "And without controversy great is the mystery of godliness: God was manifested in the flesh" (1 Timothy 3:16). Relying upon Jesus' finished work transfers an individual from darkness into the kingdom of light. John states, "But as many as received Him, to them He gave the right to become children of God" (John 1:12).

EMPLOYMENT POINT: *Believe on Jesus' finished work, and marvel at the incarnation.*

MAY 8

1 KINGS 16–18, WITH JOHN 1:29–51

And my God shall supply all your need according to His riches in glory by Christ Jesus (Philippians 4:19).

DO YOU TRUST GOD TO PROVIDE DURING DIFFICULT TIMES?

Baal worship is firmly established under Ahab. Yet Elijah, being in the minority numerically, confronts the powerful king, "As the LORD God of Israel lives, before whom I stand, there shall not be dew nor rain these years, except at my word" (1 Kings 17:1). God sends Elijah to the Brook Cherith to hide the prophet and supernaturally meet his needs. Subsequently He leads the obedient prophet to Sidon to care for, and to be cared for by, an impoverished widow. The single parent tells Elijah, "As the LORD your God lives, I do not have bread" (1 Kings 17:12). She refers to God as "your God." Elijah's great faith moves her to embrace the promises of God, and the Lord meets her needs.

EMPLOYMENT POINT: *Serve God, knowing that He will provide for you.*

MAY 9

1 KINGS 19–20, WITH JOHN 2

———◦◦◦———

The LORD is on my side; I will not fear. What can man do to me? (Psalm 118:6).

DO YOU LIVE LIKE YOU ARE IN THE MAJORITY WHEN YOU ARE A MINORITY?

Elijah exhibits the unmistakable characteristics of burn out. He had just done battle with the prophets of Baal and then "ran ahead of Ahab to the entrance of Jezreel" (1 Kings 18:46), which would be an approximate twenty-mile run. Next, Jezebel warns Elijah that as he had executed the prophets of Baal that she would "make your life as the life of one of them by tomorrow about this time" (1 Kings 19:2). The man of God loses his spiritual nerve. God encourages the prophet by manifesting His power and presence. After passing before Elijah He displays His person and work through a mighty wind, earthquake, fire, and communicates to him with "a still small voice" (1 Kings 19:11–12).

EMPLOYMENT POINT: *Seek God's renewing power and presence after spiritual battles.*

———◦◦◦———

MAY 10

1 KINGS 21–22, WITH
JOHN 3:1–21

Do not marvel that I said to you, you must be born again (John 3:7).

HAVE YOU BEEN BORN A SECOND TIME?

Jesus is omniscient, "for He knew what was in man" (John 2:25). For this reason, He comprehends that Nicodemus needs salvation. The Greek term for "born again" means *to be born from above* or *to be born again*. Our Lord explains to Nicodemus two births—one physical and the other spiritual. To begin, Jesus connects the mother's womb (first birth) with "born of water" and "born of flesh" (John 3:4–6). The second birth is for Nicodemus (the first "you" in John 3:7 is singular and refers to Nicodemus) and for everyone (the second "you" in John 3:7 is plural and points to all people). Jesus then uses an Old Testament illustration, emphasizing faith in the "only begotten Son" to be saved (John 3:14–16).

EMPLOYMENT POINT: *Believe in Jesus, who died for your sin and conquered death to be born a second time.*

MAY 11

2 KINGS 1–3, WITH JOHN 3:22–36

And the things that you have heard from me among many witnesses, commit these to faithful men who will be able to teach others also (2 Timothy 2:2).

WHERE IS THE LORD GOD OF ELIJAH? (2 KINGS 2:14).

Elijah knows that his ministry will end soon; his servant Elisha knows that he is entrusted with the enormous task of filling Elijah's sandals at his departure. Three times Elijah tests Elisha as he is traveling by saying, "stay here" (2 Kings 2:2, 4, 6). Similarly, three times the disciple responds: "As the LORD lives, and as your soul lives, I will not leave you!" (2 Kings 2:2, 4, 6). Elisha desires to be equipped for his new role. He asks his predecessor, "Please let a double portion of your spirit be upon me" (2 Kings 2:9). God honors Elisha, who stayed on Elijah like glue. We also need to attach ourselves to godly spiritual mentors who train us for God's service.

EMPLOYMENT POINT: *Stay close to your spiritual mentor, to be equipped for ministry.*

MAY 12

2 KINGS 4–5, WITH JOHN 4:1–30

And many of the Samaritans of that city believed in Him because of the word of the woman who testified, "He told me all that I ever did" (John 4:39).

ARE YOU WITNESSING TO OTHERS ABOUT JESUS' GREATNESS?

Jesus breaks the norms of His day to save one soul. He travels to, not around, Samaria. Israel's ancient enemy, the Assyrians, conquered that city centuries earlier; and some Jews intermarried with Assyrians, creating the Samaritans. Also, Jesus breaks another cultural norm by engaging a woman in conversation. Today's text reveals, "the Son of Man has come to seek and to save that which was lost" (Luke 19:10). Jesus unmasks the woman's questionable lifestyle by stating, "for you have had five husbands, and the one whom you now have is not your husband" (John 4:18). That revelation was instrumental in bringing her to the realization that Jesus is the Messiah.

EMPLOYMENT POINT: *Testify to the greatness of Jesus so that others may be saved.*

MAY 13

2 KINGS 6–8, WITH JOHN 4:31–54

———※———

And Elisha prayed, and said, "LORD, I pray, open his eyes that he may see" (2 Kings 6:17).

HOW GOOD IS YOUR SPIRITUAL ADDITION?

Elisha continually informs the king of Israel about the plans of the king of Syria; therefore, a large army is dispatched to arrest Elisha. His servant wakes up early one morning and sees their camp surrounded. The servant does his physical math by counting or estimating the enemy and says to Elisha, "Alas, my master! What shall we do?" (2 Kings 6:15). The man of God then does the spiritual math and says, "Do not fear, for those who are with us are more than those who are with them" (2 Kings 6:16). Elisha prays and the servant sees the host of angels protecting them (2 Kings 6:17). Perhaps today we should ask, "If God is for us, who can be against us?" (Romans 8:31).

EMPLOYMENT POINT: *Keep your eyes upon the Lord during life's trials for the right outlook on life.*

———※———

MAY 14

2 KINGS 9–11, WITH JOHN 5:1–24

———◆———

And your house and your kingdom shall be established forever before you. Your throne shall be established forever (2 Samuel 7:16).

CAN YOU TRUST GOD TO FULFILL HIS WORD, DESPITE WICKED OPPOSITION?

The Lord promises David an eternal house, throne, and kingdom (2 Samuel 7:12–16). Yet wicked Athaliah, the daughter of Ahab and Jezebel, seeks to destroy David's line. "When Athaliah the mother of Ahaziah saw that her son was dead, she arose and destroyed all the royal heirs" (2 Kings 11:1). Protection is given to Joash during the holocaust and subsequently he is crowned king; therefore, her wicked devices are thwarted and God's promise remains. The murderous Athaliah who seeks to cut off the line of David rightly perishes with the sword (2 Kings 11:20). Moses' words still ring true, revealing God's timeless truths. He writes, "be sure your sin will find you out" (Numbers 32:23).

EMPLOYMENT POINT: *Persevere doing what is right, knowing that God's Word will be fulfilled despite wicked opposition.*

———◆———

MAY 15

2 KINGS 12–14, WITH JOHN 5:25–47

By the mouth of two or three witnesses the matter shall be established (Deuteronomy 19:15).

ARE YOU AMONG THOSE WHO FAITHFULLY WITNESS TO JESUS' DEITY?

There exists a plethora of witnesses to the deity of Jesus. Based upon the principle from Deuteronomy 19:15, Jesus cites several. He says, "There is another who bears witness of Me" (John 5:32). "Another" means *another of the same kind* and points to God the Father; He testifies to Jesus being God. Next, Jesus lists John the Baptist among the witnesses who "was the burning and shining lamp" (John 5:35). Our Lord includes Himself in the mix. He shares, "But I have a greater witness than John's" (John 5:36). He then refers to the Scriptures "which testify of Me" (John 5:39). The many witnesses have a unified theme: the deity of Jesus Christ. Let our works also demonstrate to a dark world that Jesus is God!

EMPLOYMENT POINT: *Be a modern witness to the deity of Jesus.*

MAY 16

2 KINGS 15–17, WITH
JOHN 6:1–21

───※◈※───

But this He said to test him, for He Himself knew what He would do (John 6:6).

HE SAID TO PHILIP, "WHERE SHALL WE BUY BREAD, THAT THESE MAY EAT?" (JOHN 6:5).

Jesus doesn't ask the above question to Philip because He needs an answer; our Lord knows all things. The Good Shepherd's question has a twofold effect: It shows the inability of men to meet the needs of mankind, and displays the impossibility to feed the vast multitude. Philip should have turned to Jesus and said, "For with God nothing will be impossible" (Luke 1:37). This is the first miracle the disciples participate in with the Lord. Amazingly, Jesus provides "as much [bread and fish] as they wanted" (John 6:11). The verb "they wanted" occurs in the imperfect tense showing continual action in past time. Jesus also had "twelve baskets with the fragments" left over to feed the apostles (John 6:13).

EMPLOYMENT POINT: *Turn to Jesus during your next test, and trust in His provision.*

───※◈※───

MAY 17

2 KINGS 18–19, WITH JOHN 6:22–44

———◦———

And as Moses lifted up the serpent in the wilderness, even so must the Son of Man be lifted up (John 3:14).

HAVE YOU TURNED SOMETHING GOOD INTO AN IDOL?

God had used a bronze serpent for the Israelites bitten by snakes to look upon, to be healed (Numbers 21:4–9). Centuries later, they twisted the original use of the bronze serpent and turned it into an idol. The writer of 2 Kings explains that Hezekiah "broke in pieces the bronze serpent that Moses had made; for until those days the children of Israel burned incense to it, and called it Nehushtan" (2 Kings 18:4).

Christians are admonished by Paul how to prevent themselves from the practice of covetousness, which he equates with idolatry. He writes, "Therefore put to death your members which are on the earth: fornication, uncleanness, passion, evil desire, and covetousness, which is idolatry" (Colossians 3:5).

EMPLOYMENT POINT: *Keep Jesus on the throne of your heart by executing the deeds of the flesh.*

———◦———

MAY 18

2 KINGS 20–22, WITH JOHN 6:45–71

———◦———

Whoever eats My flesh and drinks My blood has eternal life, and I will raise him up at the last day (John 6:54).

WHY WOULD JESUS ASK HIS DISCIPLES TO EAT HIS FLESH AND DRINK HIS BLOOD, WHICH WOULD VIOLATE SCRIPTURE (LEVITICUS 3:17)?

Jesus' terse statement moves a portion of His followers to walk away from Him. John writes, "From that time many of His disciples went back and walked with Him no more" (John 6:66). Clearly Jesus isn't talking about literally eating His flesh and drinking His blood. He Himself says, "Do not think that I came to destroy the Law or the Prophets. I did not come to destroy but to fulfill" (Matthew 5:17). The person who metaphorically eats Jesus' flesh and drinks His blood is the individual who believes on Him and receives the gift of eternal life (John 6:54).

EMPLOYMENT POINT: *Believe on Jesus, who offered His body and blood for our salvation, and follow Him for length of days.*

———◦———

MAY 19

2 KINGS 23–25, WITH
JOHN 7:1–31

Now before him there was no king like him, who turned to the LORD with all his heart, with all his soul, and with all his might, according to all the Law of Moses; nor after him did any arise like him (2 Kings 23:25).

WHAT IS EATING YOU UP?

The unnamed man of God predicts the birth and zeal of Josiah. First Kings 13:2 unveils, "Behold, a child, Josiah by name, shall be born to the house of David; and on you he shall sacrifice the priests of the high places who burn incense on you, and men's bones shall be burned on you." Six centuries after the death of Josiah comes a King whose birth and zeal are also predicted. When Jesus cleanses the Temple His disciples remember Psalm 69:9, which is quoted in John 2:17: "Zeal for Your house has eaten Me up." Josiah's and Jesus' zeal are exemplary.

EMPLOYMENT POINT: *Be consumed by zeal for the work of the Lord.*

MAY 20

1 CHRONICLES 1–2, WITH JOHN 7:32–53

———◆———

For as in Adam all die, even so in Christ all shall be made alive (1 Corinthians 15:22).

HAVE YOU CONSIDERED THE IMPACT THAT ADAM AND JESUS HAVE ON MANKIND?

Adam's name appears first in 1 Chronicles 1:1. He was our federal head or representative in the Garden of Eden. Paul describes the implications of his disobedience as follows: "Therefore, just as through one man sin entered the world, and death through sin, and thus death spread to all men, because all sinned" (Romans 5:12). Paul uses the past tense verb "sinned" (in the words "because all sinned") of us because when Adam sinned as our representative so did we.

Conversely, Jesus takes upon Himself the sin of the world, so that all who believe in Him shall live eternally. The apostle gives the contrast, "For since by man came death, by Man also came the resurrection of the dead" (1 Corinthians 15:21).

EMPLOYMENT POINT: *Live for Jesus, who makes all who believe in Him spiritually alive.*

———◆———

MAY 21

1 CHRONICLES 3–5, WITH JOHN 8:1–20

God is light and in Him is no darkness at all (1 John 1:5).

ARE YOU WALKING IN GOD'S LIGHT?

Jesus arrives at the Temple early one morning. He is rudely inter-rupted by the scribes and Pharisees who "brought to Him a woman caught in adultery" (John 8:3). They seek to entrap Jesus, by pointing out that Moses' Law demands the death penalty for this act. If He encourages her to be stoned then the Romans would be upset because only they can enact capital punishment. On the other hand, if He ignores the Law, then His own people will disown Him. What Jesus writes on the ground isn't as important as how He writes. He writes with the finger of God, which is how the Law was written (Exodus 31:18). The woman who was in the dark repents and now lives in the light. No wonder Jesus says, "I am the light of the world" (John 8:12).

EMPLOYMENT POINT: *Remain in the light by following Jesus.*

MAY 22

1 CHRONICLES 6–7, WITH JOHN 8:21–36

This is My beloved Son, in whom I am well pleased (Matthew 3:17).

DO YOU ACCURATELY TEACH AND OBEY THE BIBLE, TO PLEASE GOD?

Jesus is the greatest Bible teacher who ever lived. Even those from His hometown of Nazareth acknowledge His ability. Luke records, "So all bore witness to Him, and marveled at the gracious words" (Luke 4:22). After Jesus preached the Sermon on the Mount comes another stellar report. Matthew shares, "that the people were astonished at His teaching, for He taught them as one having authority, and not as the scribes" (Matthew 7:28–29). Unlike the scribes who quoted from other so-called authorities when they teach, Jesus speaks the very Word of God. He Himself claims, "but as My Father taught Me, I speak these things" (John 8:28). He derives His Bible lessons from the Father. Jesus then adds, "for I always do those things that please Him" (John 8:29).

EMPLOYMENT POINT: *Please God by accurately teaching and obeying His Word.*

MAY 23

1 CHRONICLES 8–10, WITH JOHN 8:37–59

Most assuredly, I say to you, before Abraham was, I AM (John 8:58).

DO YOU REGULARLY PROCLAIM THE DEITY OF JESUS TO OTHERS?

Jesus claims to be God. The "I am" statements in John connect to Exodus 3:14, which show Jesus' equality with the Father. He is hated because of making this connection and the Jewish leaders "took up stones to throw at Him" (John 8:59). Later Jesus says, "I and My Father are one" (John 10:30). Observe the word "again" in the next verse: "Then the Jews took up stones again to stone Him." Why did they try to stone Him again? They respond to Him with the following statement: "For a good work we do not stone You, but for blasphemy, and because You, being a Man, make Yourself God" (John 10:33). John writes these things so that the world "may believe that Jesus is the Christ, the Son of God" (John 20:31).

EMPLOYMENT POINT: *Herald Jesus' deity to the unsaved.*

MAY 24

1 CHRONICLES 11–13, WITH JOHN 9:1–23

And David said with longing, "Oh, that someone would give me a drink of water from the well of Bethlehem, which is by the gate!" (1 Chronicles 11:17).

HOW LOYAL ARE YOU TO GOD'S LEADERS?

David yearns for a drink of water from Bethlehem, which is his place of birth; however, the Philistines block the way. Three of David's mighty men risk their lives to fulfill his desire. First Chronicles reports, "So the three broke through the camp of the Philistines, drew water from the well of Bethlehem that was by the gate, and took it and brought it to David" (1 Chronicles 11:18). Now that's loyalty! David is a man of war; he needs faithful and loyal men by his side. Through the ages, loyal servants have stood with men of God. Think about the following list of loyal assistants to their leader: Joshua, Caleb, Elisha, Timothy, Epaproditus, the apostles.

EMPLOYMENT POINT: *Be loyal to the men of God in your life.*

MAY 25

1 CHRONICLES 14–16, WITH JOHN 9:24–41

———◦———

For because you did not do it the first time, the LORD our God broke out against us, because we did not consult Him about the proper order (1 Chronicles 15:13).

DO YOU TURN TO GOD FOR DIRECTION, SO THAT YOU CAN DO THINGS RIGHT?

David does not do so concerning the moving of the ark and the consequence is fatal. God gives us His Word to bring Him glory through observing His ways. The Lord guides us to order and not chaos. Paul writes to a chaotic church, "Let all things be done decently and in order" (1 Corinthians 14:40). First Chronicles 15:13 refers to "the proper order" of worship. The Hebrew term for "proper order" occurs in the context to describe the plans and instruction for the tabernacle (Exodus 35–40). It also occurs for the specifications of the Temple (1 Kings 6:38). Moreover, it emerges concerning the rearing of Samson (Judges 13:12).

EMPLOYMENT POINT: *Consult the Lord through the Word and prayer, to honor His ways.*

———◦———

MAY 26

1 CHRONICLES 17–19, WITH JOHN 10:1–21

I am the good shepherd. The good shepherd gives His life for the sheep (John 10:11).

DO YOU DEEPLY APPRECIATE THE FATHER AND SON'S SACRIFICE?

The good shepherd soon will literally sacrifice Himself for the sheep. God's love becomes evident through the gift of Jesus to die for our sin. John writes, "For God so loved the world that He gave His only begotten Son" (John 3:16). Moreover, Paul concurs, "But God demonstrates His own love toward us, in that while we were still sinners, Christ died for us" (Romans 5:8). Shortly before Jesus offers Himself as the substitute for our sin, He says, "Greater love has no one than this, than to lay down one's life for his friends" (John 15:13). Both Father and Son possess an eternal love for us that is manifested through the gift of Jesus Christ in our behalf; "Thanks be to God for His indescribable gift!" (2 Corinthians 9:15).

EMPLOYMENT POINT: *Marvel at the love of the Father and Son through Jesus' sacrifice.*

May 27

1 Chronicles 20–22, with John 10:22–42

Pride goes before destruction, and a haughty spirit before a fall (Proverbs 16:18).

Are you yielding to pride?

Satan has perfected the art of temptation; he has used three allurements for thousands of years. The Wicked One employed them on Adam and Eve, Jesus, and similarly to David. John describes them as follows: "For all that is in the world—the lust of the flesh, the lust of the eyes, and the pride of life" (1 John 2:16). The last temptation consists of "the pride of life," which means *self-boasting about one's own accomplishments*, and labels David's sin. Prideful David dispatches a reluctant Joab to take a census (1 Chronicles 21:2–6). Generally speaking, there is nothing wrong with numbering people. After all, we have a book in the Bible entitled Numbers! It seems that David wants to boast about the military prowess of the nation, which leads to God chastening Israel.

Employment Point: *Praise God for His accomplishments in your life, and avoid self-boasting.*

MAY 28

1 CHRONICLES 23–25, WITH JOHN 11:1–17

Wait on the LORD; be of good courage, and He shall strengthen your heart; wait, I say, on the LORD! (Psalm 27:14).

DO YOU PATIENTLY WAIT FOR GOD'S PERFECT TIMING?

There was a Jewish tradition in Jesus' day that the soul of the deceased hovered over the body for three days, hoping for life to be restored. Jesus, knowing that Lazarus had died, doesn't visit the family until four days after his passing (John 11:17). Our Lord tells the disciples, "This sickness is not unto death, but for the glory of God, that the Son of God may be glorified through it" (John 11:4). Jesus, being eternally God, is the author, sustainer, and controller of both time and life. Paul describes Him as "before all things, and in Him all things consist" (Colossians 1:17). Jesus' appearance in Bethany and resurrection of Lazarus are according to His divine plan. His timing is always perfect.

EMPLOYMENT POINT: *Wait on the Lord's perfect timing in all matters in your life.*

MAY 29

1 CHRONICLES 26–27, WITH JOHN 11:18–46

———◆———

Jesus said to her, "Your brother will rise again" (John 11:23).

DO YOU BELIEVE IN JESUS' ABILITY TO RAISE THE DEAD?

Job suffers much. Yet he trusts in God's ability to raise the dead. He shares, "And after my skin is destroyed, this I know, that in my flesh I shall see God" (Job 19:26). Mary also believes in the future resurrection of the dead; however, Jesus has an immediate resurrection in mind. He assures her, "I am the resurrection and the life. He who believes in Me, though he may die, he shall live, and whoever lives and believes in Me shall never die. Do you believe this?" (John 11:25–26). Friend, do you believe this? Moreover, Paul stresses the importance of the saints' resurrection. Based upon this truth, he pens, "But thanks be to God, who gives us the victory through our Lord Jesus Christ" (1 Corinthians 15:57).

EMPLOYMENT POINT: *Believe on Jesus' promise and power to raise the dead.*

———◆———

MAY 30

1 CHRONICLES 28–29, WITH JOHN 11:47–57

He who calls you is faithful, who also will do it (1 Thessalonians 5:24).

DO YOU BELIEVE THAT GOD'S CALLING IS HIS ENABLING?

Solomon is tasked with a daunting responsibility: He is to build a Temple to house the living God. David makes great preparation for this enormous undertaking. Having personally experienced the Lord's faithfulness to His promises, the aging king encourages Solomon with sage advice: "Be strong and of good courage, and do it; do not fear nor be dismayed, for the LORD God—my God—will be with you. He will not leave you nor forsake you, until you have finished all the work for the service of the house of the LORD" (1 Chronicles 28:20). It doesn't matter whether God's promises to complete a work in us relate to sanctification (1 Thessalonians 5:24) or bringing a ministry assignment to fruition like Solomon received. His Word never fails!

EMPLOYMENT POINT: *Trust the Lord to complete the tasks He assigns to you.*

MAY 31

2 CHRONICLES 1–3, WITH JOHN 12:1–19

Now Solomon began to build the house of the LORD at Jerusalem on Mount Moriah (2 Chronicles 3:1).

ARE YOU OFFERING SACRIFICES WORTHY OF GOD?

A command is given to Abraham centuries before the erecting of the Temple. God said, "Take now your son, your only son Isaac, whom you love, and go to the land of Moriah, and offer him there as a burnt offering" (Genesis 22:2). Two millennia later another offering would be given in this same location, now called Calvary. Yet the sacrifice of Jesus would not be halted. Mary offers a sacrifice in preparation for the death of Jesus just days before his crucifixion. She "took a pound of very costly oil of spikenard, [and] anointed the feet of Jesus" (John 12:3). The price of her sacrifice would equal one year's pay for the average day laborer. Like Abraham, Solomon, and Mary, offer sacrifices worthy of our King!

EMPLOYMENT POINT: *Honor Jesus with sacrifices worthy of His great sacrifice.*

June 1

2 Chronicles 4–6, with John 12:20–50

———◆———

When Solomon had finished praying, fire came down from heaven and consumed the burnt offering and the sacrifices; and the glory of the LORD filled the temple (2 Chronicles 7:1).

Are you offering sacrifices that please God?

King Solomon finishes building the Temple and dedicates it to the Lord. Many had sacrificially given so this huge undertaking could be finished. David, who was not permitted to build the ark, gave from his personal treasury for this project. "And Solomon brought in the things which his father David had dedicated: the silver and the gold and all the furnishings" (2 Chronicles 5:1). David lives up to Paul's words, "For the children ought not to lay up for the parents, but the parents for the children" (2 Corinthians 12:14). Solomon and the congregation also "were sacrificing sheep and oxen that could not be counted" (2 Chronicles 5:6). God's holy fire consumes the cumulative sacrifices of His people to show His pleasure.

EMPLOYMENT POINT: *Please God by sacrificially giving to His work.*

———◆———

June 2

2 Chronicles 7–9, with John 13:1–17

For I have given you an example, that you should do as I have done to you (John 13:15).

Is Jesus just concerned about washing one another's feet?

The slave in a home had the responsibility to wash the guests' feet. Jesus takes upon Himself this role. Paul describes His mindset as follows: "But [He] made Himself of no reputation, taking the form of a bondservant" (Philippians 2:7). Jesus seems to have a broader application than just to wash one another's feet. He is about to die for their sins and reminds them about the world's hatred (John 15:18–19). Also, Jesus is aware about their bickering concerning who will be the greatest (Luke 22:24). He redirects them by sharing, "Greater love has no one than this, than to lay down one's life for his friends" (John 15:13). Jesus desires each disciple to be willing to die for the other.

Employment Point: *Follow Jesus by willingly laying down your life for the brethren.*

JUNE 3

2 CHRONICLES 10–12, WITH JOHN 13:18–38

———◦◉◦———

When he humbled himself, the wrath of the LORD turned from him, so as not to destroy him completely; and things also went well in Judah (2 Chronicles 12:12).

DO YOU NEED TO HUMBLE YOURSELF BEFORE THE LORD?

King Rehoboam exudes arrogance when Judah becomes strong. The Lord takes him down a notch by sending the Egyptians to chasten his kingdom "because they had transgressed against the LORD" (2 Kings 12:2). "God resists the proud," writes Peter, "but gives grace to the humble" (1 Peter 5:5). He approves of those who exhibit the following three characteristics: "On him who is poor and of a contrite spirit, and who trembles at My word" (Isaiah 66:2). To be "poor" conveys *to be bowed down* while "a contrite spirit" means *to have a crushed* or *smashed spirit*. The term "crushed" is used of Mephibosheth on account of his nurse dropping him, which crushed his feet (2 Samuel 4:4; 9:3).

EMPLOYMENT POINT: *Remain humble before the Lord to receive His approval of your life.*

———◦◉◦———

JUNE 4

2 CHRONICLES 13–16, WITH JOHN 14

———※———

For the eyes of the LORD run to and fro throughout the whole earth, to show Himself strong on behalf of those whose heart is loyal to Him (2 Chronicles 16:9).

DO YOU SERVE GOD WITH AN UNDIVIDED HEART?

King Asa exhibits great faith while serving the Lord. His army consists of 580,000 men (2 Chronicles 14:8). "Then Zerah the Ethiopian came out against them with an army of a million men" (2 Chronicles 14:9). By faith Asa leads his troops to victory against overwhelming odds. Yet later he makes an agreement with the king of Syria for military protection against another foe instead of trusting in the Lord (2 Chronicles 16:7–8). God's eyes scan the globe looking for a servant "whose heart is loyal to Him" (2 Chronicles 16:9). "Loyal" means *to be complete, whole,* and *undivided.* Completely follow the Lord, unlike Asa who did not in his sunset years (2 Chronicles 16:12).

EMPLOYMENT POINT: *Loyally follow God with an undivided heart, even when the enemy vastly outnumbers you.*

———※———

June 5

2 Chronicles 17–19, with John 15

You did not choose Me, but I chose you and appointed you that you should go and bear fruit (John 15:16).

Why has God chosen you for His service?

Jesus teaches His followers, "You did not choose Me." The verb "choose" occurs in the middle voice and carries the idea that "You did not choose Me for yourselves." Our Lord then gives the adversative "but," which shows a strong contrast. He continues, "but I chose you and appointed you that you should go and bear fruit." Again the verb "chose" appears in the middle voice, and shows that Jesus called His apostles for His own purpose. Paul also uses the middle voice verb concerning our calling. He writes, "just as He chose us in Him before the foundation of the world, that we should be holy and without blame before Him in love" (Ephesians 1:4). Our purpose in life derives from Him!

Employment Point: *Follow the Lord, who has called you to Himself.*

JUNE 6

2 CHRONICLES 20–22, WITH JOHN 16:1–15

Do not be afraid nor dismayed because of this great multitude, for the battle is not yours, but God's (2 Chronicles 20:15).

DO YOU TRUST IN THE LORD TO FIGHT YOUR BATTLES?

Fear is the natural response to being overwhelmed when you are outnumbered by the enemy. Jehoshaphat is no different, but observe what he does in response to his fear: "And Jehoshaphat feared, and set himself to seek the LORD, and proclaimed a fast throughout all Judah" (2 Chronicles 20:3). He chooses to follow the Lord and let Him fight the battle. Our Lord is a mighty warrior. The church also will return with Jesus at His Second Coming. John writes, "And the armies in heaven, clothed in fine linen, white and clean, followed Him on white horses" (Revelation 19:14). Jesus returns with a two-edged sword to defeat His enemies (Revelation 19:15), and we are depicted as following Him. We experience victory like Jehoshaphat by following the Lord.

EMPLOYMENT POINT: *Follow closely behind the Lord and let Him fight your battles.*

June 7

2 Chronicles 23–25, with John 16:16–33

These things I have spoken to you, that in Me you may have peace. In the world you will have tribulation; but be of good cheer, I have overcome the world (John 16:33).

Do you experience the peace of Jesus when under pressure?

Peace comes from relying upon God and experiencing the fruit of the Spirit. The term "fruit" is singular in Galatians 5:22, which shows that the nine fruit mentioned in Galatians 5:22–23 are a package deal. That is, you experience all of "love, joy, peace, longsuffering, kindness, goodness, faithfulness, gentleness, self-control" as you walk with God. Yet, before you can experience God's peace you need to be born again. Paul writes, "Therefore, having been justified by faith, we have peace with God through our Lord Jesus Christ" (Romans 5:1). Jesus, who is our peace (Ephesians 2:14), imparts peace to us even during times of distress when we trust in Him.

Employment Point: *Enjoy peace through the Holy Spirit's power as you walk with Jesus.*

JUNE 8

2 CHRONICLES 26–28, WITH JOHN 17

And as long as he sought the LORD, God made him prosper (2 Chronicles 26:5).

HAVE YOU BECOME AN INDEPENDENT SPIRIT, AND DO YOU WALK IN PRIDE?

King Uzziah knew the blessing of the Lord while he walked with Him. He experienced military victories, other nations honoring him, building projects success, increase in possessions, and governed a large military (2 Chronicles 26:5–14). Sadly, he doesn't give all glory to God and becomes proud. He crosses the line by attempting to take on the role of a priest, which he is not qualified to do (2 Chronicles 26:16–19). The Lord humbles him while he attempts to burn incense for the Lord. Second Chronicles 26:19 reports the following as the priests expelled him from the Temple: "leprosy broke out on his forehead, before the priests in the house of the LORD, beside the incense altar." Please slowly read the following: "For he was marvelously helped till he become strong" (2 Chronicles 26:15).

EMPLOYMENT POINT: *Thrive under the Lord by humbly serving Jesus for length of days.*

JUNE 9

2 CHRONICLES 29–31, WITH JOHN 18:1–23

Then Simon Peter, having a sword, drew it and struck the high priest's servant, and cut off his right ear (John 18:10).

DO YOU YIELD TO GOD'S WAY OF REACHING THE UNSAVED?

Judas comes with approximately six hundred Roman soldiers to arrest Jesus (John 18:3). Peter boldly steps forward and lops off the right ear of Malchus in defense of his Lord. "So Jesus said to Peter, 'Put your sword into the sheath. Shall I not drink the cup which My Father has given Me?'" (John 18:11).

Jesus submits to the will of God to be crucified. He later tells Pilate, "My kingdom is not of this world. If My kingdom were of this world, My servants would fight, so that I should not be delivered to the Jews" (John 18:36). Peter learned his lesson and later preaches about "Him [Jesus], being delivered by the determined purpose and foreknowledge of God" (Acts 2:23).

EMPLOYMENT POINT: *Submit to God's will and way to reach the unsaved.*

JUNE 10

2 CHRONICLES 32–33, WITH JOHN 18:24–40

Be strong and courageous; do not be afraid nor dismayed before the king of Assyria, nor before all the multitude that is with him; for there are more with us than with him (2 Chronicles 32:7).

DO YOUR WORDS ENCOURAGE PEOPLE TO TRUST IN THE POWER OF THE LORD?

Sennacherib is a mighty king with a vast army. He has conquered other nations and now threatens Hezekiah. Godly Hezekiah exhorts his people facing impending danger from Sennacherib, with the following words: "With him is an arm of flesh; but with us is the LORD our God, to help us and to fight our battles" (2 Chronicles 32:8). Directing the saints to the Almighty imparts courage. The response to Hezekiah's words is given. Second Chronicles 32:8 concludes, "And the people were strengthened by the words of Hezekiah king of Judah." Let's consider how we use our tongues because "death and life are in the power of the tongue" (Proverbs 18:21).

EMPLOYMENT POINT: *Strengthen believers by speaking about God's unlimited power.*

June 11

2 Chronicles 34–36, with John 19:1–22

I have fought the good fight, I have finished the race, I have kept the faith (2 Timothy 4:7).

What's your plan to complete your Christian journey well?

Josiah began his life focused on the Lord. Second Chronicles 34:2 reports, "And he did what was right in the sight of the LORD, and walked in the ways of his father David; he did not turn aside to the right hand or to the left." However, the older king deviated from the path of righteousness when "Necho king of Egypt came up to fight against Carchemish by the Euphrates; and Josiah went out against him" (2 Chronicles 35:20). Josiah is dissuaded to battle "and did not heed the words of Necho from the mouth of God" (2 Chronicles 35:22). Sadly, Josiah dies from a wound in the battle. Several godly kings like Asa, Uzziah, and Hezekiah made bad decisions in their latter years by self-reliance. Let's finish like Paul instead.

Employment Point: *Conclude your life strong by daily seeking the Lord.*

JUNE 12

EZRA 1–2, WITH
JOHN 19:23–42

———◦———

It is finished (John 19:30).

HAVE YOU TAKEN TO HEART JESUS' PHYSICALLY PAINFUL STATEMENTS MADE UPON THE CROSS?

Perhaps you've heard preached at a Good Friday service the last seven statements of Jesus from the cross. His last words uttered upon the cross are excruciatingly painful to speak, because the physical movement to draw air would aggravate His afflictions. Yet an obedient Jesus to the Father's will cries out, "It is finished." The single Greek term is found on tax bills paid in Jesus' day and carries the notion of *being paid in full*. John writes that the Lord satisfies the wrath of God (called "propitiation") through the shedding of His blood and pays the penalty for the sin of mankind through His offering. He pens, "And He Himself is the propitiation for our sins, and not for ours only but also for the whole world" (1 John 2:2).

EMPLOYMENT POINT: *Believe in Jesus, whose death pays the full price for your sin.*

———◦———

JUNE 13

EZRA 3–5, WITH JOHN 20

———◆———

Now when He rose early on the first day of the week, He appeared first to Mary Magdalene, out of whom He had cast seven demons (Mark 16:9).

WHY WOULD JESUS' FIRST RESURRECTION APPEARANCE BE TO MARY, WHEN HER TESTIMONY WOULDN'T BE LEGALLY VALID?

Jesus fulfills His own words about death and life. John writes, "I have power to lay it down, and I have power to take it again" (John 10:18). After Jesus defeats death He first manifests Himself to Mary. As a dedicated follower she comes early to the tomb to anoint Jesus' body for burial (John 20:1). She is honored for faithfully following Jesus; however, a woman's testimony isn't considered valid according to the law of the land. (Observe how Paul doesn't include Mary in his legal defense of Jesus' resurrection in 1 Corinthians 15.) Yet the Lord honors Mary, who honors Jesus.

EMPLOYMENT POINT: *Loyally follow Jesus, who is no respecter of persons, to be richly rewarded.*

———◆———

JUNE 14

EZRA 6–8, WITH JOHN 21

For Ezra had prepared his heart to seek the Law of the LORD, and to do it, and to teach statutes and ordinances in Israel (Ezra 7:10).

DOES YOUR BIBLE STUDY METHOD INCLUDE STUDYING THE WORD, EMPLOYING WHAT YOU'VE LEARNED, AND TEACHING OTHERS?

I have devised my F.I.R.E. method—which stands for familiarity, interpretation, relationship, and employment—from my study of the Bible. Ezra, as a scribe, would be familiar with the Old Testament Scriptures because of reading and rereading them. Moreover, he carefully exegeted the Bible to understand its meaning. In order to grasp the broader implications of the Scriptures he would have looked at the wider context of the passage under study. He concludes the process by employing or applying what he has learned. James writes, "But be doers of the word, and not hearers only, deceiving yourselves" (James 1:22). We should daily strive to do the same!

EMPLOYMENT POINT: *Prepare your hearts to study and employ God's Word.*

JUNE 15

EZRA 9–10, WITH
ACTS 1

—————◦◉◦—————

And He said to them, "Go into all the world and preach the gospel to every creature" (Mark 16:15).

HOW CAN YOU FULFILL JESUS' COMMAND TO PROCLAIM THE GOSPEL UNIVERSALLY?

Jesus shares with His disciples how to accomplish their mission. "But you shall receive power when the Holy Spirit has come upon you; and you shall be witnesses to Me in Jerusalem, and in all Judea and Samaria, and to the end of the earth" (Acts 1:8). Today, all born-again believers are baptized with the Spirit at the moment of their conversion. It is the indwelling Spirit who equips us to be faithful witnesses. Moreover, as we daily walk with Jesus we are also filled (or controlled) by the Holy Spirit (Ephesians 5:18–21). Observe, as you read the Book of Acts, the examples of the disciples being filled with the Spirit and proclaiming the gospel. We need to go and do likewise!

EMPLOYMENT POINT: *Witness regularly through the power of the indwelling Holy Spirit.*

—————◦◉◦—————

JUNE 16

NEHEMIAH 1–3, WITH ACTS 2:1–13

———

Pray without ceasing (1 Thessalonians 5:17).

HOW DO YOU RESPOND TO AN IMPENDING CRISIS?

Nehemiah is broken, because his beloved city of Jerusalem lies in shambles. After hearing about its dire condition he turns to the Lord, "fasting and praying" (Nehemiah 1:4). This choice servant of the Lord regularly launches missile prayers. Nehemiah, as a cupbearer, would be in a place of influence since he regularly tasted the king's food to make sure it wasn't poisoned. One day Nehemiah appears before the king exhibiting a sad countenance, which could result in his demise. After revealing to his sovereign the situation in Jerusalem, "Then the king said to me. 'What do you request?' So I prayed to the God of heaven" (Nehemiah 2:4). Again, he lifts up a rapid petition to the Lord that opens an amazing door for Nehemiah to return to Jerusalem. We should also remain in this posture of prayer.

EMPLOYMENT POINT: *Be ready to launch a missile prayer at all times.*

———

JUNE 17

NEHEMIAH 4–6, WITH ACTS 2:14–47

And [pray] for me, that utterance may be given to me, that I may open my mouth boldly to make known the mystery of the gospel (Ephesians 6:19).

DO YOU FEARLESSLY PROCLAIM THE GOSPEL TO OTHERS?

Peter has publicly denied the Lord three times and Jesus confronts him three times about his love for Him (John 21:15–19). Pentecost has arrived, and Peter is both baptized and filled with the Spirit (Acts 2:4; 11:15–16). The timid fisherman comes to understand the following words of Jesus: "Follow Me, and I will make you fishers of men" (Matthew 4:19). Peter, standing before a large crowd, heralds, "Him, being delivered by the determined purpose and foreknowledge of God, you have taken by lawless hands, have crucified, and put to death; whom God raised up" (Acts 2:23–24). The result of the message is that three thousand souls are saved (Acts 2:41). Let's also pursue the calling of catching men.

EMPLOYMENT POINT: *Walk with Jesus and seek His power to boldly proclaim the gospel.*

JUNE 18

NEHEMIAH 7–8, WITH ACTS 3

Knowing this first, that no prophecy of Scripture is of any private interpretation (2 Peter 1:20).

DO YOU SIT AT THE FEET OF CAPABLE BIBLE TEACHERS?

Not only the physical wall of Jerusalem needed repair, but the people also require a spiritual renovation. For this reason Ezra the scribe, along with qualified Bible teachers, do the following before the people: "So they read distinctly from the book, in the Law of God; and they gave the sense, and helped them to understand the reading" (Nehemiah 8:8). Likewise, Jesus provides able teachers in the church age. Paul writes, "And He Himself gave some to be apostles, some prophets, some evangelists, and some pastors and teachers, for the equipping of the saints for the work of ministry" (Ephesians 4:11–12). The Lord has graciously provided capable instructors of His Word; it is our responsibility to learn from them.

EMPLOYMENT POINT: *Posture yourself to receive godly instruction from qualified teachers.*

JUNE 19

NEHEMIAH 9–11, WITH
ACTS 4:1–22

Jesus said to him, "I am the way, the truth, and the life. No one comes to the Father except through Me" (John 14:6).

DO YOU PROCLAIM THAT JESUS IS THE ONLY WAY TO HEAVEN?

The apostles are faithful to their calling because "they taught the people and preached in Jesus the resurrection from the dead" (Acts 4:2). This message infuriates the Sadducees, who do not believe in a bodily resurrection. For this reason they have Peter arrested to appear before the Sanhedrin, which make up the Jewish supreme court. Nonetheless, Peter boldly proclaims Jesus' death and resurrection (Acts 4:10). Moreover, he heralds that Jesus is the only way to the Father. "Nor is there salvation in any other," declares the apostle, "for there is no other name under heaven given among men by which we must be saved" (Acts 4:12).

EMPLOYMENT POINT: *Trumpet the message that believing on Jesus' death and resurrection is the only way to heaven.*

JUNE 20

NEHEMIAH 12–13, WITH
ACTS 4:23–37

———◈———

Remember me, O my God, for good! (Nehemiah 13:31).

WILL YOU BEGIN AND END YOUR MINISTRY WITH PRAYER?

The Book of Nehemiah commences with the governor of Jerusalem praying, and ends on the same note. Prudently, Nehemiah confesses his sins and that of the nation when he begins to undertake the physical renovation of the wall and the spiritual renovation of the people (Nehemiah 1:5–11). He concludes by asking God to remember his benevolent life. Several years ago, while reading through the Bible, I highlighted every biblical prayer. There are a lot of highlighted sections in the Book of Nehemiah. If someone were to follow you daily, recording every prayer you made, how much ink would they use documenting your prayer life? Our ultimate example of praying comes from Jesus. He cultivates the example on earth (Mark 1:35) and continues it in heaven (Hebrews 7:25).

EMPLOYMENT POINT: *Develop a prayer life that is as natural as your breathing.*

———◈———

JUNE 21

ESTHER 1–3, WITH
ACTS 5:1–16

These six things the LORD hates, yes, seven are an abomination to Him: a proud look, a lying tongue, hands that shed innocent blood, a heart that devises wicked plans, feet that are swift in running to evil, a false witness who speaks lies, and one who sows discord among brethren (Proverbs 6:16–19).

DO YOU SPEAK DECEPTIVELY TO MAKE YOURSELF LOOK GOOD?

Ananias and Sapphira are contrasted to Barnabas in the Book of Acts. He is noted for his generosity (Acts 4:34–37). Luke writes about him, "having land, sold it, and brought the money and laid it at the apostles' feet" (Acts 4:37). Conversely, the satanically influenced couple concocts a hypocritical plan, which costs them their lives (Acts 5:1–10). God hates "a lying tongue," which literally means "a tongue of deception" (Proverbs 6:17). We need to speak truth and not craft words to manipulate people to think highly of us.

EMPLOYMENT POINT: *Avoid deceiving others by a deceptive tongue.*

JUNE 22

ESTHER 4–6, WITH
ACTS 5:17–42

———※◎※———

Yet who knows whether you have come to the kingdom for such a time as this? (Esther 4:14).

DO YOU COURAGEOUSLY FULFILL YOUR GOD-GIVEN ROLE?

Haman hatches a plot to exterminate the Jews. King Ahasuerus gives authorization to the dastardly plot not knowing the details of Haman's plan. Uncle Mordecai calls Esther, who is in a position of influence as queen, to approach Ahasuerus to rectify the situation. No one can see the king without being summoned; violating the standard would result in death lest the king offers a pardon. Esther turns to the Lord before entering Ahasuerus' presence. She tells Mordecai the following: "My maids and I will fast likewise" (Esther 4:16). Fasting, accompanied with prayer, elicits boldness in Esther and moves the hand of God, which touches the heart of Ahasuerus. "The king's heart is in the hand of the LORD" (Proverbs 21:1).

EMPLOYMENT POINT: *Seek God's power through prayer and fasting, to fulfill your God-given mission.*

———※◎※———

JUNE 23

ESTHER 7–10, WITH ACTS 6

But we will give ourselves continually to prayer and to the ministry of the word (Acts 6:4).

DO YOU HELP OR HAMPER YOUR CHURCH'S PASTORAL STAFF TO ACCOMPLISH THEIR MINISTRY?

God gives at least one spiritual gift to every believer. Peter writes, "As each one has received a gift, minister it to one another, as good stewards of the manifold grace of God" (1 Peter 4:10). A spiritual gift is a supernatural ability given by God to the believer at the moment of salvation for the edification of the body of Christ. Luke chronicles that when the church is growing certain needs arise (Acts 6:1). He discloses that the apostles employ seven faithful Spirit-filled men to care for the widows, so they can maintain their priorities (Acts 6:2–4). The end result is "the word of God spread, and the number of the disciples multiplied greatly" (Acts 6:7).

EMPLOYMENT POINT: *Apply your spiritual gift to serve others in the church.*

JUNE 24

JOB 1–3, WITH
ACTS 7:1–19

Have you considered My servant Job, that there is none like him on the earth, a blameless and upright man, one who fears God and shuns evil? (Job 1:8).

DO YOU FEAR GOD AND SHUN EVIL LIKE JOB?

Job is a man of *integrity*, which is the meaning of the term "blameless." Moreover, he is "upright" signifying that Job does what is right morally. His godly fear is exemplified by turning away from wickedness. Clearly Job guards his heart by choosing to only look upon those things that please God. He says, "I have made a covenant with my eyes; why then should I look upon a young woman?" (Job 31:1).

James sums up the patriarch's life as follows: "Indeed we count them blessed who endure. You have heard of the perseverance of Job and seen the end intended by the Lord" (James 5:11).

EMPLOYMENT POINT: *Please God by leading a life of integrity, which includes turning away from evil.*

JUNE 25

JOB 4–6, WITH
ACTS 7:20–43

Teach me, and I will hold my tongue; cause me to understand wherein I have erred (Job 6:24).

ARE YOU TEACHABLE?

Job seeks to know why the Almighty permits him to suffer. His so-called friends don't illuminate him on this matter. God exposes the folly of their counsel with the following: "The LORD said to Eliphaz the Temanite, 'My wrath is aroused against you and your two friends, for you have not spoken of Me what is right, as My servant Job has'" (Job 42:7). The Book of Job culminates with God teaching His servant a valuable lesson. Job learns that it is better to understand *who* God is rather than *why* these things have happened. He displays a teachable spirit. He says, "I have heard of You by the hearing of the ear, but now my eye sees You. Therefore I abhor myself, and repent in dust and ashes" (Job 42:5–6).

EMPLOYMENT POINT: *Seek God and remain teachable during a trial.*

JUNE 26

JOB 7–9, WITH
ACTS 7:44–60

———※———

But he, being full of the Holy Spirit, gazed into heaven and saw the glory of God, and Jesus standing at the right hand of God (Acts 7:55).

WHY IS JESUS NOT SITTING AT THE RIGHT HAND OF GOD?

The Old Testament high priest each year on the Day of Atonement (Yom Kippur) offered a temporary sacrifice for the sins of the people, but it needed to be repeated annually. The high priest never could sit down in the tabernacle or Temple because the work of salvation was not completed. Conversely, forty days after Jesus was raised from the dead, He ascended to heaven and sat down, which signifies that the work of salvation is complete. This is why He is normally pictured as sitting at the right hand of God. Stephen becomes the church's first martyr. Twice Jesus is described as standing (Acts 7:55–56), and He does so to welcome him home.

EMPLOYMENT POINT: *Serve Jesus well, anticipating a warm welcome home.*

———※———

JUNE 27

JOB 10–12, WITH
ACTS 8:1–25

———◆———

He does great things past finding out, yes, wonders without number
(Job 9:10).

ARE YOU ABLE TO NUMBER ALL THE WORKS OF GOD?

The works of the Lord are innumerable. David uses Job's term "finding out," which means *to inquire* or *to search* in Psalm 145:3, and is
translated "unsearchable." He pens, "Great is the LORD, and greatly
to be praised; and His greatness is unsearchable" (Psalm 145:3). Isaiah
concurs with Job and David about the vastness of God's resources.
He asks and answers, "Have you not known? Have you not heard?
The everlasting God, the LORD, the Creator of the ends of the earth,
neither faints nor is weary. His understanding is unsearchable" (Isaiah 40:28). Likewise Paul ponders, "How unsearchable are His judgments and His ways past finding out!" (Romans 11:33). Let's stand in
awe of God like Job, David, Isaiah, and Paul.

EMPLOYMENT POINT: *Probe the works of the Lord and marvel at His
unlimited power.*

———◆———

JOB 13–15, WITH ACTS 8:26–40

Then Philip opened his mouth, and beginning at this Scripture, preached Jesus to him (Acts 8:35).

DO YOU POINT PEOPLE TO JESUS FROM THE SCRIPTURES?

The Lord calls Philip the evangelist away from a bustling ministry in Samaria (Acts 8:5–6) to one man that he will meet "along the road which goes down from Jerusalem to Gaza" (Acts 8:26). Philip obeys and encounters an unnamed man serving "under Candace the queen of the Ethiopians" (Acts 8:27). The obedient evangelist heeds the voice of the Spirit, and finds the man perplexed while trying to understand a passage in Isaiah 53. "Then Philip opened his mouth," writes Luke, "and beginning at this Scripture, preached Jesus to him" (Acts 8:35). Philip imitates the Lord Jesus. "And beginning at Moses and all the Prophets, He expounded to them [two unnamed disciples going to Emmaus] in all the Scriptures the things concerning Himself" (Luke 24:27).

EMPLOYMENT POINT: *Direct people to Jesus using the Scriptures.*

JUNE 29

JOB 16–18, WITH
ACTS 9:1–22

———◦———

Then Job answered and said: "I have heard many such things; miserable comforters are you all!" (Job 16:1–2).

WHAT KIND OF FRIEND AND COUNSELOR ARE YOU?

Job's friends and counselors are both insensitive and inaccurate concerning his plight. God Himself assesses their counseling with the following: "For you have not spoken of Me what is right" (Job 42:7). These so-called friends take the wrong approach to Job. Paul writes, "Brethren, if a man is overtaken in any trespass, you who are spiritual restore such a one in a spirit of gentleness, considering yourself lest you also be tempted" (Galatians 6:1). The term "restore" occurs outside the Bible, and refers to gently setting broken bones. Job's friends seek to accuse and not restore him. Moreover, they don't speak the truth about God like Job. Truth must be accompanied with love. Paul encourages the Ephesians that they should be "speaking the truth in love" (Ephesians 4:15).

EMPLOYMENT POINT: *Communicate God's truth accurately and with love.*

———◦———

June 30

Job 19–20, with
Acts 9:23–43

But I was let down in a basket through a window in the wall, and escaped from his hands (2 Corinthians 11:33).

Do you share your personal testimony with humility?

Paul is the greatest missionary who ever lived, yet prior to coming to Jesus he persecuted the church. Shortly after being saved "he preached the Christ in the synagogues, that He is the Son of God" (Acts 9:20). Consequently, his life is imperiled and "the disciples took him by night and let him down through the wall in a large basket" (Acts 9:25). The apostle himself shares this story to the Corinthian believers at the culmination of 2 Corinthians 11. Paul defends his apostleship by listing the many difficulties he faced and endured in ministry, which verifies his authenticity. With humility, the embattled apostle communicates the power of God through his infirmities. Let's do likewise.

EMPLOYMENT POINT: *Share your personal testimony, exalting the power of God through human frailty.*

JULY 1

JOB 21–22, WITH
ACTS 10:1–23

———◆———

But God has shown me that I should not call any man common or unclean (Acts 10:28).

DO YOU HAVE A HEART FOR ALL PEOPLE TO BE SAVED?

Biblically there is one race; it is the human race. Paul preaches, "And He has made from one blood every nation of men" in Acts 17:26. The human race derives from Adam. Furthermore, Paul writes, "For if by the one man's offense death reigned through the one [Adam], much more those who receive abundance of grace and of the gift of righteousness will reign in life through the One, Jesus Christ" (Romans 5:17). Peter, the apostle to the Jews, receives a vision from God about killing and eating unclean animals (Acts 10:1–13). The object lesson conveys to Peter, "What God has cleansed you must not call common" (Acts 10:15). In essence, Jesus died for all people, and the message of the gospel is for them.

EMPLOYMENT POINT: *Proclaim the gospel to all people without partiality.*

———◆———

JULY 2

JOB 23–25, WITH ACTS 10:24–48

I have not departed from the commandment of His lips; I have treasured the words of His mouth more than my necessary food (Job 23:12).

WHAT IS YOUR PERSONAL TESTIMONY CONCERNING OBEDIENCE TO GOD'S WORD?

Job is perplexed as he shares his innocence before his friends. He knows that he has honored the commands of God, and yet suffers great affliction. Generally speaking, to obey God's Word is to know His blessing. The same verb "departed" in the expression "I have not departed from the commandment of His lips" emerges in Joshua 1:8: "This book of the Law shall not depart from your mouth." He is promised success for submitting to its teachings, which he experiences. The Lord stretches Job's faith and blesses him again abundantly after his trial (James 5:11). We need to also obey God's Word, knowing that eventual blessings will come.

EMPLOYMENT POINT: *Treasure God's Word and be rewarded according to His perfect timing.*

July 3

Job 26–28, with Acts 11

My righteousness I hold fast, and will not let it go; my heart shall not reproach me as long as I live (Job 27:6).

How have you determined to live until you die?

The verb "hold fast" in Job 27:6 literally means *to be strong*. Job determines to strongly apply himself to live righteously for length of days. Moreover, he strives to have a clear conscience. Great servants of God have this aspiration. Paul shares, "I myself always strive to have a conscience without offense toward God and men" (Acts 24:16). God honors saints like Job, who are determined to live with integrity: "Till I die I will not put away my integrity from me" (Job 27:5). The following verse from Paul gives a worthy standard to imitate: "For to me, to live is Christ, and to die is gain" (Philippians 1:21).

Employment Point: *Be determined that, by God's grace, you'll live righteously and with a clear conscience.*

July 4

Job 29–30, with Acts 12

Therefore, whether you eat or drink, or whatever you do, do all to the glory of God (1 Corinthians 10:31).

Do you daily live for the glory of God?

Herod Agrippa, the grandson of Herod the Great, exudes wickedness: "He killed James the brother of John with the sword" (Acts 12:2). Then he incarcerates Peter "and delivered him to four squads of soldiers to keep him, intending to bring him before the people after Passover" (Acts 12:4). God miraculously frees the apostle but holds Herod accountable for his deeds. One day as he was before the people "arrayed in royal apparel, [he] sat on his throne and gave an oration to them" (Acts 12:21). Then he receives their accolades for being a god (Acts 12:22). The "angel of the Lord struck him, because he did not give glory to God" (Acts 12:23). He attempted to steal what rightly belongs to the Lord!

EMPLOYMENT POINT: *Attribute all glory to God, who alone is worthy.*

JULY 5

JOB 31–32, WITH
ACTS 13:1–23

———◆———

I have made a covenant with my eyes; why then should I look upon a young woman? (Job 31:1).

HAVE YOU DEDICATED YOUR EYES TO THE LORD?

Jesus makes a connection between the eyes and the heart in Matthew 5:28. He states, "But I say to you that whoever looks at a woman to lust for her has already committed adultery with her in his heart." Jesus then uses hyperbole to show the extent that we should protect our heart. He adds, "If your right eye causes you to sin, pluck it out and cast if from you; for it is more profitable for you that one of your members perish, than for your whole body to be cast into hell" (Matthew 5:29). We must protect our hearts at all costs. Wisdom cries out, "Keep your heart with all diligence, for out of it spring the issues of life" (Proverbs 4:23).

EMPLOYMENT POINT: *Dedicate your eyes to glorify the Lord.*

———◆———

JULY 6

JOB 33–34, WITH
ACTS 13:24–52

Then Paul stood up, and motioning with his hand said, "Men of Israel, and you who fear God, listen" (Acts 13:16).

HOW CLEAR IS YOUR GOSPEL PRESENTATION?

Paul concisely trumpets the gospel. He walks his audience through the Old Testament connecting David and Jesus. Paul proclaims, "And we declare to you glad tidings—that promise which was made to the fathers. God has fulfilled this for us their children, in that He has raised up Jesus. As it is also written in the second Psalm: 'You are My Son, today I have begotten You'" (Acts 13:32–33). Repeatedly the articulate apostle declares the death and resurrection of Jesus (Acts 13:29–30, 33, 34, 37). We need to also stay on message as Paul did, who tells the Corinthians, "For I determined not to know anything among you except Jesus Christ and Him crucified" (1 Corinthians 2:2). The souls of men are at stake!

EMPLOYMENT POINT: *Herald the truths of the gospel with precision.*

JULY 7

JOB 35–37, WITH
ACTS 14

———※———

But I will tarry in Ephesus until Pentecost. For a great and effective door has opened to me (1 Corinthians 16:8–9).

DO YOU TAKE ADVANTAGE WHEN GOD OPENS A DOOR?

Paul's ambition is to "preach the gospel, not where Christ was named" (Romans 15:20). He asks others to pray, "that God would open to us a door for the word" (Colossians 4:3). Moreover, Luke reports, "And a vision appeared to Paul in the night. A man of Macedonia stood and pleaded with him, saying, 'Come over to Macedonia and help us.' Now after he had seen the vision, immediately we sought to go to Macedonia" (Acts 16:9–10). Paul loves gathering the saints to tell them what God is doing. He shares with his sending church, "that He had opened the door of faith to the Gentiles" (Acts 14:27). Paul then "stayed there a long time with the disciples" (Acts 14:28).

EMPLOYMENT POINT: *Tarry in God's open door and serve Him well.*

———※———

July 8

Job 38–39, with
Acts 15:1–21

Now prepare yourself like a man; I will question you, and you shall answer Me (Job 38:3).

Can you trust in God, who governs the universe?

The Lord responds to Job "out of the whirlwind," which both masks and unveils His person and work (Job 38:1). In Job's bewilderment, God asks him questions about creation like the following: "Where were you when I laid the foundations of the earth? Tell Me, if you have understanding. Who determined its measurements? Surely you know! Or who stretched the line upon it? To what were its foundations fastened?" (Job 38:4–6). Simply put, God is teaching the finite Job to trust in His infinite power. Paul writes about Jesus, "He is before all things, and in Him all things consist" (Colossians 1:17). Our God both creates and sustains every detail in this vast universe; we can depend upon Him to govern our lives.

Employment Point: *Marvel at the Master of the universe, and trust in Him always.*

JULY 9

JOB 40–42, WITH
ACTS 15:22–41

———◆———

I have heard of You by the hearing of the ear, but now my eye sees You.
Therefore I abhor myself, and repent in dust and ashes (Job 42:5–6).

DO YOU ALLOW THE HOLY ONE TO HUMBLE YOU?

After being confronted by God, Job better grasps His glory. He
exclaims, "I know that You can do everything, and that no purpose
of Yours can be withheld from You" (Job 42:2). The humbled man
of God has his eyes opened to the awesome nature of the Lord. Getting a glimpse at God's glory brings us to our knees. Isaiah has a
similar experience when he "saw the Lord sitting on a throne, high
and lifted up" (Isaiah 6:1). Like Job, he encounters his own sinfulness. He declares, "Woe is me, for I am undone . . . for my eyes have
seen the King, the LORD of hosts" (Isaiah 6:5). We should similarly
seek His face!

EMPLOYMENT POINT: *Marvel at God's glory and humble yourself
before Him.*

———◆———

JULY 10

PSALMS 1–3, WITH ACTS 16:1–15

And the things that you have heard from me among many witnesses, commit these to faithful men who will be able to teach others also (2 Timothy 2:2).

HOW DO YOU CHOOSE THE RIGHT PEOPLE TO TRAIN FOR MINISTRY?

Paul looks for faithful, available, and teachable (FAT) men to train for the work of ministry. He chooses Timothy to replace John Mark (Acts 16:1–5). Timothy is a *faithful* disciple who "was well spoken of by the brethren" (Acts 16:2). The young man, whose name means "to value God," makes himself *available* and is *teachable*. First Corinthians 4:17 shows these two traits: "For this reason I have sent Timothy to you, who is my beloved and faithful son in the Lord, who will remind you of my ways in Christ." Paul could dispatch Timothy to a troubled Corinthian church because he was faithful, available, and teachable. We should also strive to be FAT.

EMPLOYMENT POINT: *Invest in faithful, available, and teachable servants.*

JULY 11

PSALMS 4–6, WITH
ACTS 16:16–40

For You, O LORD, will bless the righteous; with favor You will surround him as with a shield (Psalm 5:12).

TO WHOM DO YOU TURN FOR BLESSING AND PROTECTION?

Abraham rescues his nephew Lot from captivity (Genesis 14). Perhaps the father of faith is concerned that those who detained Lot will retaliate for freeing him. Moses reports, "After these things the word of the LORD came to Abram in a vision, saying, 'Do not be afraid, Abram. I am your shield, your exceedingly great reward'" (Genesis 15:1). God assures Abraham of His protection and continued blessing; He is the only One who can produce these things. This is why David turns to God while fleeing from his son Absalom. The king on the lam cries out, "But You, O LORD, are a shield for me, my glory and the One who lifts up my head" (Psalm 3:3). Let's also look to Him.

EMPLOYMENT POINT: *Trust in the Lord for His blessing and protection.*

July 12

Psalms 7–9, with Acts 17:1–15

———⊙———

And you became followers of us and of the Lord, having received the word in much affliction, with joy of the Holy Spirit (1 Thessalonians 1:6).

Do people see Jesus in you?

Paul and Silas have a reputation that precedes them. As they minister in Thessalonica, the city leaders exclaim, "These who have turned the world upside down have come here too" (Acts 17:6). Why are Paul and Silas (not to mention Paul's other associates) world-changers? These godly men could say, "Imitate me, just as I also imitate Christ" (1 Corinthians 11:1). Did you note the order of the lead verse? The people became *imitators*, which is the literally meaning of the Greek term translated "followers" and is also found in 1 Corinthians 11:1, "of us and of the Lord." Those in Thessalonica beheld the Christlike lives of Paul and Silas and became followers of Jesus. Let's imitate the set standard!

Employment Point: *Imitate Jesus to turn this world upside down.*

———⊙———

JULY 13

PSALMS 10–12, WITH
ACTS 17:16–34

For the LORD is righteous, He loves righteousness; His countenance beholds the upright (Psalm 11:7).

DO YOU LOVE AND PRACTICE RIGHTEOUSNESS?

Abraham asks God in Genesis 18:25, "Shall not the Judge of all the earth do right?" He knows that he can appeal to his righteous Father for Sodom. Moreover, our heavenly Father declares us righteous when we put our faith in the gospel. Paul heralds, "For in it [the gospel] the righteousness of God is revealed from faith to faith; as it is written, 'The just shall live by faith'" (Romans 1:17). Furthermore, God imparts His blessing to the saints who long for His righteousness. Jesus teaches on the Sermon on the Mount, "Blessed are those who hunger and thirst for righteousness, for they shall be filled" (Matthew 5:6). Let's "flee also youthful lusts; but pursue righteousness, faith, love, peace with those who call on the Lord out of a pure heart" (2 Timothy 2:22).

EMPLOYMENT POINT: *Love and pursue God's righteousness.*

July 14

Psalms 13–16, with Acts 18

Now a certain Jew named Apollos, born at Alexandria, an eloquent man and mighty in the Scriptures, came to Ephesus (Acts 18:24).

What three qualities worthy of imitation did Apollos exhibit?

Apollos is born in Egypt in the city of Alexandria, which is renowned for its vast library. The first term we could apply to Apollos is *learned* (Acts 18:24–25). He diligently studied and articulated the Old Testament Scripture. Moreover, his second admirable trait is *listening,* which conveys that he learns from others. "When Aquila and Priscilla heard him, they took him aside and explained to him the way of God more accurately" (Acts 18:26). The learned teacher having received a fuller education about Jesus now employs his skill set, which demonstrates that he is thirdly *laborious* (Acts 18:27-28). As he travels to Achaia "he vigorously refuted the Jews publicly, showing from the Scriptures that Jesus is the Christ" (Acts 18:28).

Employment Point: *Strive to be biblically learned, listening, and laborious.*

JULY 15

PSALMS 17–18, WITH
ACTS 19:1–20

———※———

As for God, His way is perfect; the word of the LORD is proven; He is a shield to all who trust in Him (Psalm 18:30).

HAVE YOU EXPERIENCED THAT GOD'S WORD IS TRIED AND TRUE?

David writes Psalm 18 after escaping from the clutches of Saul. The Lord had years earlier anointed the sweet psalmist of Israel to be Israel's future king (1 Samuel 16). Yet David endures many assassination attempts against his life from Saul. Agur concurs with the sentiments of David: "Every word of God is pure; He is a shield to those who put their trust in Him" (Proverbs 30:5). God stretches David's faith and the king in waiting exalts his Lord. He says, "You have delivered me from the violent man. Therefore I will give thanks to You, O LORD, among the Gentiles, and sing praises to Your name" (Psalm 18:48–49).

EMPLOYMENT POINT: *Trust in God to experience His perfect way, proven Word, and marvelous protection.*

———※———

JULY 16

PSALMS 19–21, WITH ACTS 19:21–41

So not only is this trade of ours in danger of falling into disrepute, but also the temple of the great goddess Diana may be despised and her magnificence destroyed, whom all Asia and the world worship (Acts 19:27).

HAS YOUR INFLUENCE FOR CHRIST IMPACTED THE REVENUES THAT THE UNSAVED RECEIVE?

Ephesus is an ungodly city that houses one of the seven ancient wonders of the world. The temple of Diana and its system of worship promote promiscuity. Paul's commitment to preach Christ where He hasn't been proclaimed causes many to turn to God from idols, and hits the proprietors of idols where it counts most—in their wallets. Are there less people frequenting bars because of your Christian influence? Have the number of purchased CDs and DVDs containing godless lyrics and images declined since you've come to Christ and bear His image?

EMPLOYMENT POINT: *Influence the spending habits of many through your Christian life and witness.*

JULY 17

PSALMS 22–24, WITH ACTS 20:1–16

The LORD is my shepherd; I shall not want (Psalm 23:1).

DO YOU RELY UPON THE GOOD SHEPHERD TO MEET YOUR EVERY NEED?

God is the great provider; as the good shepherd He cares for all your spiritual, physical, and emotional needs. The sacrificial Philippian church is told the following by Paul: "And my God shall supply all your need according to His riches in glory by Christ Jesus" (Philippians 4:19). You can fully trust the One who says, "I am the good shepherd. The good shepherd gives His life for the sheep" (John 10:11). We can have confidence in His desire and ability to sustain us holistically. Because David understands God as his shepherd, he declares, "Surely goodness and mercy shall follow me all the days of my life; and I will dwell in the house of the LORD forever" (Psalm 23:6).

EMPLOYMENT POINT: *Look to the heart and hand of the Good Shepherd to care for you.*

JULY 18

PSALMS 25–27, WITH
ACTS 20:17–38

———◆———

For I have not shunned to declare to you the whole counsel of God (Acts 20:27).

DOES YOUR INSTRUCTION TO BELIEVERS ENCOMPASS THE TOTALITY OF GOD'S WORD?

We need to boldly tell the saints not just what they want to hear, but also the challenges they can expect from identifying with Christ. Paul informs the Ephesian leaders, "For I know this, that after my departure savage wolves will come in among you, not sparing the flock" (Acts 20:29). God equips us to take on the difficult role. The apostle reminds Timothy who will pastor the flock at Ephesus, "For God has not given us a spirit of fear, but of power and of love and of a sound mind" (2 Timothy 1:7). Paul encourages Timothy not to "fear," which means *to exhibit cowardice, timidity,* or *reticence.* Let's serve our Christian family well with a full serving of God's truth.

EMPLOYMENT POINT: *Equip the saints by teaching them the entirety of God's Word.*

———◆———

July 19

Psalms 28–30, with
Acts 21:1–14

Give unto the LORD, O you mighty ones, give unto the LORD glory
and strength. Give unto the LORD the glory due to His name; worship
the LORD in the beauty of holiness (Psalm 29:1–2).

Can you give something to God that He already possesses?

The Hebrew term translated "give" three times in Psalm 29:1–2 literally means *ascribe*. Ascribing glory to God carries the notion of referring to the cause that which He owns or possesses. Our Lord possesses
all glory and strength; therefore, it is our privilege to acknowledge in
worship and praise who God is. Each use of the word "give" emerges as
an imperative in Psalm 29:1–2. Likewise, Moses employs the imperative in Deuteronomy 32:3. He writes, "For I proclaim the name of the
LORD; ascribe greatness to our God." Daily we should acknowledge
the awesome nature of our God by ascribing glory to Him.

Employment Point: *Ascribe glory and strength to our God, for He
is great.*

JULY 20

PSALMS 31–33, WITH ACTS 21:15–40

If we confess our sins, He is faithful and just to forgive us our sins and to cleanse us from all unrighteousness (1 John 1:9).

DO YOU HAVE ANY UNCONFESSED SIN IN YOUR LIFE?

"Blessed is he whose transgression is forgiven, whose sin is covered," writes David, "Blessed is the man to whom the LORD does not impute iniquity" (Psalm 32:1–2). The man after God's own heart did not acknowledge his sin to God. He recounts the penalty for this act: "When I kept silent, my bones grew old. . . . for day and night Your hand was heavy upon me; my vitality was turned into the drought of summer" (Psalm 32:3–4). God graciously and consistently applied pressure until David relented. The three synonyms for sin of Psalm 32:1–2 (transgression, sin, and iniquity) occur again in Psalm 32:5, when David acknowledges his disobedience to the Lord. Subsequently he is forgiven and relieved.

EMPLOYMENT POINT: *Confess any known sin to God without delay.*

JULY 21

PSALMS 34–35, WITH ACTS 22

I persecuted this Way to the death, binding and delivering into prisons both men and women (Acts 22:4).

HOW PREPARED ARE YOU TO SHARE YOUR PERSONAL TESTIMONY AS A WITNESS FOR JESUS?

Personal testimonies are captivating. People are intrigued to hear about the lives of others. You can take advantage of the natural curiosity within the unsaved heart to tell your story. Paul does it well; he also does it often, as recorded in the Book of Acts. Pay careful attention to the frequency he tells his story about personally encountering Jesus. Paul connects with his Jewish audience in Acts 22:1–3, informing them that he is a fellow Jew and trained for ministry under Gamaliel. Once he hooks them, the experienced personal storyteller informs his captive audience that Jesus is alive and personally commissioned him: "For you will be His witness to all men of what you have seen and heard" (Acts 22:15).

EMPLOYMENT POINT: *Prepare and share your personal testimony.*

JULY 22

PSALMS 36–37, WITH
ACTS 23:1–11

Mark the blameless man, and observe the upright; for the future of that man is peace (Psalm 37:37).

ARE YOU STRIVING TO LEAD A BLAMELESS LIFE?

David gives the following wise counsel: "Do not fret because of evil-doers, nor be envious of the workers of iniquity" (Psalm 37:1). Here, "fret" means be warmed, fume, or be incensed. The wicked only thrive for a short time and "they shall soon be cut down like the grass" (Psalm 37:2). Conversely, David desires his readers to focus upon "the blameless man," which term means *given to integrity*. He points out "for the future of that man is peace." Evil men do not experience the peace of God. Isaiah writes, "The way of peace they have not known, and there is no justice in their ways; they have made them-selves crooked paths; whoever takes that way shall not know peace" (Isaiah 59:8). Let's pursue the path of peace through righteous living.

EMPLOYMENT POINT: *Observe and imitate the blameless man to know God's peace.*

July 23

Psalms 38–40, with
Acts 23:12–35

He has put a new song in my mouth—praise to our God; many will see it and fear; and will trust in the LORD (Psalm 40:3).

How has God's deliverance in your life changed your music?

Once again, the Lord snatches David from being destroyed (Psalm 40:1–2). Similarly, God has snatched us from the clutches of the wicked one and saved us. In 1984 my wife and I took a group of teens on a retreat to West Virginia. My teaching topic was on music and the songs in the Bible. We examined the lyrics to Exodus 15, Deuteronomy 32, and Revelation 15. The teens decided by the end of the retreat to glorify God through their music. Moreover, we had two young people put their faith in Jesus for salvation. David's words are true about the new song, "Many will see it and fear; and will trust in the LORD."

EMPLOYMENT POINT: *Glorify God for your deliverance with a new song.*

July 24

Psalms 41–43, with Acts 24

———※———

As the deer pants for the water brooks, so pants my soul for You, O God (Psalm 42:1).

Are you daily panting after God?

The Hebrew term for "panting" conveys *a strong and audible thirsting.* With passion the author exclaims the following: "My soul thirsts for God, for the living God. When shall I come and appear before God?" (Psalm 42:2). Jesus' preaching elevates the Word of the Lord in the Sermon on the Mount, and reveals the blessings that come from seeking after God. He begins, "Blessed are the poor in sprit, for theirs is the kingdom of heaven" (Matthew 5:3). When the Bible is exalted, it brings the believer to his knees. Moreover, Jesus proclaims, "Blessed are those who hunger and thirst for righteousness, for they shall be filled" (Matthew 5:6). We should hunger and thirst for the living God who solely fulfills our deepest longings.

Employment Point: *Seek the living God, who alone can satisfy the craving of the soul.*

———※———

July 25

Psalms 44–46, with Acts 25

If the world hates you, you know that it hated Me before it hated you (John 15:18).

Do those who hate Jesus hate you?

The Jewish hierarchy loathes Paul. Luke records, "Then the high priest and the chief men of the Jews informed him [Festus] against Paul" (Acts 25:2). What is their request? They seek to have Paul transferred to Jerusalem so that they can ambush him (Acts 25:3). Why does the apostle draw fire from the Jewish high priest and leaders? He answers this question when writing to Timothy. Paul pens, "Yes, and all who desire to live godly in Christ Jesus will suffer persecution" (2 Timothy 3:12). This faithful servant of the Lord endured much for Jesus, as recorded in 2 Corinthians 11:22–33. Both his past suffering and our present persecution testify to being united with Jesus. We are called to follow in His steps.

EMPLOYMENT POINT: *Please Jesus at all costs, and expect the world to also hate you.*

JULY 26

PSALMS 47–49, WITH ACTS 26

<hr>

For the redemption of their souls is costly, and it shall cease forever (Psalm 49:8).

WHAT IS THE ONE THING THAT MONEY CAN'T BUY?

Proverbs 22:7 teaches us, "The rich rules over the poor." Their wealth often deceives them into believing that they are superior to others; however, all the money in the world cannot purchase the salvation of just one person. "None of them can by any means redeem his brother," writes the psalmist, "nor give to God a ransom for him" (Psalm 49:7). Moreover, the psalmist reveals the haughtiness of the rich, "Their inner thought is that their houses will last forever, their dwelling places to all generations; they call their lands after their own names" (Psalm 49:11). Our Lord Jesus penetrates the naiveté of the rich and asks, "For what will it profit a man if he gains the whole world, and loses his own soul?" (Mark 8:36).

EMPLOYMENT POINT: *Trust in Jesus, who alone can redeem your soul.*

<hr>

July 27

Psalms 50–52, with Acts 27:1–25

Therefore take heart, men, for I believe God that it will be just as it was told me (Acts 27:25).

Where do you turn to have your spiritual spine stiffened during a storm?

Paul travels to Rome with a military escort; however, God first has an appointment for him to keep. The ship is lost during a storm but no lives are, thanks to the Lord. An angel had told Paul before the wreck, "You must be brought before Caesar; and indeed God has granted you all those who sail with you" (Acts 27:24). Earlier during a mission trip to Corinth "the Lord spoke to Paul in the night by a vision, 'Do not be afraid, but speak, and do not keep silent; for I am with you, and no one will attack you to hurt you'" (Acts 18:9–10). We can rely upon Jesus who says, "I am with you always" (Matthew 28:20).

Employment Point: *Depend upon Jesus and His Word, even during a storm.*

July 28

Psalms 53–55, with
Acts 27:26–44

―――◦◉◦―――

Evening and morning and at noon I will pray, and cry aloud, and He shall hear my voice (Psalm 55:17).

How can you be prepared to endure a betrayal?

David experiences a painful betrayal. Betrayals occur by a one-time friend who turns into an enemy. The grieving psalmist writes, "For it is not an enemy who reproaches me; then I could bear it. Nor is it one who hates me who has exalted himself against me; then I could hide from him. But it was you, a man my equal, my companion and my acquaintance" (Psalm 55:12–13). Similarly our Lord sustains a painful betrayal at Gethsemane. Jesus responds by asking Judas, "Friend, why have you come?" (Matthew 26:50). Unlike David, Jesus knew His betrayer who dined with Him (John 13:18–19). Yet both Jesus and David maintain a healthy prayer life, which sustains them (Psalm 55:17; Mark 14:35). We should do the same!

Employment Point: *Pray regularly to be prepared for any crisis.*

―――◦◉◦―――

July 29

Psalms 56–58, with Acts 28:1–15

I will cry out to God Most High, to God who performs all things for me (Psalm 57:2).

What should you do from a cave?

Psalms 57 and 142 have the setting of David hiding in a cave for protection. Wisely he turns to the Lord in prayer, "Be merciful to me, O God, be merciful to me! For my soul trusts in You" (Psalm 57:1). He knows that the Lord is on his side. "I will cry out to God Most High," writes David, "to God who performs all things for me" (Psalm 57:2). During a perilous time he acknowledges that his "soul is among lions" (Psalm 57:4), but exclaims, "Be exalted, O God, above the heavens; let Your glory be above all the earth" (Psalm 57:5). Like Joseph who saw God working for him (Genesis 50:20), David also trusts "that all things work together for good to those who love God" (Romans 8:28).

Employment Point: *Praise God, anticipating His deliverance while in a cave.*

JULY 30

PSALMS 59–61, WITH
ACTS 28:16–31

———◦❖◦———

Then Paul dwelt two whole years in his own rented house (Acts 28:30).

HOW DO YOU RESPOND WHEN GOD LIMITS THE GOALS THAT YOU'VE SET FOR HIM?

Paul desires to preach Jesus where the gospel hasn't been heralded (Romans 15:20). Yet God permits him to be placed under house arrest for two years. Why would God limit the apostle whose goal is to spread the gospel prolifically? We need to remember the following words of the Lord from Isaiah 55:8, "For My thoughts are not your thoughts, nor are your ways My ways." Amazingly, the Lord expands Paul's outreach by limiting him. During Paul's imprisonment he pens Ephesians, Philippians, Colossians, and Philemon. Think about the breadth of outreach these letters have brought over two millennia. Moreover, Paul writes while imprisoned, "that the things which happened to me have actually turned out for the furtherance of the gospel" (Philippians 1:12). Only God could do this!

EMPLOYMENT POINT: *Trust God to broaden your ministry, even while being limited.*

———◦❖◦———

July 31

Psalms 62–64, with Romans 1

My soul, wait silently for God alone, for my expectation is from Him (Psalm 62:5).

How should you talk to yourself?

David has learned the fine art of when and how to talk to himself. He addresses his entire being, as shown by the words "my soul." Boldly the man after God's own heart tells himself what to do. "My soul," commands David, "wait silently for God alone." The restless man of God points his entire being to rely only upon the Lord because He is "my rock, my salvation, my defense, my glory, my strength, and my refuge" (Psalm 62:6–7). How have you personalized your relationship with God? How often do you call upon Him using the word *my*? Like David, Paul has a personal relationship with God. He is not ashamed of the gospel (Romans 1:16), but calls the message about Jesus' life, death, and resurrection *my* gospel (Romans 2:16).

Employment Point: *Personalize your relationship with God, trusting Him at all times.*

August 1

Psalms 65–67, with Romans 2

Therefore you are inexcusable, O man, whoever you are who judge, for in whatever you judge another you condemn yourself; for you who judge practice the same things (Romans 2:1).

Do you practice what you preach?

Paul shows the Roman believers the sinfulness of all men from Romans 1:18–3:20. He also uses a series of questions exposing their own sin and hypocrisy. Pointedly he asks, "You, therefore, who teach another, do you not teach yourself? You who preach that a man should not steal, do you steal? You who say, 'Do not commit adultery,' do you commit adultery? You who abhor idols, do you rob temples?" (Romans 2:21–22). Masterfully the wise apostle unveils the duplicity of the Jews who have not lived up to their name. The name "Jew" means *praise*. Yet God expects all of us to bring praise to His name (Romans 2:28–29).

Employment Point: *Practice what you preach, which will cause your life to bring praise to God.*

AUGUST 2

PSALMS 68–69, WITH ROMANS 3

For all have sinned and fall short of the glory of God (Romans 3:23).

DO YOU UNDERSTAND THE IMPLICATIONS OF ADAM'S LIFE?

The Greek verb "have sinned" comes from the aorist tense, which shows past time. Adam became our representative in the Garden of Eden, and when he sinned we did likewise. Paul connects the dots with the following assessment: "Therefore, just as through one man sin entered the world, and death through sin, and thus death spread to all men, because all sinned" (Romans 5:12). Again the term "sinned" occurs in the aorist (past) tense. Thankfully the story doesn't end there. Paul writes, "For as in Adam all die, even so in Christ all shall be made alive" (1 Corinthians 15:22). The apostle leads us past the first man (Adam) to our sin-bearer (Jesus). Our mission is to proclaim Adam's impact on mankind and how Jesus took the fall for us.

EMPLOYMENT POINT: *Guide sinners beyond Adam's transgression to Jesus' reconciliation.*

AUGUST 3

PSALMS 70–72, WITH ROMANS 4

For You are my hope, O Lord GOD; You are my trust from my youth (Psalm 71:5).

HOW DO YOU PROTECT YOURSELF FROM THE FEARS ASSOCIATED WITH AGING?

"By You I have been upheld from birth;" writes the psalmist, "You are He who took me out of my mother's womb" (Psalm 71:6). The writer of this psalm rehearses God's faithfulness to him from birth in order to combat his fears of growing old. He reflects upon his past, "O God, You have taught me from my youth; and to this day I declare Your wondrous works" (Psalm 71:17). Solomon's following admonition to youth should be heeded: "Remember now your Creator in the days of your youth, Before the difficult days comes, And the years draw near when you say, 'I have no pleasure in them'" (Ecclesiastes 12:1). Learning valuable faith lessons while young will help sustain you later.

EMPLOYMENT POINT: *Build a lasting godly foundation in your youth that will endure the test of time.*

August 4

Psalms 73–74, with Romans 5

Therefore, having been justified by faith, we have peace with God through our Lord Jesus Christ (Romans 5:1).

Does the peace of Jesus permeate your life?

Only through believing in Jesus' finished work can an individual experience peace with God. Paul goes as far as to say the following about Jesus: "For He Himself is our peace" (Ephesians 2:14). Jesus often extended a greeting of peace when He appeared to His saints. Now that He is at the right hand of God, we are given the Holy Spirit who brings us peace. The apostle writes, "But the fruit of the Spirit is love, joy, peace" (Galatians 5:22), which the believer experiences when he walks with God. Also, sure footing is granted to the child of God who carries the peace of God to others. Paul pens, "having shod your feet with the preparation of the gospel of peace" (Ephesians 6:15).

EMPLOYMENT POINT: *Experience and promote God's peace through the indwelling Holy Spirit.*

AUGUST 5

PSALMS 75–77, WITH ROMANS 6

For he who has died has been freed from sin (Romans 6:7).

ARE YOU AMONG THE LIVING DEAD?

Positionally, we have been crucified with Jesus and sit with Him in heavenly places. You and I are elevated to God's right hand because of our relationship with Jesus. Our salvation has "raised us up together, and made us sit together in the heavenly places in Christ Jesus" (Ephesians 2:6). For this reason God "has blessed us with every spiritual blessing in the heavenly places in Christ" (Ephesians 1:3). Understanding our positional sanctification enables us not to yield to temptation. Paul shares, "I have been crucified with Christ; it is no longer I who live, but Christ lives in me; and the life which I now live in the flesh I live by faith in the Son of God, who loved me and gave Himself for me" (Galatians 2:20).

EMPLOYMENT POINT: *Experience victory over the old nature, because of your union with Jesus.*

August 6

Psalm 78, with Romans 7

We will not hide them from their children, telling to the generation to come the praises of the LORD, and His strength and His wonderful works that He has done (Psalm 78:4).

ARE YOU TELLING THE STORY TO THE NEXT GENERATION?

God gave the Law of Moses to the children of Israel. The essence of the Law reveals the person and work of God. In other words, it teaches the people about the very nature of the Lord, and based upon His nature, what the Israelites were to do. God "commanded our fathers, that they should make them known to their children" (Psalm 78:5). Moses pens about the words of the Law, "You shall teach them diligently to your children, and shall talk of them when you sit in your house, when you walk by the way, when you lie down, and when you rise up" (Deuteronomy 6:7).

EMPLOYMENT POINT: *Teach the next generation about God's person and work, as revealed in the Bible.*

AUGUST 7

PSALMS 79–81, WITH ROMANS 8:1–18

For I consider that the sufferings of this present time are not worthy to be compared with the glory which shall be revealed in us (Romans 8:18).

HAVE YOU WEIGHED YOUR PRESENT SUFFERINGS FOR JESUS IN LIGHT OF THE COMING GLORY?

Paul suffered much! Observe that the word "suffering" is plural in Romans 8:18. He informs the Corinthians about his ministry in Asia, "that we were burdened beyond measure, above strength, so that we despaired even of life. Yes, we had the sentence of death in ourselves" (2 Corinthians 1:8–9). He catalogues the many afflictions he endured in 2 Corinthians 11:23–33. Yet he writes, "For our light affliction, which is but for a moment, is working for us a far more exceeding and eternal weight of glory" (2 Corinthians 4:17). Paul's eternal perspective "that all things work together for good" (Romans 8:28) has served him well. We should similarly adopt this mindset.

EMPLOYMENT POINT: *Evaluate your present trials in light of your future glory.*

AUGUST 8

PSALMS 82–84, WITH ROMANS 8:19–39

For the LORD God is a sun and shield; the LORD will give grace and glory; no good thing will He withhold from those who walk uprightly (Psalm 84:11).

HAVE YOU CONSIDERED THE BENEFITS OF WALKING WITH GOD?

The psalmist writes, "For a day in Your courts is better than a thousand. I would rather be a doorkeeper in the house of my God than dwell in the tents of wickedness" (Psalm 84:10). The writer then gives the reason for his desire to be with the Lord in Psalm 84:11, "For the LORD God is a sun and shield." Consider the following benefits granted to those who abide in God: He gives direction and protection, His favor and glory descend upon you, and He withholds nothing good from you. These perks lead me to Psalm 37:4. David shares, "Delight yourself also in the LORD, and He shall give you the desires of your heart."

EMPLOYMENT POINT: *Walk with God and personally experience His goodness.*

AUGUST 9

PSALMS 85–87, WITH
ROMANS 9

—◦—

For I could wish that I myself were accursed from Christ for my brethren, my countrymen according to the flesh (Romans 9:3).

WHAT SACRIFICE WOULD YOU BE WILLING TO MAKE FOR THE LOST TO BE SAVED?

Jesus sacrificed His life for us in order that we might be saved. The apostle Paul yearns for his fellow Jews to be saved; he'd be willing to give his soul for theirs. "Accursed" carries the idea that Paul would sacrificially dedicate himself to destruction for God's sake. Clearly the man after God's own heart imitates the love of his Lord. Elsewhere he writes, "Christ has redeemed us from the curse of the law, having become a curse for us" (Galatians 3:13). Moreover, his passion reflects the heart of God "who desires all men to be saved and to come to the knowledge of the truth" (1 Timothy 2:4).

EMPLOYMENT POINT: *Align your heart with God's heart and long for the lost to be found.*

—◦—

August 10

Psalms 88–89, with Romans 10

For Christ is the end of the law for righteousness to everyone who believes (Romans 10:4).

Have you fulfilled the Law through a personal relationship with Jesus?

The first word in the Greek sentence in Romans 10:4 is "end." Paul emphasizes that Jesus is the goal or completion of the Old Testament Law leading to our righteousness. Our Lord joins two perplexed disciples as they walk to Emmaus. They are struggling to understand how the Messiah could die. Jesus restrains them from knowing who He is as He travels with them (Luke 24:16). The living Word unfolds the purpose of the Law to them. Luke records, "And beginning at Moses and all the Prophets, He expounded to them in all the Scriptures the things concerning Himself" (Luke 24:27). Jesus fulfills the Law (Matthew 5:17) and imparts God's righteousness to all who believe in Him (2 Corinthians 5:21).

Employment Point: *Fulfill the Law by believing in Jesus, who alone kept the Law.*

AUGUST 11

PSALMS 90–92, WITH ROMANS 11:1–21

So teach us to number our days, that we may gain a heart of wisdom (Psalm 90:12).

ARE YOU GROWING IN WISDOM BY MAKING EACH DAY COUNT FOR GOD?

Moses reminds us that the eternal God is our security (Psalm 90:1–2). He alone is eternal and has "been our dwelling place in all generations" (Psalm 90:1). Conversely, man is frail. "You turn man to destruction," pens Moses (Psalm 90:3). Moses uses the Hebrew word that means *man in his frailty*. James concurs with Moses about the brevity of life. "It is even a vapor that appears for a little time and then vanishes away" (James 4:14). Moses and James would encourage us to do the math concerning our brief earthly stay. "So teach us to number our days," writes Moses, "that we may gain a heart of wisdom" (Psalm 90:12). God's wisdom is available for those who live for Him.

EMPLOYMENT POINT: *Make each day count for God, and glean His wisdom.*

AUGUST 12

PSALMS 93–95, WITH
ROMANS 11:22–36

Today, if you will hear His voice: Do not harden your hearts, as in the rebellion (Psalm 95:7–8).

HAVE YOU ENTERED INTO GOD'S REST?

"For the LORD is the great God," writes the psalmist, "and the great King above all gods" (Psalm 95:3). We are to "worship and bow down; let us kneel before the LORD our Maker. For He is our God" (Psalm 95:6–7). The author of Hebrews exhorts the Jews to whom he's writing (called "brethren" in Hebrews 3:12) not to turn away from Jesus, as the Israelites did to God after witnessing His power in the wilderness. That generation could not enter into the rest of the land of Canaan because of their disobedience. Likewise we can know that Jesus is eternally God and still not believe upon His finished work in order to be saved. Sadly, Moses' generation "could not enter in because of unbelief" (Hebrews 3:19).

EMPLOYMENT POINT: *Don't turn away from Jesus, who alone can save your soul.*

AUGUST 13

PSALMS 96–98, WITH ROMANS 12

And do not be conformed to this world, but be transformed by the renewing of your mind (Romans 12:2).

WHAT ARE YOU PUTTING INTO YOUR MIND?

You have heard it said that physically you are what you eat. Biblically speaking, spiritually you are what you think. Paul desires the believers at Rome to offer themselves as "a living sacrifice" to God (Romans 12:1). The soul, spirit, and body should be dedicated to God. Believers are not to be squeezed into the mold of this world's system, which means participating in the lust of the flesh, the lust of the eyes, and the pride of life. Rather, "bringing every thought into captivity to the obedience of Christ" (2 Corinthians 10:5) should be our goal. We are now to put off the old man and put on the new (Ephesians 4:22, 24). Moreover, "be renewed in the spirit of your mind" writes Paul (Ephesians 4:23).

EMPLOYMENT POINT: *Transform your mind through filling it with God's Word.*

August 14

Psalms 99–102, with Romans 13

I will set nothing wicked before my eyes (Psalm 101:3).

How are you safeguarding your mind?

David walks with integrity and surrounds himself with people who practice the same. He says, "I will behave wisely in a perfect way" (Psalm 101:2). He determines to live skillfully *on a road of integrity*, which is the literal meaning of "in perfect way." Furthermore, he declares, "I will set nothing wicked before my eyes" (Psalm 101:3). The term "wicked" means *worthless*. When my three sons lived under our roof, my wife and I printed out and placed on top of every television and computer screen the following: "I will set nothing wicked before my eyes." Our family strived to please God by only viewing those things that pleased Him; we didn't squander our time. Purpose to protect your mind by printing out and placing Psalm 101:3 above all your viewing devices.

Employment Point: *Guard your mind by only viewing those things that please the Lord.*

AUGUST 15

PSALMS 103–104, WITH ROMANS 14

———

As far as the east is from the west, so far has He removed our transgressions from us (Psalm 103:12).

ARE YOU LIVING IN LIGHT OF THE MERISM IN PSALM 103:12?

David, the psalmist, uses a merism to describe the mercy of God. A merism consists of two contrasting words that depict the completeness or entirety of something. The words "east" and "west" show two extremes and convey the vastness of God's mercy to pardon our sin. Another example of the extent of God's loving kindness to His children is given in the previous verse. "For as the heavens are high above the earth," pens David, "So great is His mercy toward those who fear Him" (Psalm 103:11). One of God's attributes is mercy. Since the Lord is eternal in nature, there is no limit to the mercy He can offer to His children.

EMPLOYMENT POINT: *Bless the Lord for the many benefits He shares with us, including extending His mercy to us.*

———

AUGUST 16

PSALMS 105–106, WITH ROMANS 15:1–20

And so I have made it my aim to preach the gospel, not where Christ was named (Romans 15:20).

WHAT IS YOUR AMBITION FOR JESUS?

Our Lord Jesus lays out the mission for the church through the Great Commission (Matthew 28:18–20). Moreover, He sets out a strategy for the early church, "and you shall be witnesses to Me in Jerusalem, and in all Judea and Samaria, and to the end of the earth" (Acts 1:8). Paul's goal as derived from Jesus' strategy for the church is to "preach the gospel, not where Christ was named." Three times Paul uses the word "aim" in his writings (Romans 15:20; 2 Corinthians 5:9; 1 Thessalonians 4:11). The Greek term "aim" means *to love honor*. Its New Testament uses imply loving honor for God. We similarly should be ambitious for Jesus, and ask Him to give us goals worthy of His glory!

EMPLOYMENT POINT: *Love to honor God, through having an action plan derived from the Lord.*

AUGUST 17

PSALMS 107–108, WITH
ROMANS 15:21–33

For He satisfies the longing soul, and fills the hungry soul with goodness (Psalm 107:9).

HAS GOD SATISFIED YOUR SOUL?

The psalmist understands that only God brings contentment to the soul, which is the entire person. Yet He desires us to seek Him, so that He alone can fulfill our deepest needs. "Satisfies" means *to be satisfied, have enough,* or *too much.* Jesus addresses this topic in the Beatitudes. Our Lord preaches, "Blessed are those who hunger and thirst for righteousness, for they shall be filled" (Matthew 5:6). Only the Lord can satiate the hunger and quench the thirst of our inner being. James gives the following command: "Draw near to God and He will draw near to you" (James 4:8). The half-brother of the Lord grasps the truth that God rewards those who approach Him. After all, "He is a rewarder of those who diligently seek Him" (Hebrews 11:6).

EMPLOYMENT POINT: *Draw near to the Lord to have His goodness satisfy your soul.*

August 18

Psalms 109–111, with Romans 16

And the God of peace will crush Satan under your feet shortly (Romans 16:20).

Are you longing for Satan's crushing?

A battle has been raging for thousands of years. After Eve partakes of the forbidden fruit, God speaks, "And I will put enmity between you and the woman, and between your seed and her Seed; He shall bruise your head, and you shall bruise His heel" (Genesis 3:15). The woman's Seed is Jesus and the serpent's seed is the devil's followers throughout the ages, including both people and demons. We are called to partner with Jesus. Paul writes about his own ministry, "to open their [the unsaved] eyes, in order to turn them from darkness to light, and from the power of Satan to God" (Acts 26:18). Satan's final destination is the lake of fire (Revelation 20:10); however, our mission is to cross enemy lines and bring the lost to the God of peace.

Employment Point: *Rescue the perishing while anticipating Satan's demise.*

AUGUST 19

PSALMS 112–115, WITH
1 CORINTHIANS 1

Praise the LORD! Blessed is the man who fears the LORD, who delights greatly in His commandments (Psalm 112:1).

ARE YOU EXPERIENCING THE BLESSINGS OF THE LORD?

To fear the Lord is to have a deep reverence for His person and work. The psalmist lays out particular blessings upon the individual who fears God and keeps His commandments. First, the Lord imparts both physical and lasting spiritual blessings. "Wealth and riches will be in his house," conveys the psalmist, "and his righteousness endures forever" (Psalm 112:3). Indeed, he will experience light instead of darkness. "Unto the upright there arises light in the darkness" (Psalm 112:4). The man who fears the Lord is generous, which causes the Lord to bless him abundantly (Psalm 112:5, 9). "He has dispersed abroad, He has given to the poor; His righteousness endures forever; His horn will be exalted with honor" (Psalm 112:9). Let's fear Him for length of days!

EMPLOYMENT POINT: *Fear the Lord and know His multifaceted blessings.*

AUGUST 20

PSALMS 116–118, WITH
1 CORINTHIANS 2

But he who is spiritual judges all things, yet he himself is rightly judged by no one (1 Corinthians 2:15).

ARE YOU A SPIRITUALLY MINDED PERSON?

Paul founded the church at Corinth in about AD 51. He writes this letter to those saints in about AD 56. Sadly, after five years of being saved, he writes, "And I, brethren, could not speak to you as to spiritual people but as to carnal, as to babes in Christ" (1 Corinthians 3:1). The apostle differentiates between three kinds of people in 1 Corinthians 2:14–3:3. First, he writes about "the natural man [who] does not receive the things of the Spirit of God" (1 Corinthians 2:14). Paul's term "natural" literally means *soulish*; this man is unsaved. We've also seen him address the Corinthians' immaturity. He calls them "carnal," which means fleshly. The apostle desires both the Corinthian saints and us to be mature and evaluate everything by God's Word.

EMPLOYMENT POINT: *Become spiritual by evaluating all things by the Bible.*

AUGUST 21

PSALM 119:1–48, WITH
1 CORINTHIANS 3

Your word I have hidden in my heart, that I might not sin against You (Psalm 119:11).

HOW CAN A YOUNG PERSON HAVE VICTORY OVER SIN?

The psalmist asks and answers the following: "How can a young man cleanse his way? By taking heed according to Your word" (Psalm 119:9). Pursuing God to know Him up close and personal takes maximum effort. "With my whole heart I have sought You;" continues the poet, "Oh, let me not wander from Your commandments!" (Psalm 119:10). Jesus, in His humanity, exemplifies a passion to know and please His Father. Before entering the ministry our Lord "fasted forty days and forty nights" (Matthew 4:2) in His quest to walk with the Father and glorify Him through overcoming temptation. When tempted by Satan, He quotes from Deuteronomy 8:3: "Man shall not live by bread alone, but by every word that proceeds from the mouth of God" (Matthew 4:4). We should imitate Him!

EMPLOYMENT POINT: *Live victoriously through the power of God's Word.*

August 22

Psalm 119:49–104, with 1 Corinthians 4

But with me it is a very small thing that I should be judged by you or by a human court. In fact, I do not even judge myself (1 Corinthians 4:3).

Do you worry about how people regard you?

Paul explains God's judgment of believers in 1 Corinthians 3. He alone tests each one's life work to determine whether a Christian will receive a reward (1 Corinthians 3:11–15). The Corinthians unfairly judge Paul; however, he isn't concerned because Jesus will reward his faithful service. He concludes, "Therefore judge nothing before the time, until the Lord comes, who will both bring to light the hidden things of darkness and reveal the counsels of the hearts. Then each one's praise will come from God" (1 Corinthians 4:5). Paul uses the term "comes" as in "the Lord comes" in the past tense; Jesus certainly will return and reward Paul.

Employment Point: *Live confidently that only Jesus is qualified to judge you, and to reward you accordingly.*

AUGUST 23

PSALM 119:105–176, WITH 1 CORINTHIANS 5

Direct my steps by Your word, and let no iniquity have dominion over me (Psalm 119:133).

HOW CONFIDENT ARE YOU IN THE INTEGRITY OF GOD'S WORD?

The psalmist displays an absolute confidence in the Bible. He believes that the same God who guided Abraham, who led the Israelites as a nation, and who leads us today by His Spirit (Romans 8:14) can give us direction through the Scriptures. He writes, "Your word is very pure; therefore Your servant loves it" (Psalm 119:140). Agur displays a similar view of the Bible. He says, "Every word of God is pure; He is a shield to those who put their trust in Him" (Proverbs 30:5). We can believe without reservation that the Scripture is "given by inspiration of God, and is profitable for doctrine, for reproof, for correction, for instruction in righteousness" (2 Timothy 3:16). After all, "the entirety of Your word is truth" (Psalm 119:160).

EMPLOYMENT POINT: *Seek God's direction through the trusted Word of God.*

AUGUST 24

PSALMS 120–123, WITH 1 CORINTHIANS 6

For you were bought at a price; therefore glorify God in your body and in your spirit, which are God's (1 Corinthians 6:20).

DO YOU LIVE AS IF THE HOLY SPIRIT DWELLS WITHIN YOU?

Perhaps the Corinthians adopted the following slogan to justify their immorality: "Foods for the stomach and the stomach for foods" (1 Corinthians 6:13). Were they suggesting that because God made food to satisfy hunger, He similarly permits sexual passion in any context to be fulfilled? The Corinthians were aware of the temple of Aphrodite, which housed one thousand temple prostitutes. Some of them perhaps frequented the temple during their former pagan practices. Paul explains that we are to lead pure lives because God's Spirit is housed in the temple of our physical bodies (1 Corinthians 6:19). For this reason, we are to bring glory to God by appropriately using our temple. His residence within us is costly; it's accomplished through Jesus' death.

EMPLOYMENT POINT: *Glorify God through holy living.*

August 25

Psalms 124–127, with 1 Corinthians 7:1–24

———

Behold, children are a heritage from the LORD, the fruit of the womb is a reward (Psalm 127:3).

Do you honor children as a gift from God?

God's Word places great emphasis upon the value of children. Unlike the other nations, the Israelites were to despise child sacrifice (Deuteronomy 12:31). Moreover, parents and grandparents are given the task to school their children and grandchildren in the ways of the Lord (Deuteronomy 6:1–9). Also, Jesus made time out of His busy schedule to bless the children. Mark 10:13 reveals that the disciples "brought little children to Him, that He might touch them; but the disciples rebuked those who brought them." Our Lord corrects His followers and commands, "Let the little children come to Me, and do not forbid them; for of such is the kingdom of God" (Mark 10:14). Jesus' statement shows that even those unwanted children aborted by their parents are welcome in heaven.

EMPLOYMENT POINT: *Make time to bless children through your words and deeds.*

———

August 26

Psalms 128–131, with 1 Corinthians 7:25–40

Blessed is every one who fears the Lord, who walks in His ways (Psalm 128:1).

Are you walking in God's ways?

God is no respecter of persons; He blesses each individual who fears Him. The wise man informs us, "The blessing of the Lord makes one rich, and He adds no sorrow with it" (Proverbs 10:22). God honors the work of our hands (Psalm 128:2) and our family when we revere Him. We are told, "Your wife shall be like a fruitful vine in the very heart of your house; your children like olive plants all around your table" (Psalm 128:3). "Your wife shall be like a fruitful vine," writes the poet about the godly man, and "your children like olive plants." Unlike grass, which quickly grows and dies, he equates the godly with a "fruitful vine" and "olive plants" that have staying power. Remember, "thus shall the man be blessed who fears the Lord" (Psalm 128:4).

Employment Point: *Revere God, and He'll bless your family.*

AUGUST 27

PSALMS 132–135, WITH
1 CORINTHIANS 8

Therefore, if food makes my brother stumble, I will never again eat meat, lest I make my brother stumble (1 Corinthians 8:13).

DO YOU REGULATE YOUR FOOD AND DRINK CHOICES BY CHRISTIAN LOVE?

The Corinthians had a couple of choices to purchase their meat. They could go to the market and pay the full price for meat. Their other option is to purchase the leftover meat not used in the sacrifices at the local temple. The latter choice comes at a discount, but some believers would want nothing to do with this option or food because of its association with idols. Although God has declared all food clean, we shouldn't partake of anything that causes a brother to stumble. The apostle writes, "It is good neither to eat meat nor drink wine nor do anything by which your brother stumbles or is offended or is made weak" (Romans 14:21).

EMPLOYMENT POINT: *Let love for your brothers and sisters in Christ govern your Christian liberty.*

August 28

Psalms 136–138, with 1 Corinthians 9

But I discipline my body and bring it into subjection, lest, when I have preached to others, I myself should become disqualified (1 Corinthians 9:27).

What's your strategy to complete the Christian race?

Paul's audience is aware of both the Olympic and isthmian games. Corinth hosted the latter and strict training rules are imposed for the participants. Any violation from the standards results in being disqualified to compete. In this setting Paul asks the following question, which expects a positive answer: "Do you not know that those who run in a race all run, but one receives the prize?" He continues, "Run in such a way that you may obtain it" (1 Corinthians 9:24). We are similarly to discipline ourselves for the Christian life; focus is essential to complete the mission entrusted to us. The battle in the ring of life doesn't compare to shadow boxing (1 Corinthians 9:26), but a regiment of strict discipline and training.

Employment Point: *Sacrifice self-indulgence and await your reward.*

August 29

Psalms 139–141, with 1 Corinthians 10:1–13

———❧———

I will praise You, for I am fearfully and wonderfully made; marvelous are Your works, and that my soul knows very well (Psalm 139:14).

Do you focus upon self-image, or being made in God's image?

The reading of Psalm 139 should cause the worshiper to stand in awe of God. He is omniscient (Psalm 139:1–6). Our heavenly Father knows everything past, present, and future. "For there is not a word on my tongue," writes the poet, "But behold, O LORD, you know it altogether" (Psalm 139:4). He even knows every word that we speak or will ever utter. Moreover, He is omnipotent (Psalm 139:13–18). By God's mighty power we were woven together in our mother's womb (Psalm 139:13). He put and developed our bones within her womb (Psalm 139:15). No wonder the psalmist exclaims: "I will praise You, for I am fearfully and wonderfully made" (Psalm 139:14).

EMPLOYMENT POINT: *Focus upon the God who formed you in the womb for His glory.*

———❧———

AUGUST 30

PSALMS 142–144, WITH
1 CORINTHIANS 10:14–33

Therefore, my beloved, flee from idolatry (1 Corinthians 10:14).

ARE YOU FLEEING FROM IDOLS, WHILE RUNNING TO GOD?

Five times Paul uses the word "all" in 1 Corinthians 10:1–4. He shows the privileges that the entire nation of Israel had to see God's vast power, as they were extricated from the captivity in Egypt and had their needs supernaturally met. Yet the majority of them turned to idols. An idol is not a neutral object. Behind the material creation lies a supernatural power. Paul exposes the hidden danger of idolatry. He writes, "that the things which the Gentiles sacrifice they sacrifice to demons and not to God" (1 Corinthians 10:20). Jesus makes the following observation: "No one can serve two masters" (Matthew 6:24). Furthermore, Paul equates covetousness with idolatry (Colossians 3:5). Every child of God should heed John's prescription. He pens, "Little children, keep yourselves from idols" (1 John 5:21).

EMPLOYMENT POINT: *Flee from idolatry and run to the living God.*

August 31

Psalms 145–147, with
1 Corinthians 11:1–15

Great is the LORD, and greatly to be praised; and His greatness is unsearchable (Psalm 145:3).

Are you pursuing the infinite greatness of the living God?

David writes Psalm 145 with each verse beginning with a succeeding letter of the Hebrew alphabet, which labels it as an acrostic psalm. He praises the Lord for both His goodness and greatness. God is good. Men who know him "shall utter the memory of Your great goodness" (Psalm 145:7). Moreover the psalmist writes, "The LORD is good to all, and His tender mercies are over all His works" (Psalm 145:9). Our Lord is not only good, but also He's great. "His greatness is unsearchable," pens the poet (Psalm 145:3). "Unsearchable" also appears in Isaiah 40:28 and Job 9:10. Job comments, "He does great things past finding out, Yes, wonders without number" (Job 9:10). Let's ponder both the goodness and greatness of God today!

Employment Point: *Enjoy the goodness of God while searching out His greatness.*

255

September 1

Psalms 148–150, with
1 Corinthians 11:16–34

For if we would judge ourselves, we would not be judged (1 Corinthians 11:31).

When was your last self-examination?

Socrates said that the unexamined life is not worth living. Paul reports that the unexamined life might cost your life. The Corinthians are admonished to scrutinize their lives and confess any known sin before participating in communion. Apparently some of the saints didn't apply this principle. That is why Paul writes, "For this reason many are weak and sick among you, and many sleep [have died]" (1 Corinthians 11:30). The Lord's Table is to be treated with the utmost respect. As the body of Christ gathers for the memorial of Jesus' death, a time of self-examination should precede this ordinance. "If we confess our sins, He is faithful and just to forgive us our sins and to cleanse us from all unrighteousness," writes John (1 John 1:9).

EMPLOYMENT POINT: *Examine your life and confess any known sin before participating in communion.*

SEPTEMBER 2

PROVERBS 1–2, WITH
1 CORINTHIANS 12

———————

The fear of the LORD is the beginning of knowledge, but fools despise wisdom and instruction (Proverbs 1:7).

ARE YOU LIVING IN THE FEAR OF THE LORD?

"The fear of the Lord" means *to reverently and obediently walk with God.* Employing this lifestyle will cause you to grow in the knowledge and wisdom of God. Observe the connection between fearing the Lord and wisdom in Psalm 111:10. "The fear of the LORD is the beginning of wisdom; a good understanding have all those who do His commandments." Job understands the linkage. He says, "Behold, the fear of the Lord, that is wisdom, and to depart from evil is understanding" (Job 28:28). The godly patriarch exhibits wisdom and knowledge by fearing the Lord and is juxtaposed with two men of faith. Ezekiel places him next to Noah and Daniel as models of righteousness (Ezekiel 14:14, 20).

EMPLOYMENT POINT: *Walk in the fear of the Lord and grow in the knowledge and wisdom of God.*

———————

September 3

Proverbs 3–4, with
1 Corinthians 13

Though I speak with the tongues of men and of angels, but have not love, I have become sounding brass or a clanging cymbal (1 Corinthians 13:1).

Are you using your spiritual gift with the attitude of love?

Paul states multiple hyperboles (overstatements) to make his point that love is more important than spiritual gifts (1 Corinthians 13:1–3). He didn't possess "all mysteries" and "all knowledge" and "have all faith" (1 Corinthians 13:2). Yet if he did, and didn't minister with love, the entire work would be fruitless. Spiritual gifts, which are a supernatural ability given by God to believers at the moment of salvation for the building up of the body of Christ, are temporal. They exist for a time, but love is eternal. That's why Paul shares, "And now abide faith, hope, love, these three; but the greatest of these is love" (1 Corinthians 13:13).

Employment Point: *Serve the body of Christ, using your spiritual gifts with love.*

September 4

Proverbs 5–6, with
1 Corinthians 14:1–20

———◦◦◦———

Go the ant, you sluggard! Consider her ways and be wise (Proverbs 6:6).

Are you a diligent worker like the ant?

God loves work; we begin the Bible learning about His work during the first six days of creation. Our heavenly Father found satisfaction in labor. Moses records what God did after day six. He writes, "Then God saw everything that He had made, and indeed it was very good" (Genesis 1:31). Moreover, the Lord blesses Adam by placing him in the Garden of Eden (Genesis 2:8–15). We are privileged to work and provide for our needs and that of our family. Indeed, a good work ethic is just what the thief needs to replace a bad habit. Paul counsels, "Let him who stole steal no longer, but rather let him labor, working with his hands what is good, that he may have something to give him who has need" (Ephesians 4:28).

Employment Point: *Maintain a good work ethic to please God and to serve others.*

———◦◦◦———

September 5

Proverbs 7–8, with 1 Corinthians 14:21–40

Say to wisdom, "You are my sister," and call understanding your nearest kin (Proverbs 7:4).

Do you tread the path of wisdom?

The wise man says, "For at the window of my house I looked through my lattice, and saw among the simple, I perceived among the youths, a young man devoid of understanding, passing along the street near her corner; and he took the path to her house" (Proverbs 7:6–8). Our author describes a dead man walking; he lacks discretion and takes a deadly path. "Her house is the way to hell," writes the wise man, "Descending to the chambers of death" (Proverbs 7:27). There are many avenues leading to this dark corridor. One wrong click of the mouse, a poor movie choice, or physically traveling the wrong road can lead to your demise. Your life is precious to God, so choose to walk the path of wisdom!

Employment Point: *Journey down the path of wisdom to avoid self-destruction.*

September 6

Proverbs 9–10, with
1 Corinthians 15:1–32

Then last of all He was seen by me also, as by one born out of due time (1 Corinthians 15:8).

Have you considered the evidence in Paul's defense of Jesus' resurrection?

Our Lord first appears to Mary Magdalene after conquering death (Mark 16:9). Yet Paul doesn't include her in his list of witnesses. He is establishing a legal defense of Jesus' resurrection. Sadly, a woman's testimony is considered invalid during the first century. Imagine the courtroom scene. Paul calls more than five hundred eyewitnesses who had seen Jesus after He was crucified. The jury wouldn't have to rely upon circumstantial evidence in this case. Then the last witness is Paul himself, who at one time persecuted the church. He carries a powerful testimony because of his former hostilities toward Jesus and Christians. Moreover, he is the only eyewitness to see Jesus after His ascension. The host of witnesses encourages us to live for Jesus!

Employment Point: *Boldly proclaim the gospel, because Jesus is alive.*

September 7

Proverbs 11–12, with
1 Corinthians 15:33–58

Therefore, my beloved brethren, be steadfast, immovable, always abounding in the work of the Lord, knowing that your labor is not in vain in the Lord (1 Corinthians 15:58).

Are you laboring to the point of perspiration for Jesus?

Paul chooses the word "therefore" to conclude the longest chapter in the Bible on the topic of resurrection. The Greek construction gives us the meaning of *conclusion*. He concludes that since we are assured of victory over death through Jesus' resurrection that we are now to labor diligently for Him not allowing anything to distract us from the ministry. We don't fight for victory as Christians but from victory because of Jesus. Paul proclaims, "But thanks be to God, who gives us the victory through our Lord Jesus Christ" (1 Corinthians 15:57). Serve Him well, knowing that He'll return to reward you; your labor truly is not in vain!

Employment Point: *Be loyal to the Lord's work, because you are a victor through Jesus.*

SEPTEMBER 8

PROVERBS 13–14, WITH
1 CORINTHIANS 16

On the first day of the week let each of you lay something aside, storing up as he may prosper (1 Corinthians 16:2).

DO YOU REGULARLY ROB GOD?

God, through Malachi, asks the Israelites the following question: "Will a man rob God?" He then declares, "Yet you have robbed Me!" (Malachi 3:8). Israelites were robbing God by not bringing their tithes and offerings to the Temple. Paul teaches that as he had "given orders to the churches of Galatia [concerning giving], so you must do also" (1 Corinthians 16:1). As the church meets on the first day of the week, each believer is to bring his offering as God has caused him to prosper. Not attending church weekly or arriving at church after the offering has been taken is not an excuse to rob God. Whatever we have comes from God, and He is to be regularly honored through our generous giving to His work.

EMPLOYMENT POINT: *Don't rob God by weekly keeping what belongs to Him.*

September 9

Proverbs 15–16, with 2 Corinthians 1

Pride goes before destruction, and a haughty spirit before a fall (Proverbs 16:18).

Are you humbly walking with God?

Pride surfaces by not living in the fear of the Lord. "The fear of the LORD is to hate evil; pride and arrogance and the evil way," writes the wise man (Proverbs 8:13). Micah declares the following: "He has shown you, O man, what is good; and what does the LORD require of you, but to do justly, to love mercy, and to walk humbly with your God?" (Micah 6:8). Whereas pride leads to destruction, those who live in the fear of the Lord are blessed. Peter expresses the importance of replacing pride for humility. He writes, "and be clothed with humility, for 'God resists the proud, but gives grace to the humble'" (1 Peter 5:5). Those who exalt themselves will be humbled (Proverbs 16:18) and those who humble themselves, God exalts (1 Peter 5:6).

Employment Point: *Humbly walk in fear of the Lord to avoid falling.*

September 10

Proverbs 17–18, with
2 Corinthians 2

Now thanks be to God who always leads us in triumph in Christ, and through us diffuses the fragrance of His knowledge in every place (2 Corinthians 2:14).

Are you emitting the sweet aroma of Jesus to every place that you travel?

From the moment we believe in Jesus and are declared righteous until the instant that we are fully conformed to His image, we are triumphant in Christ. Paul reminds us, "we are more than conquerors through Him who loved us" (Romans 8:37). In 2 Corinthians 2:14, the apostle depicts the imagery of a Roman general who had just experienced triumph over his enemies and would subsequently lead a victorious procession. It was a custom in Paul's day that the triumphal procession would be accompanied by the release of sweet smells from the burning spices in the streets. Our Christian lives should also emit the sweet aroma of Jesus.

EMPLOYMENT POINT: *Dispense the aroma of Jesus to every location where He leads you.*

September 11

Proverbs 19–20, with 2 Corinthians 3

The discretion of a man makes him slow to anger, and his glory is to overlook a transgression (Proverbs 19:11).

Do you exercise good sense in your dealings with people?

"Discretion" is translated from a Hebrew noun and means *intelligence* or *good sense*. This *intelligence* doesn't derive from the wisdom of the world or from higher education. A believer who exercises skillful living will make "him slow to anger." He has learned that "a soft answer turns away wrath, but a harsh word stirs up anger" (Proverbs 15:1). Moreover, a person of discretion will "overlook a transgression." Paul makes the case for forgiving others. He imparts the following wisdom: "And be kind to one another, tenderhearted, forgiving one another, even as God in Christ forgave you" (Ephesians 4:32). The Lord has forgiven our past, present, and future sins through the death of Jesus. Let's live skillfully and exhibit patience, while forgiving others.

Employment Point: *Show discretion by being slow to anger and forgiving others.*

SEPTEMBER 12

PROVERBS 21–22, WITH
2 CORINTHIANS 4

Therefore we do not lose heart. Even though our outward man is perishing, yet the inward man is being renewed day by day (2 Corinthians 4:16).

HOW DO YOU CONTINUE SERVING THE LORD IN SPITE OF MANY AFFLICTIONS?

We are ministers of the new covenant (2 Corinthians 3:6). With the heavenly assignment comes opposition from Satan. Paul endures temporal adversity for serving the Lord; however, he compares it with eternity: "For our light affliction, which is but for a moment, is working for us a far more exceeding and eternal weight of glory" (2 Corinthians 4:17). Ponder Paul's difficulties (2 Corinthians 11:16–33). Yet he calls them a "light affliction." How does he arrive at this conclusion? The great apostle gives the answer in Romans 8:18, "For I consider that the sufferings of this present time are not worthy to be compared with the glory which shall be revealed in us."

EMPLOYMENT POINT: *Endure all things for Jesus by having an eternal perspective.*

September 13

Proverbs 23–24, with 2 Corinthians 5

Do not let your heart envy sinners, but be zealous for the fear of the LORD all the day (Proverbs 23:17).

Are you protecting your heart from sinner envy?

Satan loves to show Christians all the fun they could be enjoying. He appeals to his three allies: the lust of the flesh, the lust of the eyes, and the pride of life. The devil takes Jesus on a tour of the world (Luke 4:5). Then he pompously makes the following offer: "All this authority I will give You, and their glory; for this has been delivered to me, and I give it to whomever I wish" (Luke 4:6). Jesus doesn't yield. Consider Isaiah 50:10, "Who among you fears the LORD? Who obeys the voice of His Servant? Who walks in darkness and has no light? Let him trust in the name of the LORD and rely upon his God."

EMPLOYMENT POINT: *Live in the fear of the Lord, and don't submit to sinner envy.*

September 14

Proverbs 25–27, with 2 Corinthians 6

Do not be unequally yoked together with unbelievers. For what fellowship has righteousness with lawlessness? And what communion has light with darkness? And what accord has Christ with Belial? Or what part has a believer with an unbeliever? And what agreement has the temple of God with idols? (2 Corinthians 6:14–16).

Have you separated yourself from false teachers?

Paul asks five rhetorical questions in 2 Corinthians 6:14–16 to make the following point: Jesus and Satan don't mix. False teachers have permeated the Corinthian church. For this reason, Paul gives three commands, "Come out from among them and be separate, says the Lord. Do not touch what is unclean, and I will receive you" (2 Corinthians 6:17). Paul warns his children in the faith that if they will leave the false teachers and cleave to God, then He will treat them again like blessed sons and daughters.

Employment Point: *Do not sit at the feet of false teachers, but separate from them.*

September 15

Proverbs 28–29, with 2 Corinthians 7

He who trusts in his own heart is a fool, but whoever walks wisely will be delivered (Proverbs 28:26).

Why can't you trust your own heart?

We have all received a fallen nature from Adam. For this reason we should not live under the dictates of our heart. Jeremiah elaborates upon this, "The heart is deceitful above all things, and desperately wicked; who can know it?" (Jeremiah 17:9). Rather, we need to allow the Lord to guide us through His Word, prayer, godly counsel, and by His orchestration of the circumstances in our life. "I, the LORD, search the heart," continues Jeremiah, "I test the mind, even to give every man according to his ways, according to the fruit of his doings" (Jeremiah 17:10). Since only God knows us thoroughly, we should yield to His direction. The wise man shares, "Trust in the LORD with all your heart, and lean not on your own understanding" (Proverbs 3:5).

EMPLOYMENT POINT: *Allow God, not your heart, to guide you.*

September 16

Proverbs 30–31, with 2 Corinthians 8

Now godliness with contentment is great gain (1 Timothy 6:6).

What Two Things Should You Pray For?

We are introduced to Agur in Proverbs 30. He understands the power of the Word and prayer. He writes, "Every word of God is pure; He is a shield to those who put their trust in Him" (Proverbs 30:5). Next, he prays to be kept from deception. He requests, "Two things I request of You (deprive me not before I die): Remove falsehood and lies far from me" (Proverbs 30:7–8a). Prudently he seeks the Lord to protect him from being deceived. Next, he shows that we should pray to obtain Godward dependence. He continues, "Give me neither poverty nor riches—feed me with the food allotted to me; lest I be full and deny You, and say, 'Who is the Lord?' Or lest I be poor and steal, and profane the name of my God" (Proverbs 30:8b–9).

Employment Point: *Pray to be kept from deception, and to practice Godward dependence.*

SEPTEMBER 17

ECCLESIASTES 1–3, WITH 2 CORINTHIANS 9

Thanks be to God for His indescribable gift! (2 Corinthians 9:15).

DO YOU SACRIFICIALLY GIVE TO THE LORD'S WORK?

The Macedonian believers knew great poverty, yet gave generously to meet the needs of the poor saints in Jerusalem. Paul holds them up as an example to the Corinthian saints to imitate. He writes, "that in a great trial of affliction the abundance of their joy and their deep poverty abounded in the riches of their liberality" (2 Corinthians 8:2). In essence, the Macedonians further impoverished themselves in order to meet the *needs* of poor believers (2 Corinthians 8:4; 9:12).

Jesus did the same. He left the glories of heaven to become like us, so one day we would be like Him. Our Lord temporarily gave up the treasures of heaven to make us rich. We need to follow in the footsteps of the Macedonians and Jesus, who made themselves poor for the sake of others.

EMPLOYMENT POINT: *Care for the needs of the saints through sacrificial giving.*

SEPTEMBER 18

ECCLESIASTES 4–6, WITH
2 CORINTHIANS 10

When you make a vow to God, do not delay to pay it; for He has no pleasure in fools. Pay what you have vowed—better not to vow than to vow and not pay (Ecclesiastes 5:4–5).

ARE YOU HONORING YOUR VOWS TO GOD?

A vow is a sacred commitment to God. For instance, marriage is a sacred institution, and the bride and groom commit to honor their vows before God and the witnesses present. Solomon cautions us not to rashly take a vow. He says, "Better not to vow than to vow and not pay" (Ecclesiastes 5:5). Regardless of the circumstance that led you to make a vow to God, it should be honored. The psalmist writes, "I will go into Your house with burnt offerings; I will pay You my vows, which my lips have uttered and my mouth has spoken when I was in trouble" (Psalm 66:13–14).

EMPLOYMENT POINT: *Honor God by keeping the vows that you've made before Him.*

September 19

Ecclesiastes 7–9, with 2 Corinthians 11:1–15

For such are false apostles, deceitful workers, transforming themselves into apostles of Christ (2 Corinthians 11:13).

Are you discerning the false from the true?

Jesus repeatedly warns His followers to be aware of deceivers (Matthew 24:4, 5, 11, 24). The term "deceive" that Jesus uses derives from the verb meaning *to wander*. Our English word planet comes from this term. False teachers and apostles lead people astray. Technically speaking, there are not any apostles today. To qualify to be an apostle, an individual had to be a witness of Jesus' resurrection (Acts 1:22), and Paul clearly states that he was the last one to see the risen Lord (1 Corinthians 15:8). Paul uses a different word than Jesus in 2 Corinthians 11:13 to describe those who infiltrate the church. He calls them "deceitful," which means *to beguile through deception* or *to defraud by deception*. Paul exposes their masquerade since they didn't live up to biblical standards.

Employment Point: *Evaluate church leaders by their beliefs and lifestyle.*

September 20

Ecclesiastes 10–12, with 2 Corinthians 11:16–33

Remember now your Creator in the days of your youth, before the difficult days come, and the years draw near when you say, "I have no pleasure in them" (Ecclesiastes 12:1).

Do you use time wisely?

Solomon, who is older and wiser by the time he pens Ecclesiastes, commands younger people not to fritter away their youth, but serve the Creator. The Hebrew term "Creator" is plural and could be translated "Creators." God in Trinity is involved in creation and must be served. Solomon graphically depicts the aging process to warn young people that their vim and vigor will fade (Ecclesiastes 12:2–7), so they should prudently use their time. Moses, who contrasts the eternality of God with frail man (Psalm 90:1–11), writes, "So teach us to number our days, that we may gain a heart of wisdom" (Psalm 90:12). Paul gives an additional reason: "redeeming the time, because the days are evil" (Ephesians 5:16). Wise youth serve their Creators!

Employment Point: *Serve God in your youth.*

September 21

Song of Solomon 1–3, with 2 Corinthians 12

I charge you, O daughters of Jerusalem, by the gazelles or by the does of the field, do not stir up nor awaken love until it pleases (Song of Solomon 2:7).

Do you encourage young people to use their time wisely?

The Song of Solomon is a poetic writing about the love of Solomon and the Shulamite. God wonderfully creates sex for a husband and wife to enjoy; however, waiting until the right season to enjoy this intimacy is His plan. For this reason the Song of Solomon on three occasions warns about stirring passion until the right season (Song of Solomon 2:7; 3:5; 8:4). Christian parents need to guide their children to use their youth wisely and not prematurely "stir up nor awaken love until it pleases." Paul gives sage advice, "But put on the Lord Jesus Christ, and make no provision for the flesh to fulfill its lusts" (Romans 13:14).

EMPLOYMENT POINT: *Walk in wisdom by understanding God's season for your life, and act appropriately.*

September 22

Song of Solomon 4–5, with 2 Corinthians 13

Examine yourselves as to whether you are in the faith. Test yourselves. Do you not know yourselves, that Jesus Christ is in you?—unless indeed you are disqualified (2 Corinthians 13:5).

Do you give yourself regular self-examinations?

Paul issues two commands to the saints at Corinth, which also applies to us. The imperatives are "examine" and "test" yourselves. Sadly, the Corinthians had scrutinized Paul, but had not looked carefully at their own lives. Socrates said that the unexamined life wasn't worth living. Wisely the apostle navigates the critical believers to consider who resides in them. His question expects a positive response: "Do you not know yourselves, that Jesus Christ is in you?" In the former letter to the same group Paul asked a similar question (1 Corinthians 6:19), and then told them "to glorify God in your body and in your spirit, which are God's" (1 Corinthians 6:20).

Employment Point: *Examine your life, and make any necessary changes to please God.*

September 23

Song of Solomon 6–8, with Galatians 1

But even if we, or an angel from heaven, preach any other gospel to you than what we have preached to you, let him be accursed (Galatians 1:8).

Are you proclaiming the true gospel?

Infiltrators influence the Galatian saints. These Judaizers are false teachers who mix the Law with grace, which ruins the message of grace. Paul continually marvels, which is the meaning of the present tense verb "marvel" in Galatians 1:6, "that you are turning away so soon from Him who called you in the grace of Christ, to a different gospel." The gospel is the good news that Jesus died for our sins and rose again, and that anyone who places faith in His finished work is saved. Strongly Paul declares that an individual trumpeting a false message is "accursed," which means *dedicated to destruction*. To show the gravity of the situation Paul repeats the condemnation upon the purveyors of heresy (Galatians 1:9).

Employment Point: *Don't corrupt the gospel of grace by adding works.*

SEPTEMBER 24

ISAIAH 1–3, WITH GALATIANS 2

"Come now, and let us reason together," says the LORD, "Though your sins are like scarlet, they shall be as white as snow; though they are red like crimson, they shall be as wool" (Isaiah 1:18).

ARE YOU MAINTAINING YOUR WALK WITH THE LORD?

Isaiah confronts a people given to compromise. Although the Lord cares for Israel and calls her His vineyard (Isaiah 5:1, 7), she has adopted sinful practices. "Woe to those who call evil good and good evil," proclaims Isaiah, "who put darkness for light, and light for darkness; who put bitter for sweet, and sweet for bitter!" (Isaiah 5:20). The erring people need to seek the God of Light and repent of their sin. John writes, "If we confess our sins, He is faithful and just to forgive us our sins and to cleanse us from all unrighteousness" (1 John 1:9). Repenting from known sin is essential to walking with God.

EMPLOYMENT POINT: *Repent and confess your sin, to restore fellowship with God.*

SEPTEMBER 25

ISAIAH 4–6, WITH GALATIANS 3

So I said: "Woe is me, for I am undone! Because I am a man of unclean lips, and I dwell in the midst of a people of unclean lips; for my eyes have seen the King, the LORD of hosts" (Isaiah 6:5).

HAS THE HOLINESS OF GOD DRIVEN YOU TO YOUR KNEES?

Isaiah receives a vision of God who is "high and lifted up" (Isaiah 6:1). He then observes the seraphim (literally "burning ones"). "And one cried to another and said: 'Holy, holy, holy is the LORD of hosts; the whole earth is full of His glory!'" (Isaiah 6:3). Thrice the word "holy" is attributed to God and appears as a superlative; He alone is holy! Isaiah understands his own sinfulness and the peoples as a result of the vision. He is cleansed of his sin (Isaiah 6:7) and responds to the call of God: "Here am I! Send me" (Isaiah 6:8).

EMPLOYMENT POINT: *Allow God's holiness to humble you and to prepare you for service.*

September 26

Isaiah 7–9, with Galatians 4

But when the fullness of the time had come, God sent forth His Son, born of a woman, born under the law (Galatians 4:4).

Have you considered the timing and purpose of Jesus' arrival?

Moses becomes the first biblical writer pointing to the virgin birth. As God addresses Satan for his manipulation of Eve, He says, "And I will put enmity Between you and the woman, And between your seed and her Seed" (Genesis 3:15). Jesus is the seed of woman and seven centuries after Moses writes, Isaiah gives his prediction. "Behold, the virgin shall conceive and bear a Son, and shall call His name Immanuel" (Isaiah 7:14). Paul cites two purposes of Jesus' birth. He came "to redeem those who were under the law, that we might receive the adoption as sons" (Galatians 4:5). Our Lord came to redeem sinners and to give them the status of sons.

Employment Point: *Live for the One who redeems you and places you into the family of God.*

September 27

Isaiah 10–12, with Galatians 5

The wolf also shall dwell with the lamb, the leopard shall lie down with the young goat, the calf and the young lion and the fatling together; and a little child shall lead them (Isaiah 11:6).

Are you anticipating the return of the Prince of Peace?

Isaiah depicts both comings of Jesus. "For unto us a Child is born, unto us a Son is given; and the government will be upon His shoulder. And His name will be called Wonderful, Counselor, Mighty God, Everlasting Father, Prince of Peace" (Isaiah 9:6). One of the titles for Jesus is "Everlasting Father," which literally means *Father of Eternity*. Since God created time, He chose when Jesus would first be born of a virgin and decides when He'll return a second time to establish worldwide peace. Today, children of God look for the Rapture (Titus 2:13). After the Rapture will be the Tribulation and Jesus' Second Coming.

Employment Point: *Walk with God, anticipating Jesus' future reign of peace.*

September 28

Isaiah 13–15, with Galatians 6

———— ⊙ ————

Brethren, if a man is overtaken in any trespass, you who are spiritual restore such a one in a spirit of gentleness, considering yourself lest you also be tempted (Galatians 6:1).

Am I my brother's keeper?

Paul addresses the Galatian believers as "brethren" nine times in this epistle. The implication is that since all Christians are eternally related then we have a responsibility to one another. When a growing Christian observes a fellow believer who has stumbled in his faith, we are to "restore such a one in a spirit of gentleness." The apostle commands us to help the fallen family member. "Restore" is a present imperative and the term appears in secular writings of setting broken bones. Doctor Paul prescribes the restoration to be done "in a spirit of gentleness." Contained within the list of the fruit of the Spirit (Galatians 5:22–23) is "gentleness," which carries the notion of meekness or mildness. Let's humbly serve one another!

Employment Point: *Restore spiritual health to fallen brethren with meekness.*

———— ⊙ ————

September 29

Isaiah 16–18, with Ephesians 1

Blessed be the God and Father of our Lord Jesus Christ, who has blessed us with every spiritual blessing in the heavenly places in Christ (Ephesians 1:3).

ARE YOU LIVING UP TO YOUR HEAVENLY STATUS?

Paul addresses the Ephesian believers about their elevated status in Ephesians 1:1–3:21. Positionally, they are seated with Jesus. The apostle to the Gentiles reminds the saints that God "raised us up together, and made us sit together in the heavenly places in Christ Jesus" (Ephesians 2:6). Not only are we crucified with Christ (Galatians 2:20), but also because of His resurrection "should walk in newness of life" (Romans 6:4). Now that we positionally sit with Jesus in heaven, we enjoy "the riches of His grace" (Ephesians 1:7) and mercy (Ephesians 2:4). In essence, all the spiritual blessings of Jesus are shared with us because we are "heirs of God and joint heirs with Christ" (Romans 8:17).

EMPLOYMENT POINT: *Live up to your riches in Christ because of your heavenly seat.*

September 30

Isaiah 19–21, with Ephesians 2

And He came and preached peace to you who were afar off and to those who were near (Ephesians 2:17).

Do you know that Jesus proclaims the gospel through the lips of the saints?

The church of Ephesus consisted mainly of Gentiles. They are the ones Paul characterizes as "afar off." Unlike the Jews, Gentiles traditionally were not exposed to the Old Testament teachings. On the other hand, Paul describes the Jews as "those who were near." The apostle to the Gentiles explains how privileged the Jews are from Romans 9:4. He writes, "who are Israelites, to whom pertain the adoption, the glory, the covenants, the giving of the law, the service of God, and the promises." Whether to Jews or Gentiles, Jesus speaks to them when we herald the good news about His death and resurrection. We need to seek opportunities to have Him speak through us!

Employment Point: *Represent the Prince of Peace by having Him share the gospel of peace through you.*

October 1

Isaiah 22–23, with Ephesians 3

And in that day the Lord GOD of hosts called for weeping and for mourning, for baldness and for girding with sackcloth (Isaiah 22:12).

Do you repent of your sin during a crisis?

King Sennacherib of Assyria laid a siege against Jerusalem in 701 BC. Perhaps Isaiah 22 refers to this incident (2 Kings 18–19). If so, God supernaturally thwarted the enemy by striking many of their soldiers, which caused the army to depart from Jerusalem. The Lord used the situation not only to display His vast power, but also to drive His children to repent of their vast sins. Isaiah records their pathetic response: "But instead, joy and gladness, slaying oxen and killing sheep, eating meat and drinking wine: 'Let us eat and drink, for tomorrow we die!'" (Isaiah 22:13). Sadly, the children of Israel celebrated their physical deliverance, but didn't turn from their sin.

EMPLOYMENT POINT: *Depend upon God in a crisis, while repenting of any known sin.*

October 2

Isaiah 24–26, with Ephesians 4

———●———

I, therefore, the prisoner of the Lord, beseech you to walk worthy of the calling with which you were called (Ephesians 4:1).

Is your Christian walk matching your heavenly status?

Eight times Paul uses the term "walk" in Ephesians. Since believers positionally sit with Jesus in heaven (Ephesians 1:3; 2:6), we are not to walk according to this world's system (Ephesians 2:1–3; 4:17), and should be a redeemed people practicing good works (Ephesians 2:10). Moreover, we are to walk in love (Ephesians 5:2) and light (Ephesians 5:8) circumspectly (Ephesians 5:15). The child of God is also to endeavor "to keep the unity of the Spirit in the bond of peace" (Ephesians 4:3). We have an example to follow in the Trinity. Father, Son, and Holy Spirit have a perfect oneness (Ephesians 4:4–6), and we are to model that same unity. Let's live according to our elevated status as God's children, not imitating the world but the Lord.

Employment Point: *Walk worthily of your heavenly calling.*

———●———

October 3

Isaiah 27–28, with Ephesians 5

———◦———

For precept must be upon precept, precept upon precept, line upon line, line upon line, here a little, there a little (Isaiah 28:10).

What is your Responsibility Concerning the Word of God?

Israel is a spiritual mess. The people are characterized as drunkards (Isaiah 28:1–3). Not only are the people given to wine, so are the priests and the prophets (Isaiah 28:7). Both the prophets and the priests are to systematically instruct the saints layer by layer from God's Word; however, the clergy and laity are alike and in no position to teach or be taught. For this reason, God sends the Assyrians to judge the prophets, priests, and people. Now they will be subject to foreigners instructing them. Isaiah writes, "For with stammering lips and another tongue He will speak to this people" (Isaiah 28:11). God's leaders should honor the Lord by teaching His people, and the saints ought to submit to that instruction.

Employment Point: *Teach and learn God's Word, lest you lose that sacred privilege.*

———◦———

October 4

Isaiah 29–30, with Ephesians 6

Put on the whole armor of God, that you may be able to stand against the wiles of the devil (Ephesians 6:11).

Do you dress for Christian success?

Paul commands the child of God to "put on the whole armor of God." He cites three things we need to defeat the enemy: power, protection, and prayer. Our strength derives from the Lord. That is why the apostle commences the closing of our epistle with, "Finally, my brethren, be strong in the Lord and in the power of His might" (Ephesians 6:10). We need God's power accompanied with His protection. The various pieces of the Roman soldier's armor, applied to the Christian life, will keep us spiritually covered (Ephesians 6:13–17). Prayer is the last element of the essential triad. Paul writes, "praying always with all prayer and supplication in the Spirit" (Ephesians 6:18). Let's honor our commander in chief by applying these elements in our Christian life.

Employment Point: *Live victoriously through God's power, protection, and much prayer.*

October 5

Isaiah 31–33, with Philippians 1

———————

Woe to those who go down to Egypt for help, and rely on horses, who trust in chariots because they are many, and in horsemen because they are very strong, but who do not look to the Holy One of Israel, nor seek the LORD! (Isaiah 31:1).

Whom do you trust in a crisis?

When the Assyrians under the leadership of Sennacherib threatened the southern kingdom of Judah, some Israelites turned to Egypt for help. God put this pressure on His people so that they might repent of their sin and rely solely upon Him. Isaiah writes, "Return to Him against whom the children of Israel have deeply revolted. For in that day every man shall throw away his idols of silver and his idols of gold" (Isaiah 31:6–7). Ultimately, the victory over the enemy comes from the Lord. The Lord predicts the Assyrians demise and their fleeing from Judah (Isaiah 31:8).

EMPLOYMENT POINT: *Turn to the Lord, and rely upon His strength during a crisis.*

———————

October 6

Isaiah 34–36, with Philippians 2

———— ◈ ————

Let this mind be in you which was also in Christ Jesus (Philippians 2:5).

Do you have the mind of Jesus?

Paul commands the saints at Philippi to have the attitude of Jesus. The passage (Philippians 2:5–11) is referred to as the *kenosis*, which is the Greek term meaning *to empty oneself*. Jesus left heaven in order to be made like us; therefore, the day is hastening when we'll be like Him (Philippians 3:20–21). Our Lord chose not to exercise some of His attributes when He took on flesh. Although being fully God, He submitted to the Roman cross and didn't display His authority to extricate Himself. Moreover, He made Himself the servant of all by dying on the cross for us. The end result is that "God also has highly exalted Him and given Him the name which is above every name" (Philippians 2:9). Our future greatness depends upon our present service.

Employment Point: *Adopt the mind of Jesus and become the servant of all.*

———— ◈ ————

OCTOBER 7

ISAIAH 37–38, WITH PHILIPPIANS 3

———◆———

Then Hezekiah turned his face toward the wall, and prayed to the LORD (Isaiah 38:2).

WHERE DO YOU TURN WHEN YOU HAVE A PERSONAL HEALTH CRISIS?

King Hezekiah trusts in the Lord as the entire nation experiences an imminent threat from the powerful king of Assyria (Isaiah 37:1). God honors Hezekiah's faith and supernaturally delivers His people. Next, the king suffers from failing health and nears death (Isaiah 38:1). Once again he draws close to the Lord, seeking to have his health restored (Isaiah 38:2–3). The giver and sustainer of life graciously imparts fifteen additional years to the king and confirms this with a sign on the sundial (Isaiah 38:8).

Unfortunately, Hezekiah doesn't use that time wisely and seemingly becomes self-centered (Isaiah 39:8). Unlike Asa who didn't seek the Lord during a physical illness (2 Chronicles 16:12), Hezekiah does. Yet the Lord is to be trusted unto death.

EMPLOYMENT POINT: *Trust the Lord during a personal health crisis, and until He calls you home.*

———◆———

October 8

Isaiah 39–40, with Philippians 4

Rejoice in the Lord always. Again I will say, rejoice! (Philippians 4:4).

Do you always rejoice in the Lord?

Paul writes Ephesians, Philippians, Colossians, and Philemon while being under house arrest (Acts 28:30–31). Although in chains, he exhorts the saints at Philippi to continually rejoice. Circumstances didn't prevent the prisoner for Jesus from being filled with the Spirit and constantly enjoying His presence, which produces joy! Paul and Silas model that joy is a result of walking with the Lord and doesn't come because life's circumstances are favorable. After wrongfully being imprisoned in Philippi, Paul and Silas are beaten by rods and put into stocks (Acts 16:23–24). Yet "at midnight Paul and Silas were praying and singing hymns to God" (Acts 16:25). Observe that the imprisoned duo sang "hymns to God" and not "about God." We can "rejoice always" (1 Thessalonians 5:16) by trusting the Lord through every circumstance.

Employment Point: *Rejoice in the Lord continually, because He is with us throughout the trials of life.*

October 9

Isaiah 41–42, with Colossians 1

Fear not, for I am with you; be not dismayed, for I am your God. I will strengthen you, yes, I will help you, I will uphold you with My righteous right hand (Isaiah 41:10).

Are you living without fear because God is with you?

God is an ever-present help in trouble. Twice He calls Israel to be fearless and reminds them, "I will help you" (Isaiah 41:10, 14). The Lord is eternal. Isaiah pens, "I, the LORD, am the first; and with the last I am He" (Isaiah 41:4). God's eternal nature should help us to remember that He is all-powerful, knows everything, and is ever-present. Paul understands this and writes that He alone makes us capable to serve Him. He pens, "Not that we are sufficient of ourselves to think of anything as being from ourselves, but our sufficiency is from God" (2 Corinthians 3:5).

EMPLOYMENT POINT: *Fear not, because the eternal God will help you accomplish what He calls you to do.*

October 10

Isaiah 43–44, with Colossians 2

"You are my witnesses," says the LORD, "and My servant whom I have chosen, that you may know and believe Me, and understand that I am He" (Isaiah 43:10).

Have you considered the eternal nature of the Father and the Son?

The expression "I am He" used in Isaiah 43:10 speaks of deity. It similarly appears in Isaiah 41:4. There Isaiah writes, "I, the LORD, am the first; and with the last I am He." Interestingly, both are translated by a Greek expression in the Septuagint (LXX) that Jesus often uses of Himself. Seven times Jesus chooses these two Greek words as recorded by John to connect His eternality with that of the Father (John 6:35; 8:12; 10:7, 11; 11:25; 14:6; 15:1). On account of the Father and Son being eternally God, Jesus could state, "I and My Father are one" (John 10:30).

EMPLOYMENT POINT: *Believe that both God the Father and God the Son have existed forever, and give them their rightly preeminence.*

October 11

Isaiah 45–47, with Colossians 3

———

Set your mind on things above, not on things on the earth (Colossians 3:2).

Do you have an earthly or heavenly gaze?

We have been positionally crucified with Christ (Galatians 2:20; Colossians 3:3) and raised with Him (Colossians 3:1). Believers are now to enjoy their elevated status and blessings (Ephesians 1:3; 2:6). Even though God has favored the saints, they are commanded by Paul to "set your mind on things above." The imperative is given in the present tense, which means they are to continually fix their mind on heavenly things. Satan makes sure that we have many distractions in the world in which we live. Yet this world's system isn't to command our interest because "the world has been crucified to me," writes Paul in Galatians 6:14, "and I to the world." Let's live in light of our heavenly seating arrangement to please the Lord.

Employment Point: *Maintain a heavenly mindset to please the One who has freed you from the bondage of sin and Satan.*

———

October 12

Isaiah 48–49, with Colossians 4

Meanwhile praying also for us, that God would open to us a door for the word, to speak the mystery of Christ, for which I am also in chains (Colossians 4:3).

Are you praying for opportunities to share the gospel?

Spirit-filled believers look for God's connections. They seek an open door to present the life-changing message of the gospel to the unsaved. Paul is under house arrest and has limited physical mobility. During another imprisonment, he writes, "for which I suffer trouble as an evildoer, even to the point of chains; but the word of God is not chained" (2 Timothy 2:9). Paul's understanding of the unfettered Word causes him to share with the saints at Thessalonica: "Pray for us, that the word of the Lord may run swiftly and be glorified" (2 Thessalonians 3:1). Boldly walk through the open door once God honors your prayers (1 Corinthians 16:8–9).

EMPLOYMENT POINT: *Pray for an open door, and walk through it once God honors your request.*

October 13

Isaiah 50–52, with 1 Thessalonians 1

The Lord GOD has opened My ear; and I was not rebellious (Isaiah 50:5).

ARE YOU FOLLOWING IN THE STEPS OF GOD'S GREATEST SERVANT?

Isaiah pens four servant songs (Isaiah 42:1–9; 49:1–13; 50:4–11; 52:13–53:12). Although they indirectly allude to Israel at times, ultimately they point to Jesus. The New Testament confirms this linkage. Matthew quotes from the first servant song (Isaiah 42:1–9) and attributes it to Jesus (Matthew 12:18–21). He writes, "Behold! My Servant whom I have chosen, My Beloved in whom My soul is well pleased!" (Matthew 12:18). The Lord Jesus is characterized as an obedient servant who yields to His Father's will and endured great hostility from sinners on His way to the cross. The prophet writes of Jesus, "I gave My back to those who struck Me, and My cheeks to those who plucked out the beard; I did not hide My face from shame and spitting" (Isaiah 50:6).

EMPLOYMENT POINT: *Submit to the Father to also be an obedient servant.*

October 14

Isaiah 53–55, with
1 Thessalonians 2

So, affectionately longing for you, we were well pleased to impart to you not only the gospel of God, but also our own lives, because you had become dear to us (1 Thessalonians 2:8).

What sacrifices are you willing to make for others?

Paul is a rugged disciple of Jesus, but also gentle. He writes, "But we were gentle among you, just as a nursing mother cherishes her own children" (1 Thessalonians 2:7). Moreover, Paul and his associates (Silas and Timothy) not only were well pleased to preach the gospel to the Thessalonians, but also would willingly lay down their lives for them. No wonder the dynamic trio witness many converts to Christ. They imitate their Lord and Savior by sacrificing themselves for the benefit of others. No wonder Paul, Silas, and Timothy are characterized by the unbelievers at Thessalonica by the following: "these who have turned the world upside down" (Acts 17:6).

Employment Point: *Turn the world upside down through self-sacrifice and a gentle spirit.*

OCTOBER 15

ISAIAH 56–58, WITH
1 THESSALONIANS 3

"Why have we fasted," they say, "and you have not seen? Why have we afflicted our souls, and You take no notice?" In fact, in the day of your fast you find pleasure, and exploit all your laborers (Isaiah 58:3).

DO YOU HAVE SEASONS OF FASTING TO ACCOMPANY YOUR PRAYERS?

Jesus assumes that His disciples fast. He declares, "When you fast, do not be like the hypocrites, with a sad countenance" (Matthew 6:16). Observe that He says "when," and not *if* you fast. Unfortunately, many so-called followers of God have used fasting not to draw near to God, but to draw attention to themselves. Isaiah connects self-sacrifice with God's blessing. "If you extend your soul to the hungry," our author writes in Isaiah 58:10, "And satisfy the afflicted soul, then your light shall dawn in the darkness, and your darkness shall be as the noonday."

EMPLOYMENT POINT: *Let your fast include caring for the poor and needy, and then God will honor your prayers.*

October 16

Isaiah 59–61, with
1 Thessalonians 4

———◦◈◦———

For this we say to you by the word of the Lord, that we who are alive and remain until the coming of the Lord will by no means precede those who are asleep (1 Thessalonians 4:15).

Are you anticipating the imminent return of Jesus?

Paul's belief "that Jesus died and rose again" (1 Thessalonians 4:14) bolsters his confidence that Jesus will return. The verbs "died" and "rose again" are in the active voice. That is, Jesus willingly laid down His life and raised Himself from the dead just as He predicted (John 10:17–18). Twice the apostle uses the word "we," including himself in the Rapture (1 Thessalonians 4:15, 17). Paul believes that he could be alive when "the Lord Himself will descend from heaven" (1 Thessalonians 4:16). Church-age saints who die before the Rapture immediately go to heaven (2 Corinthians 5:8). These departed saints will return with Jesus to meet us (1 Thessalonians 4:17).

Employment Point: *Daily live for Jesus, while anticipating His return.*

———◦◈◦———

October 17

Isaiah 62–64, with 1 Thessalonians 5

Men have not heard nor perceived by the ear, nor has the eye seen any God besides You, who acts for the one who waits for Him (Isaiah 64:4).

Are you waiting upon the Lord, who acts for you?

David, a man after God's own heart, tells himself, "My soul, wait silently for God alone, for my expectation is from Him" (Psalm 62:5). It is difficult for us not to take matters into our own hands. For this reason we need to be reminded, "Be anxious for nothing, but in everything by prayer and supplication, with thanksgiving, let your requests be made known to God" (Philippians 4:6). God strengthens those who wait upon Him. Isaiah writes, "But those who wait on the LORD shall renew their strength" (Isaiah 40:31). Since God is working together all things for our good (Romans 8:28), we need to wait upon Him to work in our behalf.

Employment Point: *Wait upon the Lord, knowing that He acts for you.*

OCTOBER 18

ISAIAH 65–66, WITH
2 THESSALONIANS 1

Since it is a righteous thing with God to repay with tribulation those who trouble you (2 Thessalonians 1:6).

ARE YOU WAITING UPON THE LORD TO RECOMPENSE THOSE WHO AFFLICT YOU?

God's saints have been persecuted through the ages. Paul tells the Roman saints, which applies to all of us, to be "patient in tribulation" (Romans 12:12). We are to seek peace with all people, knowing that the righteous Lord will right the wrongs done to us. "Beloved, do not avenge yourselves," advises Paul, "but rather give place to wrath; for it is written, 'Vengeance is Mine, I will repay,' says the Lord" (Romans 12:19). The verb in 2 Thessalonians 1:6 translated "to repay" literally means *to give back*. Biblical history teaches us that God gives back to the Pharaoh of the Exodus, Haman the Jew-hater in the Book of Esther, and those who sought to destroy Daniel, justice in the end.

EMPLOYMENT POINT: *Wait upon God to repay those who trouble you.*

October 19

Jeremiah 1–2, with
2 Thessalonians 2

Before I formed you in the womb I knew you; before you were born I sanctified you; I ordained you a prophet to the nations (Jeremiah 1:5).

When did God call you to Himself?

God knew Jeremiah and had a special appointment for him to fulfill before he is born. The sovereign Lord also commissions Paul to a specific task from his conception. He writes, "it pleased God, who separated me from my mother's womb and called me through His grace, to reveal His Son in me, that I might preach Him among the Gentiles" (Galatians 1:15–16). Likewise, we have a sacred calling. Paul informs the Ephesians, "just as He chose us in Him before the foundation of the world, that we should be holy and without blame before Him in love" (Ephesians 1:4). Since we have a high calling like Jeremiah and Paul, let us seek to honor the Lord by holy living.

Employment Point: *Dedicate your life to Him who calls you to Himself before time began.*

October 20

Jeremiah 3–4, with 2 Thessalonians 3

For even when we were with you, we commanded you this: If anyone will not work, neither shall he eat (2 Thessalonians 3:10).

Is work a curse?

God punched a time clock. He created the world in six days. "Then God saw everything that He had made, and indeed it was very good" (Genesis 1:31). Since the Creator knows that labor is good, He puts the first man to work. Moses writes, "Then the LORD God took the man and put him in the garden of Eden to tend and keep it" (Genesis 2:15).

Sadly, some of the saints at Thessalonica were gossips and not working. They didn't learn these practices from Paul and his associates. He states, "For you yourselves know how you ought to follow us, for we were not disorderly among you; nor did we eat anyone's bread free of charge, but worked with labor and toil night and day" (2 Thessalonians 3:7–8).

Employment Point: *Imitate God, Adam, and Paul, who know the blessing of work.*

October 21

Jeremiah 5–6, with
1 Timothy 1

———◈———

Thus says the LORD: "Stand in the ways and see, and ask for the old paths, where the good way is, and walk in it; then you will find rest for your souls" (Jeremiah 6:16).

Are you walking the path of obedience leading to blessing?

The psalmist depicts two paths in life. Obedience's trail leads to God's favor, while the track of disobedience ends in death. "Blessed is the man," writes the poet, "who walks not in the counsel of the ungodly, nor stands in the path of sinners" (Psalm 1:1). Those who traverse the road of obedience do so by heeding God's Word. Again the psalmist writes, "But his delight is in the law of the LORD, and in His law he meditates day and night" (Psalm 1:2). Patriarchs like Abraham walked the old path of obedience and God blessed them. Psalm 1:3 ends with these encouraging words: "And whatever he does shall prosper."

Employment Point: *Walk the pathway of obedience leading to blessing.*

———◈———

October 22

Jeremiah 7–8, with
1 Timothy 2

For there is one God and one Mediator between God and men, the Man Christ Jesus (1 Timothy 2:5).

Are you regularly approaching the throne of grace through the God-Man?

Paul encourages Timothy to pray "for kings and all who are in authority" (1 Timothy 2:2). Our prayers are to the Father through His Son. The Father acknowledges our prayers because we come to Him via Jesus' righteousness. Moreover, God "desires all men to be saved and to come to the knowledge of the truth." As we offer our prayers to the Lord they should include praying for the salvation of those in authority. Jesus "gave Himself a ransom for all" (1 Timothy 2:6), which includes "kings and all who are in authority." Furthermore, we should marvel that Jesus took on flesh (1 Timothy 3:16) and remains next to God in His glorified body to mediate for us (1 Timothy 2:5).

Employment Point: *Pray to the Father, through the Son, for the salvation of your governing authorities.*

October 23

Jeremiah 9–10, with 1 Timothy 3

But let him who glories glory in this, that he understands and knows Me, that I am the LORD, exercising lovingkindness, judgment, and righteousness in the earth. For in these I delight (Jeremiah 9:24).

How well do you know the Lord?

Jeremiah preaches throughout the book, condemning the idolatry that eventually leads to the nation's demise. Yet he expresses the things that God longs for in His people in Jeremiah 9:24. Our Lord looks for the individual who "understands and knows Me." The Hebrew term "understands" denotes *to walk in wisdom based upon insight* and the word "knows" in the Hebrew and Greek Translation of the Old Testament (LXX) is used of a *personal knowledge* (Genesis 4:1). God longs for those who live skillfully because they know Him intimately. Saints, who walk with the Lord who is given to lovingkindness, judgment, and righteousness, please Him. Let us pursue these things for God's glory.

Employment Point: *Seek to live skillfully by a deep and personal knowledge of God.*

OCTOBER 24

JEREMIAH 11–13, WITH
1 TIMOTHY 4

———◈———

Now the Spirit expressly says that in latter times some will depart from the faith, giving heed to deceiving spirits and doctrines of demons (1 Timothy 4:1).

ARE YOU AWARE OF SATAN'S DECEPTIONS?

The last days began with the first coming of Jesus Christ (Hebrews 1:1–2). Satan failed to kill Jesus at His birth (Matthew 2:1–12) and today seeks to lead astray people from worshiping Him. He is a liar (John 8:44) and influences others to do the same (Acts 5:3). Furthermore, he desires to have the saints embrace the wisdom of this world. James exposes his *modus operandi* in James 3:14–15, "But if you have bitter envy and self-seeking in your hearts, do not boast and lie against the truth. This wisdom does not descend from above, but is earthly, sensual, demonic." Moreover, Satan's missionaries are described as follows: "For such are false apostles, deceitful workers, transforming themselves into apostles of Christ" (2 Corinthians 11:13).

EMPLOYMENT POINT: *Be watchful, for Satan is a master deceiver.*

———◈———

October 25

Jeremiah 14–16, with
1 Timothy 5

Then the LORD said to me, "Even if Moses and Samuel stood before Me, My mind would not be favorable toward this people. Cast them out of My sight, and let them go forth" (Jeremiah 15:1).

HOW COMMITTED IS GOD TO JUSTICE?

God cites two great prayer warriors to depict the depth of Israel's sin. Both men of God have an intercessory ministry for the nation. The Philistines attack Israel, and Samuel prays for deliverance (1 Samuel 7). "And Samuel took a suckling lamb and offered it as a whole burnt offering to the LORD. Then Samuel cried out to the LORD for Israel, and the LORD answered him" (1 Samuel 7:9). Similarly, Moses intercedes for Israel concerning the golden calf incident, and the Lord honors his prayer (Exodus 32:11–14). Yet God would not pardon Israel during Jeremiah's ministry "because of Manasseh the son of Hezekiah, king of Judah, for what he did in Jerusalem" (Jeremiah 15:4).

EMPLOYMENT POINT: *Don't presume upon God's mercy, because He also administers justice.*

October 26

Jeremiah 17–19, with 1 Timothy 6

———◆———

Now godliness with contentment is great gain (1 Timothy 6:6).

Are you content to be godly?

Godliness is a pursuit, and being content can be learned. Paul directs Timothy, "But you, O man of God, flee these things and pursue righteousness, godliness, faith, love, patience, gentleness" (1 Timothy 6:11). The twin commands in 1 Timothy 6:11 are in the present tense. Timothy is to continually run away from harmful lusts and track down godliness. Observe also how the Lord teaches Paul to be content. While under house arrest in Rome, he writes, "Not that I speak in regard to need, for I have learned in whatever state I am, to be content" (Philippians 4:11). He continues, "I know how to be abased, and I know how to abound" (Philippians 4:12). Where did he learn these things? "I can do all things through Christ," writes Paul, "who strengthens me" (Philippians 4:13). He learned to trust the Unchanging One (Hebrews 13:8).

Employment Point: *Pursue godliness and develop contentment from Jesus.*

———◆———

October 27

Jeremiah 20–22, with 2 Timothy 1

Then I said, "I will not make mention of Him, nor speak anymore in His name." But His word was in my heart like a burning fire shut up in my bones; I was weary of holding it back, and I could not (Jeremiah 20:9).

Is God's holy Word burning within you?

For the first time in the Book of Jeremiah the prophet personally experiences violence (Jeremiah 20:2). He becomes despondent because of the opposition from those who should have heeded the message of repentance. Yet he breaks forth into praise knowing that his righteous judge will avenge him. He exclaims, "But the LORD is with me as a mighty, awesome One. Therefore my persecutors will stumble, and will not prevail. They will be greatly ashamed, for they will not prosper" (Jeremiah 20:11). Moreover, God's Word burned in his heart, and he could not quench its flames.

Employment Point: *Implant God's Word deeply into your heart so that it will burn even during dark days.*

October 28

Jeremiah 23–24, with 2 Timothy 2

Flee also youthful lusts; but pursue righteousness, faith, love, peace with those who call on the Lord out of a pure heart (2 Timothy 2:22).

Do you run away from temptation and to God's holy servants?

Joseph exhibits the command to "flee also youthful lusts." He chooses not to flirt with Potiphar's wife, but runs from the path of sin. He asks the temptress before bolting, "How then can I do this great wickedness, and sin against God?" (Genesis 39:9). Indeed, Paul exhorts his younger son in the faith to spend time with godly individuals who promote purity. The wise apostle knows the following: "He who walks with wise men will be wise, But the companion of fools will be destroyed" (Proverbs 13:20). "Do not be deceived," also writes Paul, "Evil company corrupts good habits" (1 Corinthians 15:33). Christians who move away from worldly allurements and pivot toward godly companionship will glorify God.

Employment Point: *Flee temptation, and choose friends given to holiness.*

OCTOBER 29

JEREMIAH 25–26, WITH
2 TIMOTHY 3

Then it will come to pass, when seventy years are completed, that I will punish the king of Babylon and that nation (Jeremiah 25:12).

DO YOU ANTICIPATE GOD FULFILLING ALL THE PROPHECIES IN THE BIBLE?

Nebuchadnezzar becomes king of Babylon in 605 BC, which is the same year that Daniel was deported to that country. The Lord uses this powerful king to chasten the disobedient people of Judah. Their northern counterpart went into captivity in 722/721 BC by the Assyrians, and they did not learn from God's actions. God gives the duration of the captivity as seventy years, which will be followed by the conquest of Babylon. Cyrus the Persian in 539 BC conquers Babylon as predicted. Meanwhile Jeremiah clings tightly to God because he knows that His Word is true. Similarly, we should walk with Jesus who accurately predicts the future and is Himself the fulfillment of the Law (Matthew 5:17–18).

EMPLOYMENT POINT: *Trust the integrity of God's Word while clinging to its author.*

OCTOBER 30

JEREMIAH 27–28, WITH 2 TIMOTHY 4

Be diligent to come to me quickly (2 Timothy 4:9).

TO WHOM DO YOU TURN DURING A CRISIS?

Paul understands that death knocks at his door. He writes, "For I am already being poured out as a drink offering, and the time of my departure is at hand" (2 Timothy 4:6). He calls for his son in the faith to bring him a cloak to keep his aging body warm, and his books to keep his mind spiritually acute. Thankfully Timothy remains loyal to the Lord and Paul, "for Demas has forsaken me, having loved this present world" (2 Timothy 4:10). The contrast is clear: Timothy is devoted to Paul while Demas is devoid of spiritual commitment. Paul writes about Timothy to the Corinthians, "who will remind you of my ways in Christ" (1 Corinthians 4:17). Furthermore, the apostle dispatches Timothy to Philippi saying, "For I have no one like-minded," which literally means *like souled* (Philippians 2:20).

EMPLOYMENT POINT: *Be a loyal follower of Jesus and support His servants.*

October 31

Jeremiah 29–30, with Titus 1

———◦———

For I know the thoughts that I think toward you, says the LORD, thoughts of peace and not of evil, to give you a future and a hope (Jeremiah 29:11).

DO YOU HOPE IN GOD'S MERCY?

Jeremiah has a difficult message to communicate. He essentially tells his brethren that they need to submit to Nebuchadnezzar and his army and willingly go to Babylon. The nation's prolonged disobedience is about to be met with God's justice, tempered with mercy. To those who obey God's Word the Lord gives "a future and a hope." The inhabitants in Judah currently suffer "because they have not heeded My words, says the LORD, which I sent to them by My servants the prophets, rising up early and sending them; neither would you heed, says the LORD. Therefore hear the word of the LORD, all you of the captivity, whom I have sent from Jerusalem to Babylon" (Jeremiah 29:19–20).

EMPLOYMENT POINT: *Immediate obedience to God's Word produces a bright future.*

———◦———

November 1

Jeremiah 31–32, with Titus 2

———◆———

Looking for the blessed hope and glorious appearing of our great God and Savior Jesus Christ (Titus 2:13).

Are your eyes fixed toward heaven?

Paul proclaims that believers should be anticipating the imminent return of Jesus. "Looking" is a present tense verb and conveys a continual waiting. Elsewhere the apostle refers to the Rapture as the "one hope of your calling" (Ephesians 4:4) and in our current passage as "the blessed hope." "Blessed" means *marked by favor*. Specifically, the "blessed hope" and "glorious appearing" point us to Jesus Christ whom Paul calls "our great God." Literally the Greek says, "the great God and Savior of us, Jesus Christ." One article (the) connects "God and Savior" with Jesus. Having this expectation motivates us to be morally pure and "zealous for good works" (Titus 2:14). Eyes focused upon heaven keep us pleasing God at all times!

Employment Point: *Continually look for Jesus' return, accompanied by holy living and zealously serving the Lord.*

———◆———

NOVEMBER 2

JEREMIAH 33–35, WITH TITUS 3

———————

Then I set before the sons of the house of the Rechabites bowls full of wine, and cups; and I said to them, "Drink wine" (Jeremiah 35:5).

HOW DOES YOUR CHRISTIANITY DIFFER FROM OTHERS?

Jeremiah gives an argument from the lesser to the greater in Jeremiah 35. God dispatches him to the "house of the Rechabites." They are a group of Gentiles related to the Kenites. Imagine the prophet of God gathering them into the Temple and then saying, "Drink wine." "But they said, 'We will drink no wine, for Jonadab the son of Rechab, our father, commanded us, saying, You shall drink no wine, you nor your sons forever'" (Jeremiah 35:6). The family honored their earthly father's command. Yet God the Father gave commandments to Israel. "But you have not inclined your ear, nor obeyed Me" says the Lord (Jeremiah 35:15). Although Israel is chastened for their disobedience, God rewards the Rechabites for honoring their earthly father.

EMPLOYMENT POINT: *Obey your father, and God the Father, for blessings.*

———————

November 3

Jeremiah 36–37, with Philemon

Though I might be very bold in Christ to command you what is fitting, yet for love's sake I rather appeal to you (Philemon 8–9).

How well do you use your influence for the Lord?

Paul plays a great violin. Can you hear the tune from prison that he masterfully uses to tug on Philemon's heartstrings—referring to himself as aged, a prisoner, and in chains (Philemon 9–10)? Onesimus, who is the slave of Philemon, robs his master (Philemon 18) and runs away to Rome. The Lord sovereignly guides him to the imprisoned apostle and Onesimus is spiritually set free. Paul has the authority to command Philemon to emancipate Onesimus, but chooses rather to make an appeal. It will be costly for Philemon to sacrifice his slave to serve Paul. Yet a letter written fifty years after Paul penned the Book of Philemon talked about a bishop named . . . Onesimus.

Employment Point: *Go the extra mile for the One who went the extra mile for you.*

November 4

Jeremiah 38–39, with Hebrews 1

Yes, and all who desire to live godly in Christ Jesus will suffer persecution (2 Timothy 3:12).

How have you suffered for the Lord?

Jeremiah faithfully conveys the message imparted to him from the Lord. The message could easily peg Jeremiah as not being a patriotic Jew and betraying his country. Yet he proclaims that his people need to submit to Nebuchadnezzar and his army and not fight, lest Jerusalem be destroyed. "So they took Jeremiah and cast him into the dungeon of Malchiah the king's son, which was in the court of the prison, and they let Jeremiah down with ropes. And in the dungeon there was no water, but mire. So Jeremiah sank in the mire" (Jeremiah 38:6). Jeremiah probably wonders, "How low can I go?" Hebrews chronicles some of the Old Testament saints' sufferings (Hebrews 11:36–37), then states that these heroes of Hebrews 11 "obtained a good testimony through faith" (Hebrews 11:39).

Employment Point: *Endure persecution by faith and obtain a good testimony.*

NOVEMBER 5

JEREMIAH 40–42, WITH HEBREWS 2

Inasmuch then as the children have partaken of flesh and blood, He Himself likewise shared in the same, that through death He might destroy him who had the power of death, that is, the devil (Hebrews 2:14).

DO YOU FEAR DYING?

God places Adam and Eve in the Garden of Eden. They disobey the Lord and eat the forbidden fruit from the tree of the knowledge of good and evil, so death and the fear of death permeates mankind (Genesis 2:17). For this reason Jesus becomes like us, so that one day we would be like Him. Our Lord *nullifies*—which is the meaning of "destroy" in Hebrews 2:14—Satan "who had the power of death." Through Jesus' sacrifice He would "release those who through fear of death were all their lifetime subject to bondage" (Hebrews 2:15). We can fearlessly say, "Thanks be to God, who gives us the victory through our Lord Jesus Christ" (1 Corinthians 15:57).

EMPLOYMENT POINT: *Don't fear death, because it is a defeated foe.*

November 6

Jeremiah 43–45, with Hebrews 3

———◆———

And do you seek great things for yourself? Do not seek them; for behold, I will bring adversity on all flesh (Jeremiah 45:5).

Do you understand the times in which you live?

Baruch serves Jeremiah well. He is a faithful scribe to Jeremiah during a difficult period in Israel's history. Daniel is taken into captivity to Babylon in the same year that Nebuchadnezzar ascends his throne (605 BC). Ezekiel experiences the same during the second deportation by the powerful king (597 BC). Now in 586 BC Jerusalem and its Temple are destroyed. Perhaps Baruch desires to be like Elisha the servant of Elijah and accomplish great things; however, this is not part of God's plan. He humbles His people and they have to endure a period of captivity lasting seventy years (Jeremiah 25:11). God says to Baruch, "But I will give your life to you as a prize in all places" (Jeremiah 45:5).

Employment Point: *Serve the Lord, and allow Him to reward you accordingly.*

———◆———

NOVEMBER 7

JEREMIAH 46–48, WITH HEBREWS 4

———————

For we do not have a High Priest who cannot sympathize with our weaknesses, but was in all points tempted as we are, yet without sin (Hebrews 4:15).

DO YOU TURN TO HEAVEN'S HIGH PRIEST DURING A TEMPTATION?

Jesus currently serves in the role as High Priest. The writer of Hebrews uses the present tense verb "we have" in Hebrews 4:14. He pens, "Seeing then that we have a great High Priest who has passed through the heavens, Jesus the Son of God." Our Lord is the preeminent High Priest "since He always lives to make intercession for them" (Hebrews 7:25). Only Jesus who is the perfect High Priest can empathize with our human condition, and yet He never bowed to temptation. His provision is always punctual. "Let us therefore come boldly to the throne of grace," writes the anonymous author, "that we may obtain mercy and find grace to help in time of need" (Hebrews 4:16).

EMPLOYMENT POINT: *Rely upon heaven's High Priest to overcome temptation.*

———————

NOVEMBER 8

JEREMIAH 49–50, WITH HEBREWS 5

And the land will tremble and sorrow; for every purpose of the LORD shall be performed against Babylon, to make the land of Babylon a desolation without inhabitant (Jeremiah 51:29).

WHEN WILL GOD LITERALLY DESTROY BABYLON AND FULFILL HIS PROMISE?

Jeremiah 50–51 predicts a future destruction of Babylon. Moreover, its elimination shall be permanent, unlike during 539 BC when the Medes and the Persians conquered the land. Babylon is an ancient city founded by Nimrod (Genesis 10:9–10). The Lord's future decimation will be perpetual. Jeremiah writes, "It shall be inhabited no more forever, nor shall it be dwelt in from generation to generation" (Jeremiah 50:39). The city is compared to the obliteration of Sodom and Gomorrah (Jeremiah 50:40). As two chapters are given to predict Babylon's demise, there are two chapters given to show its fulfillment (Revelation 17–18). Its permanent annihilation and heaven's future celebration are given in Revelation 18:21–19:5.

EMPLOYMENT POINT: *Honor the God who metes out justice in His perfect time.*

NOVEMBER 9

JEREMIAH 51–52, WITH HEBREWS 6

For God is not unjust to forget your work and labor of love which you have shown toward His name, in that you have ministered to the saints, and do minister (Hebrews 6:10).

ARE YOU TIRED FROM SERVING JESUS?

God is just and keeps a meticulous set of books. Those who *labor to the point of exhaustion*, which is the literal meaning of "labor," will be rewarded on the day of judgment. The Hebrew Christians who honored God, having ministered to other believers in the name of Jesus, will be compensated. We are to prioritize fellow believers to serve. Paul exhorts the saints at Galatia, "Let us do good to all, especially to those who are of the household of faith" (Galatians 6:10). Our Lord not only acknowledges our past service for Him, but also notes our present ministry. He delights in believers who have served Him in the past and continue to do so.

EMPLOYMENT POINT: *Serve God continually, while anticipating your future rewards.*

NOVEMBER 10

LAMENTATIONS 1–2, WITH HEBREWS 7

Therefore He is also able to save to the uttermost those who come to God through Him, since He always lives to make intercession for them (Hebrews 7:25).

WHY SHOULD YOU TRUST JESUS TO COMPLETE HIS WORK IN YOU?

Jesus' priesthood trumps Aaron's. Those who served from the line of Aaron were limited by death from ministering as priests. The author of Hebrews pens, "Also there were many priests, because they were prevented by death from continuing" (Hebrews 7:23). Our Lord comes from a different line than Aaron; His priesthood derives from Melchizedek. He was a king and priest in Jerusalem (Genesis 14) and becomes a type for Jesus' perpetual ministry since there is no recorded genealogy for Melchizedek's parentage (Hebrews 7:6). By way of example, Jesus comes from this enduring priestly line. Because Jesus is eternally God, His priesthood continues, and He will finish the work of salvation that He's begun in us.

EMPLOYMENT POINT: *Depend upon God's eternal High Priest to finish His work.*

NOVEMBER 11

LAMENTATIONS 3–5, WITH HEBREWS 8

***

Through the LORD's mercies we are not consumed, because His compassions fail not. They are new every morning; great is Your faithfulness (Lamentations 3:22–23).

DO YOU DAILY RELY UPON GOD'S MERCY?

Judah deserves to be totally annihilated because of her idolatrous ways. Yet the Lord preserves a remnant of the people. Jeremiah experiences a low in his life and ministry because of the devastation of the nation he loves. The weeping prophet pours out his heart to God. He prays, "Remember my affliction and roaming, the wormwood and the gall. My soul still remembers and sinks within me" (Lamentations 3:19–20). As Jeremiah turns to the Lord, he is given hope (Lamentations 3:21).

Based upon God's mercy, we should heed Paul's exhortation: "I beseech you therefore, brethren, by the mercies of God, that you present your bodies a living sacrifice, holy, acceptable to God, which is your reasonable service" (Romans 12:1).

EMPLOYMENT POINT: *Commit to serving the Lord, who daily extends mercy to you.*

***

NOVEMBER 12

EZEKIEL 1–3, WITH HEBREWS 9

———

And as it is appointed for men to die once, but after this the judgment (Hebrews 9:27).

ARE YOU READY TO MEET YOUR JUDGE?

Jesus says, "Nevertheless I tell you the truth. It is to your advantage that I go away; for if I do not go away, the Helper will not come to you" (John 16:7). The Holy Spirit would aid Jesus' followers and "will convict the world of sin, and of righteousness, and of judgment" (John 16:8). Children of God don't need to fear death and the subsequent judgment. John counsels, "And now, little children, abide in Him, that when He appears, we may have confidence and not be ashamed before Him at His coming" (1 John 2:28). God fills us with His love when we walk with Him. "Love has been perfected among us in this," writes John, "that we may have boldness in the day of judgment" (1 John 4:17).

EMPLOYMENT POINT: *Prepare to meet your Judge by walking with Jesus.*

———

November 13

Ezekiel 4–6, with Hebrews 10:1–23

Take a clay tablet and lay it before you, and portray on it a city, Jerusalem. Lay siege against it, build a siege wall against it, and heap up a mound against it; set camps against it also, and place battering rams against it all around (Ezekiel 4:1–2).

WHAT OBJECT LESSON ARE YOU COMMUNICATING TO OTHERS?

Ezekiel is taken captive by the Babylonians in 597 BC and becomes the object-lesson prophet. God instructs His servant to display a series of symbolic acts, to communicate to those still in Judah about their pending judgment (Ezekiel 4:1–6:7). With humility Ezekiel portrays to the idolatrous nation the displeasure of God through his actions. Obeying the Lord means embracing a childlike faith. Jesus says, "Therefore whoever humbles himself as this little child is the greatest in the kingdom of heaven" (Matthew 18:4). Our Lord also demonstrates great humility by washing the disciples' feet (John 13) and dying on the cross (Philippians 2:5–11).

EMPLOYMENT POINT: *Humble yourself, to become God's object lesson to others.*

November 14

Ezekiel 7–9, with
Hebrews 10:24–39

Not forsaking the assembling of ourselves together, as is the manner of some, but exhorting one another, and so much the more as you see the Day approaching (Hebrews 10:25).

Do you encourage the saints to grow spiritually at your church?

Jesus predicts the birth of the church in Matthew 16:18. He says to Peter, "I will build My church, and the gates of Hades shall not prevail against it." Death—even Jesus' death—would not stop the building of His church. Moreover, it is in the context of the church that we are to minister our spiritual gifts (1 Peter 4:10). It is also the place to be trained by spiritually gifted men. They are given "for the equipping of the saints for the work of ministry, for the edifying of the body of Christ" (Ephesians 4:12). Indeed, even our future judgment is described within the setting of the church (1 Corinthians 3:11–15).

EMPLOYMENT POINT: *Be trained and serve others through a Bible-based church.*

NOVEMBER 15

EZEKIEL 10–12, WITH HEBREWS 11:1–19

For he waited for the city which has foundations, whose builder and maker is God (Hebrews 11:10).

HOW SECURE IS YOUR FUTURE?

God commands Abraham to "Get out of your country" (Genesis 12:1) and *be a blessing,* which is the literal translation from "And you shall be a blessing" (Genesis 12:2). He obeys the Lord and departs from familiar surroundings to the land of promise. The father of faith demonstrates his salvation by being willing to sacrifice Isaac, the promised seed (Hebrews 11:17). How could Abraham leave his homeland, travel to a place he has never seen, and then be willing to sacrifice his beloved son Isaac? It is because his eyes are upon a "city which has foundations." "Foundations" is plural and shows the permanence of the New Jerusalem. John describes the New Jerusalem as follows: "Now the wall of the city had twelve foundations" (Revelation 21:14). Like Abraham, let us walk in faith, knowing that our future is secure!

EMPLOYMENT POINT: *Live by faith, knowing that your foundations will endure.*

November 16

Ezekiel 13–15, with Hebrews 11:20–40

———— ◊ ————

Even if these three men, Noah, Daniel, and Job, were in it, they would deliver only themselves by their righteousness (Ezekiel 14:14).

What is the danger of persistent disobedience?

David writes, "God is a just judge, and God is angry with the wicked every day" (Psalm 7:11). Yet, "The Lord is not slack concerning His promise, as some count slackness, but is longsuffering toward us, not willing that any should perish but that all should come to repentance" (2 Peter 3:9). We learn about God's justice and longsuffering from the Bible. Wisdom cries out that the latter should not be presumed upon. The Lord declares His displeasure in Judah. Even if the great men of God—Noah, Daniel, and Job—lived currently in Israel, He would still chasten them. Ezekiel writes, "Son of man, when a land sins against Me by persistent unfaithfulness, I will stretch out My hand against it" (Ezekiel 14:13).

Employment Point: *Obey the Lord instantly, and don't presume upon His patience.*

———— ◊ ————

NOVEMBER 17

EZEKIEL 16, WITH HEBREWS 12

Since we are surrounded by so great a cloud of witnesses, let us lay aside every weight, and the sin which so easily ensnares us, and let us run with endurance the race that is set before us, looking unto Jesus (Hebrews 12:1–2).

DO YOU HAVE A SINGULAR FOCUS IN YOUR FAITH JOURNEY?

We have the hall of faith in Hebrews 11. These men and women experienced victory over their challenges because they acted upon God's promises. The writer of Hebrews exhorts his audience to "lay aside every weight." Perhaps he is referring to Judaism, since some were tempted to abandon Jesus for their former practice. Instead of permanently looking back, they need to look forward to the One who fulfills the Old Testament and is "the author and finisher of our faith." Moreover, they must set aside "the sin which so easily ensnares us," which points to the sin of unbelief.

EMPLOYMENT POINT: *Look to Jesus by faith, to complete your journey well.*

November 18

Ezekiel 17–19, with Hebrews 13

The soul who sins shall die. The son shall not bear the guilt of the father, nor the father bear the guilt of the son (Ezekiel 18:20).

What will you leave for the next generation?

All of us are either a good or bad example. God holds accountable sinners and blesses those who choose the path of righteousness. Ezekiel finishes Ezekiel 18:20 as follows: "The righteousness of the righteous shall be upon himself, and the wickedness of the wicked shall be upon himself." The Lord takes no pleasure in the death of the wicked (Ezekiel 18:23), and desires that sinners turn from their trespasses and walk with God. Ezekiel calls disobedient Israelites in behalf of God to amend their ways. He proclaims, "Repent, and turn from all your transgressions, so that iniquity will not be your ruin" (Ezekiel 18:30). Like the Thessalonians, God longs for all people to repent and exemplify godliness to others (1 Thessalonians 1:6–10).

Employment Point: *Turn to God, and leave a godly legacy.*

NOVEMBER 19

EZEKIEL 20–21, WITH JAMES 1

—————

But be doers of the word, and not hearers only, deceiving yourselves (James 1:22).

HAVE YOU BEEN EMPLOYING WHAT YOU'VE BEEN LEARNING?

James, the half-brother of the Lord, commands the saints to apply what they have learned. Although it is true that "faith comes by hearing, and hearing by the word of God" (Romans 10:17), putting into practice what you have heard is the final step of Bible study. The wise bondservant of God doesn't want the believers to fall into Satan's trap by "deceiving yourselves." James' term "deceiving" comes from a compound Greek word from the preposition *aside*, implying misdirection, and *to reason*. He is concerned that they are falsely reasoning like the hearer of the Bible "observing his natural face in a mirror; for he observes himself, goes away, and immediately forgets what kind of man he was" (James 1:23—24). The Scripture is given for us to know God through practicing its content.

EMPLOYMENT POINT: *Intently hear God's Word and employ its message.*

—————

NOVEMBER 20

EZEKIEL 22–23, WITH JAMES 2

So I sought for a man among them who would make a wall, and stand in the gap before Me on behalf of the land, that I should not destroy it; but I found no one (Ezekiel 22:30).

ARE YOU STANDING IN THE GAP FOR OTHERS?

God set His gaze upon Sodom, Gomorrah, and the surrounding cities. The wickedness of the people had to be judged. Yet Lot lived in Sodom. Thankfully he had Abraham intercede for him (Genesis 18:22–33), which led to his deliverance (2 Peter 2:7). The Lord's eyes scan the globe looking for people of faith. We learn from 2 Chronicles 16:9, "For the eyes of the LORD run to and fro throughout the whole earth, to show Himself strong on behalf of those whose heart is loyal to Him." Passionate prayer avails God's power. He uses average people with great faith like Elijah to work wonders (James 5:17–18).

EMPLOYMENT POINT: *Stand in the gap for others with righteous living and fervent prayer.*

November 21

Ezekiel 24–26, with James 3

But the wisdom that is from above is first pure, then peaceable, gentle, willing to yield, full of mercy and good fruits, without partiality and without hypocrisy (James 3:17).

Whose wisdom are you receiving?

James exposes the wisdom of this world, which is driven by self-gratification (James 3:14–16). Conversely, God's wisdom begins with purity. The Greek word for "pure" carries the notion to be free from impurity or contamination. Whereas this world's wisdom is "self-seeking," the wisdom that derives from heaven is "gentle," which means *to be yielding* and *unassertive*. James then uses another term carrying a similar idea as translated by "willing to yield." These two terms stand in sharp contrast to "envy and self-seeking" (James 3:16). Children of God imitate the nature of the unsaved by exhibiting the latter. Paul admonishes the Corinthians, "For where there are envy, strife, and divisions among you, are you not carnal and behaving like mere men?" (1 Corinthians 3:3).

Employment Point: *Seek God's wisdom and exhibit His holy nature.*

NOVEMBER 22

EZEKIEL 27–28, WITH JAMES 4

―――⦿―――

Be sober, be vigilant; because your adversary the devil walks about like a roaring lion, seeking whom he may devour (1 Peter 5:8).

DO YOU UNDERSTAND SATAN'S STRENGTHS AND WEAKNESSES?

Ezekiel makes a transition from "the prince of Tyre" (Ezekiel 28:2) to the "king of Tyre" (Ezekiel 28:12). Satan's origin and expulsion from heaven are given under the latter section. The connecting trait of the two passages is pride. Pride brings the downfall of the earthly king, as it did Satan. The wicked one has limitations; twice Ezekiel refers to him as being "created" (Ezekiel 28:13, 15). For this reason he cannot be everywhere at all times like God. Yet his prowess must not be ignored. Michael, a powerful angel, respects his might. "In contending with the devil," writes Jude, "when he disputed about the body of Moses, dared not bring against him a reviling accusation, but said, 'The Lord rebuke you!'" (Jude 9).

EMPLOYMENT POINT: *Rely upon the strength of the Lord to overcome Satan.*

―――⦿―――

NOVEMBER 23

EZEKIEL 29–31, WITH JAMES 5

———◦◦◦———

You also be patient. Establish your hearts, for the coming of the Lord is at hand (James 5:8).

WHAT SHOULD YOU FOCUS UPON IN LIGHT OF JESUS' IMMINENT RETURN?

James gives two commands and offers encouragement in James 5:8. First, he reminds believers that the Christian race is not a 100-meter dash, but rather a 26.2-mile marathon. Therefore, James states the imperative "be patient." The church has been anticipating Jesus' return for two thousand years; even so we must patiently wait. Yet the Christian life needs to be nurtured in order to be steadfast. This is why James gives the second command: "Establish your hearts." The Greek verb "establish" conveys to be fixed or firm. It occurs in 2 Thessalonians 3:3, "But the Lord is faithful, who will establish you and guard you from the evil one." Finally, we are to obey these two commands "for the coming of the Lord is at hand."

EMPLOYMENT POINT: *Be patient and firm in your faith, because Jesus is returning.*

———◦◦◦———

November 24

Ezekiel 32–33, with 1 Peter 1

———◦———

I have no pleasure in the death of the wicked, but that the wicked turn from his way and live (Ezekiel 33:11).

Are you being a good watchperson for Jesus?

Watchmen have an important task. They are to scan the countryside and alert the people if an enemy approaches. God uses this analogy for Ezekiel to fully grasp his assignment. Concerning an invading army, God instructs the son of man, "if he blows the trumpet and warns the people, then whoever hears the sound of the trumpet and does not take warning, if the sword comes and takes him away, his blood shall be on his own head" (Ezekiel 33:3–4). Ezekiel's responsibility parallels the watchman. If he does not warn the people, then their blood is upon his hands (Ezekiel 33:6). Indeed, we have also been called to alert the people of approaching judgment if they don't turn from their sin to Jesus.

Employment Point: *Warn the unsaved to believe on Jesus to escape coming judgment.*

———◦———

NOVEMBER 25

EZEKIEL 34–35, WITH
1 PETER 2

But you are a chosen generation, a royal priesthood, a holy nation, His own special people, that you may proclaim the praises of Him who called you out of darkness into His marvelous light (1 Peter 2:9).

DO YOU PRACTICE YOUR HEAVENLY POSITION AND PURPOSE?

God has called Jesus' church to be His elect people. Moreover, we are designated as "a royal priesthood." Even as Abraham interceded for Lot, and the Old Testament priests for the people, we are to pray for the salvation of the lost and spiritual growth of the found. After all, we are "His own special people." The Greek term translated "special" means *to acquire* or *purchase*. Peter then gives the purpose for God acquiring us, "that you may proclaim the praises of Him who called you out of darkness into His marvelous light." Since we have been rescued from darkness, "let us continually offer the sacrifice of praise to God" (Hebrews 13:15).

EMPLOYMENT POINT: *Praise the Lord continually, recognizing your heavenly status.*

November 26

Ezekiel 36–37, with
1 Peter 3

———————

Again He said to me, "Prophesy to these bones, and say to them, 'O dry bones, hear the word of the LORD!'" (Ezekiel 37:4).

Do you believe that God can give life to the spiritually dead?

Ezekiel is called to do something seemingly ridiculous; the Lord calls him to speak to dry bones, which represent Israel. Although they are spiritually dead, only God's Word can bring Israel back to life. Ezekiel is confronted with the following question: Can I trust the power of God to give life to the dead? By faith Ezekiel proclaims God's Word, and the bones come to life. Moreover, we are called to proclaim the gospel to the spiritually dead. Don't forget what the Lord has done for us. "Even when we were dead in trespasses, made us alive together with Christ," writes Paul (Ephesians 2:5). Daily speak God's living Word to the dead, believing that the Lord can save them!

EMPLOYMENT POINT: *Trust God to raise the spiritually dead through the gospel.*

———————

NOVEMBER 27

EZEKIEL 38–39, WITH
1 PETER 4

———◦———

As each one has received a gift, minister it to one another, as good stewards of the manifold grace of God (1 Peter 4:10).

ARE YOU USING YOUR SPIRITUAL GIFT FOR GOD'S GLORY?

Peter testifies that each believer has received at least one spiritual gift. A spiritual gift is a supernatural ability given by God to the believer at the moment of salvation for the building up of the body of Christ. The Greek term "gift" derives from the word "grace" and has a suffix; therefore, the word means *the result of grace*. Use your grace-gift to bring God glory. Peter explains, "If anyone speaks, let him speak as the oracles of God. If anyone ministers, let him do it as with the ability which God supplies, that in all things God may be glorified through Jesus Christ" (1 Peter 4:11). Spiritual gifts are given not for self-edification, but for ministering to others.

EMPLOYMENT POINT: *Use your spiritual gift to minister to others and bring glory to God.*

———◦———

NOVEMBER 28

EZEKIEL 40, WITH
1 PETER 5

In the visions of God He took me into the land of Israel and set me on a very high mountain; on it toward the south was something like the structure of a city (Ezekiel 40:2).

WHAT IS THE STRUCTURE OF EZEKIEL 40–48?

Today we live in the church age. It began on the Day of Pentecost in Acts 2 and will end with the Rapture. Daniel 9:24–27 gives us the amazing prophecy of the seventy weeks of Daniel. It shows that the Antichrist will make a covenant with Israel for seven years. The signing of that covenant commences the Tribulation, as is recorded in Revelation 6–19. At the end of that period Jesus Christ returns to the earth (Revelation 19:11–21). Jesus' Second Coming is to defeat His enemies gathered at Armageddon and to establish the millennial kingdom as described in Revelation 20. Ezekiel's Temple is built for that period of time.

EMPLOYMENT POINT: *Worship Jesus, who will establish His kingdom on earth.*

November 29

Ezekiel 41–42, with 2 Peter 1

For prophecy never came by the will of man, but holy men of God spoke as they were moved by the Holy Spirit (2 Peter 1:21).

How confident are you in the Bible's content?

Apparently false teachers accused Peter and the apostles of pursuing myths. Peter writes, "For we did not follow cunningly devised fables when we made known to you the power and coming of our Lord Jesus Christ, but were eyewitnesses of His majesty" (2 Peter 1:16). The apostle testifies to witnessing the transfiguration of Jesus and hearing the voice of the Father, who said, "This is My beloved Son, in whom I am well pleased" (2 Peter 1:17). Moreover, Peter uses a present tense verb explaining, "we have [currently have] the prophetic word confirmed" (2 Peter 1:19). As a sailing vessel is carried across the water (Acts 27:15, 17), "holy men of God spoke as they were moved by the Holy Spirit."

EMPLOYMENT POINT: *Live confidently in Jesus' deity and the Bible's integrity.*

November 30

Ezekiel 43–44, with
2 Peter 2

Behold, the glory of the God of Israel came from the way of the east. His voice was like the sound of many waters; and the earth shone with His glory (Ezekiel 43:2).

Are you awaiting the return of the glorious One?

God's glory departed from the Temple prior to its being destroyed in 586 BC. Ezekiel writes, "And the glory of the LORD went up from the midst of the city and stood on the mountain, which is on the east side of the city" (Ezekiel 11:23). The description of Jesus "like the sound of many waters" appears in the Book of Revelation (Revelation 1:15). Jesus' Second Coming is predicted and will be fulfilled at the end of the Tribulation (Revelation 1:7; 19:11–21). Matthew depicts His advent as follows: "they will see the Son of Man coming on the clouds of heaven with power and great glory" (Matthew 24:30). Both Ezekiel and Matthew predict His glorious return.

Employment Point: *Worship and serve the all-glorious King.*

December 1

Ezekiel 45–46, with
2 Peter 3

The Lord is not slack concerning His promise, as some count slackness, but is longsuffering toward us, not willing that any should perish but that all should come to repentance (2 Peter 3:9).

Why hasn't Jesus yet returned?

There have been mockers for two thousand years asking, "Where is the promise of His coming?" (2 Peter 3:4). Their words imply that Jesus isn't coming back; however, our Lord doesn't operate based upon an earthly timetable. The Lord had Noah preach for 120 years to the people while the ark was prepared. Yet Moses records the Lord's statement: "My Spirit shall not strive with man forever, for he is indeed flesh; yet his days shall be one hundred and twenty years" (Genesis 6:3). As God set a time limit for the earthly inhabitants prior to the flood to repent or be judged, He will do the same with Jesus' return. Both situations speak about His longsuffering.

EMPLOYMENT POINT: *Faithfully witness to others, knowing that time is fleeting.*

December 2

Ezekiel 47–48, with
1 John 1

This is the message which we have heard from Him and declare to you, that God is light and in Him is no darkness at all (1 John 1:5).

Are you walking in God's light?

John writes about the importance of remaining in God's light. The reminder is necessary since there were false teachers who were expelled from the church having propagated bad doctrine and were saying one thing and practicing another (1 John 2:19). This group is exposed by the words "if we say" (1 John 1:6, 8, 10). Our author teaches us about God's light by using a positive and negative statement. "God is light," conveys that the Lord is absolutely holy. Then he reveals the same truth by writing "and in Him is no darkness at all." The Father perpetually remains without moral flaw or contamination. When we abide in His light, "we have fellowship with one another" (1 John 1:7).

EMPLOYMENT POINT: *Enjoy fellowship with God and believers by walking in the light.*

December 3

Daniel 1–2, with 1 John 2

But Daniel purposed in his heart that he would not defile himself with the portion of the king's delicacies (Daniel 1:8).

Have you determined to please the Lord?

Some saints live up to their names. Daniel (God is my judge), Hananiah (the Lord is gracious), Mishael (who is like God), and Azariah (the Lord is my help) are taken captive to Babylon in 605 BC. Clearly God-fearing parents brought up these young men, because they are unwilling to compromise under severe pressure. "Daniel purposed in his heart" to be loyal to his God. The Hebrew verb "purposed" means *to put, to set,* or *to place.* Job uses this term translated as "I would commit" in Job 5:8. "But as for me, I would seek God, and to God I would commit my cause—who does great things, and unsearchable, marvelous things without number" (Job 5:8–9). God honored the commitment of great patriarchs and will do the same for you!

Employment Point: *Purpose to always please God.*

December 4

Daniel 3–4, with 1 John 3

They do not serve your gods or worship the gold image which you have set up (Daniel 3:12).

How well do you stand up under pressure?

King Nebuchadnezzar allows the dream that he had to swell his head (Daniel 2:38). For this reason, he erects a ninety-foot idol to be worshiped. The Babylonians try to brainwash Hananiah, Mishael, and Azariah by giving them new names; however, they, like Daniel, purpose to always please the Lord. Nebuchadnezzar, who is accustomed to having his way, becomes furious when the three Jewish men don't bow to his decree. I wonder what was hotter on that day, Nebuchadnezzar or the furnace for torture to intimidate the people? Amazingly the three men of conviction turn down a second chance to bow down to the image, knowing that their God can deliver them, and if not, they will not worship an idol. Their testimony is enlarged by God's supernatural protection.

Employment Point: *Be willing to sacrifice your life to please the Lord.*

December 5

Daniel 5–6, with 1 John 4

———

Now when Daniel knew that the writing was signed, he went home. And in his upper room, with his windows open toward Jerusalem, he knelt down on his knees three times that day, and prayed (Daniel 6:10).

Do you value your prayer time more than your life?

Daniel lives with integrity. When those who are jealous of his success try to bring him down, they cannot find any blemish in him (Daniel 6:4). Could Daniel's faithful existence have to do with his prayer life? He follows the model of the psalmist in Psalm 55:17: "Evening and morning and at noon I will pray, and cry aloud, and He shall hear my voice." God honors the faith and prayers of Daniel even in the lions' den. The writer of Hebrews pens, "who through faith subdued kingdoms, worked righteousness, obtained promises, stopped the mouths of lions" (Hebrews 11:33). Daniel is rescued "because he believed in his God" (Daniel 6:23).

Employment Point: *Develop faith and faithfulness with a consistent prayer life.*

———

December 6

Daniel 7–8, with
1 John 5

For this is the love of God, that we keep His commandments. And His commandments are not burdensome (1 John 5:3).

Do you delight in keeping God's commands?

We are to guard the commandments of God like prison guards watch over their prisoners. John uses the term "keep," meaning *to guard* or *keep watch over*. It emerges in Acts 12:5–6 of Peter being kept in prison. Not only are God's commandments to be obeyed, they also should be our delight, which is conveyed by the words "are not burdensome." King David writes a prophecy about Jesus' delight in God's will. He pens, "Behold, I come; In the scroll of the book it is written of me. I delight to do Your will, O my God, and Your law is within my heart" (Psalm 40:7–8). As the writer of Hebrews describes Jesus' obedience to the Father's will (Hebrews 10:5–8), we should follow in His path!

Employment Point: *Demonstrate the love of God by keeping His Word with delight.*

DECEMBER 7

DANIEL 9–10, WITH
2 JOHN

I, Daniel, understood by the books the number of the years speci-
fied by the word of the LORD through Jeremiah the prophet, that
He would accomplish seventy years in the desolations of Jerusalem
(Daniel 9:2).

HOW WELL DO YOU KNOW THE FUTURE?

Daniel relies upon the prophecies of Scripture to understand his
times. Having a copy of the Book of Jeremiah, he learns that his
beloved people will be in Babylonian captivity for seventy years, and
then God would punish the king of Babylon (Jeremiah 25:11–12).
Sadly, the children of Israel didn't learn from Daniel's example. Daniel 9:24–27 predicts the exact day on which the Messiah would ride
into Jerusalem, offering them the kingdom. Observe the specificity of
Jesus' statement after He had wept over the nation for their unbelief:
"If you had known, even you, especially in this your day, the things
that make for your peace!" (Luke 19:42).

EMPLOYMENT POINT: *Study Bible prophecy to understand the future
and how to currently live.*

DECEMBER 8

DANIEL 11–12, WITH
3 JOHN

I wrote to the church, but Diotrephes, who loves to have the preeminence among them, does not receive us (3 John 9).

WHAT IS YOUR NUMBER ONE PRIORITY IN LIFE?

John apparently wrote an earlier letter to the church as shown by the past tense verb "I wrote." Diotrephes, who is self-centered, perhaps suppressed the letter from the congregation. He "loves to have the preeminence," which literally means *he loves to be first.* The apostle reports to Gaius that he "does not receive us." Diotrephes shunned John's apostolic authority by not welcoming those missionaries that he sent to the church. What is Diotrephes' problem? Perhaps he is jealous of John and his authority. Unlike Diotrephes, John remains under Jesus' authority. Paul writes about the Lord Jesus as the head of the church "that in all things He may have the preeminence" (Colossians 1:18). Jesus should receive top billing in our lives!

EMPLOYMENT POINT: *Keep Jesus as your main priority in life and submit to His leaders.*

December 9

Hosea 1–4, with Jude

Go again, love a woman who is loved by a lover and is committing adultery, just like the love of the LORD for the children of Israel (Hosea 3:1).

How costly is your redemption?

God has an unusual object lesson for Israel. Hosea marries a woman who is unfaithful. The human relationship depicts how Israel left the true God for idols. Graciously the Lord desires to have His chosen people to be reconciled with Him, and this is illustrated through Hosea pursuing Gomer. Through the course of her immorality, the harlot becomes enslaved and needs redemption. Hosea writes, "So I bought her for myself for fifteen shekels of silver, and one and one-half homers of barley" (Hosea 3:2). The combined price of redemption is approximately that for a slave (Exodus 21:32). Jesus has redeemed us as former captives of Satan. "In whom we have redemption through His blood," writes Paul, "the forgiveness of sins" (Colossians 1:14).

Employment Point: *Be loyal to Jesus, who redeemed you to Himself.*

DECEMBER 10

HOSEA 5–8, WITH REVELATION 1

Blessed is he who reads and those who hear the words of this prophecy, and keep those things which are written in it; for the time is near (Revelation 1:3).

ARE YOU MARKED BY GOD'S FAVOR?

Where were you on September 11, 2001? I was sitting in my office studying Revelation 1:1–3 to preach the following Sunday. How the words "for the time is near" leaped from the page on that fateful day. John gives the first of seven uses of this Greek term for "blessed," which means *marked with God's favor*. There exists a blessing to the individual who reads the Book of Revelation and those who employ its commands. Moreover, the apostle informs us that the prophecies of Revelation should be heeded with the added incentive "for the time is near," which conveys that they are within reach. John's expression shows that once the prophecies unfold, they will be enacted quickly.

EMPLOYMENT POINT: *Read, hear, and heed the Book of Revelation to be blessed.*

DECEMBER 11

HOSEA 9–11, WITH REVELATION 2

Sow for yourselves righteousness; reap in mercy; break up your fallow ground, for it is time to seek the LORD, till He comes and rains righteousness on you (Hosea 10:12).

IS IT TIME FOR YOU TO BREAK UP THE FALLOW GROUND?

Hosea uses the setting of agriculture to instruct the nation. He calls them to repentance because of their wickedness. The prophet pens, "You have plowed wickedness; you have reaped iniquity. You have eaten the fruit of lies, because you trusted in your own way" (Hosea 10:13). Hosea presses the Israelites to plant "righteousness" so that they could receive God's "mercy," which means His *lovingkindness* or *loyal love*. Centuries earlier Moses wrote about God's desire for His people. "Therefore circumcise the foreskin of your heart, and be stiff-necked no longer" (Deuteronomy 10:16). Hosea's equivalent to Moses' command is found in the expression "break up the fallow ground." Both men of God call for repentance.

EMPLOYMENT POINT: *Cultivate a heart of righteousness to harvest God's favor.*

DECEMBER 12

HOSEA 12–14, WITH REVELATION 3

Behold, I stand at the door and knock. If anyone hears My voice and opens the door, I will come in to him and dine with him, and he with Me (Revelation 3:20).

HAVE YOU INVITED JESUS TO FELLOWSHIP WITH YOU?

In approximately AD 60 the inhabitants of Laodicea experienced a severe earthquake. When the government offered to rebuild their city, the affluent citizens declined their assistance. Unfortunately, the saints in the city adopt a similar self-sufficient mindset and need Jesus' correction. The believers become like the hot water piped in from Hierapolis that turns lukewarm when it reaches its destination. As a result, the Lord threatens to "vomit you out of My mouth" (Revelation 3:16). These lukewarm saints are financially rich but spiritually bankrupt. Jesus assessment is "you are wretched, miserable, poor, blind, and naked" (Revelation 3:17). Since Jesus loves them, He rebukes them and calls them to repentance and a restoration of fellowship.

EMPLOYMENT POINT: *Repent of self-sufficiency and enjoy fellowship with Jesus.*

DECEMBER 13

JOEL, WITH REVELATION 4

So I will restore to you the years that the swarming locust has eaten, the crawling locust, the consuming locust, and the chewing locust, my great army which I sent among you (Joel 2:25).

WHEN WILL GOD FULFILL HIS PROMISE OF RESTORATION?

Disaster strikes Judah without notice. A foreboding black cloud of dreaded locusts invade the land (Joel 1). Joel transitions from an army of locusts to a human army (Joel 2). The prophet warns, "For the day of the LORD is coming, for it is at hand: a day of darkness and gloominess, a day of clouds and thick darkness, like the morning clouds spread over the mountains. A people come" (Joel 2:1–2). Unlike locusts that generally come from the south, this army approaches from the north (Joel 2:20). Revelation 6–19 depicts the Day of the Lord. It will culminate with the Second Coming of Jesus (Revelation 19:11–21) and leads to the restorative millennial kingdom (Revelation 20).

EMPLOYMENT POINT: *Anticipate the Prince of Peace, who fulfills His promises.*

DECEMBER 14

AMOS 1–3, WITH REVELATION 5

Worthy is the Lamb who was slain to receive power and riches and wisdom, and strength and honor and glory and blessing! (Revelation 5:12).

WHY IS JESUS PRAISED WITH THESE SEVEN ATTRIBUTES?

Revelation 4–5 depicts the calm before the storm of the Tribulation. God sits upon the throne and is worshiped as Creator (Revelation 4:11). Since He created the universe, including all people, the Father has the right to judge both. As He sits upon the throne, the question is offered, "Who is worthy to open the scroll and to loose its seals?" (Revelation 5:2). John weeps over the sin of the world as revealed through their unworthiness to open the scroll (Revelation 5:3–4). Suddenly Jesus emerges on the scene and takes the scroll, which will unleash the seal, trumpet, and bowl judgments upon the world. The resurrected Lamb of God then receives the sevenfold praises as the Worthy One!

EMPLOYMENT POINT: *Worship Jesus, who is worthy to be praised for all eternity.*

DECEMBER 15

AMOS 4–6, WITH REVELATION 6

———◆———

For the great day of His wrath has come, and who is able to stand? (Revelation 6:17).

HOW BAD IS THE TRIBULATION?

Amos describes himself in Amos 7:14, "I was no prophet, nor was I a son of a prophet." Yet he calls Israel to repent of their sin and also explains the Day of the Lord. He writes, "It will be darkness, and not light. It will be as though a man fled from a lion, and a bear met him! Or as though he went into the house, leaned his hand on the wall, and a serpent bit him!" (Amos 5:18–19). John records the period known as the Day of the Lord, or the Tribulation, in Revelation 6–19. One half of the world's population will die in the first half of the Tribulation (Revelation 6:8; 9:18). Thankfully the Rapture comes before the Tribulation to deliver us from God's wrath (Romans 5:9; 1 Thessalonians 1:10; 5:9).

EMPLOYMENT POINT: *Believe on Jesus' finished work to escape the wrath of God.*

———◆———

DECEMBER 16

AMOS 7–9, WITH REVELATION 7

———◆———

And I heard the number of those who were sealed. One hundred and forty-four thousand of all the tribes of the children of Israel (Revelation 7:4).

FOR THE GREAT DAY OF HIS WRATH HAS COME, AND WHO IS ABLE TO STAND? (REVELATION 6:17).

At the start of the Tribulation there will be no saints on the earth, because the church will have been raptured. Revelation 7:1–8 informs us that suddenly and miraculously 144,000 Jews are saved, sealed, and dispatched to bring the gospel to the unsaved world. The result of their ministry will be an innumerable multitude saved (Revelation 7:9). Jesus has a desire for all people to be saved. Amazingly, He identifies the unidentifiable. Since the Temple's destruction in AD 70 that housed genealogical record for the Jews, no one knows the genealogy of any Jewish person. Yet the Messiah knows, equips, and sends a spiritual army to reach the lost.

EMPLOYMENT POINT: *Align your heart with Jesus' holy heart to reach the lost.*

———◆———

DECEMBER 17

OBADIAH, WITH REVELATION 8

———◆———

Though you ascend as high as the eagle, and though you set your nest among the stars, from there I will bring you down (Obadiah 4).

WHAT IS THE OUTCOME FOR THOSE WHO DON'T HONOR THE CHILDREN OF GOD?

Isaac and Rebekah longed to have children. The child of promise, Isaac, pleads with the Lord for children, and God honors his request. Moses writes, "But the children struggled together within her" (Genesis 25:22). Thus would be the theme of Jacob and Esau, who represent two nations: Israel and Edom. Unwisely, the Edomites refuse to aid the Israelites during their wilderness wandering (Numbers 20:14–21). Faithful to His Word, God judges the Edomites. Earlier the Lord promised to Abraham, "I will bless those who bless you, and I will curse him who curses you" (Genesis 12:3). Although the Edomites thought they were secure because of their rugged and lofty landscape, God brought them down.

EMPLOYMENT POINT: *Honor God's chosen people and receive His blessing, rather than His wrath.*

———◆———

December 18

Jonah, with Revelation 9

Arise, go to Nineveh, that great city, and cry out against it; for their wickedness has come up before Me (Jonah 1:2).

Have you been given a second chance to make a first impression?

God calls Jonah to stand up, step up, and speak up for God. Quickly the disobedient prophet learns that sidestepping God's command brings you down. First, Jonah descends to the bottom of a ship to escape the Lord's command (Jonah 1:3). Next, he is hurled into the Mediterranean Sea to save the crew. He recounts how low he could go: "For You cast me into the deep, into the heart of the seas, and the floods surrounded me" (Jonah 2:3). Although the sailors literally hurl Jonah into the sea, he attributes their action to God. The Lord supernaturally rescues the drowning prophet and gives him a second chance to make a first impression. He gives the same command to the humbled prophet a second time (Jonah 3:2).

Employment Point: *Stand up, step up, and speak up for God.*

DECEMBER 19

MICAH 1–3, WITH REVELATION 10

———◦◦———

Then I took the little book out of the angel's hand and ate it, and it was as sweet as honey in my mouth. But when I had eaten it, my stomach became bitter (Revelation 10:10).

WHAT DOES GOD EXPECT YOU TO DO WITH HIS WORD?

John describes the vision given to him about a mighty angel who stands on the land and sea. The angel's strategic posture, which occurs three times, shows that the upcoming judgment will be upon land and sea (Revelation 10:2, 5, 8). Jesus earlier directs John to write the Book of Revelation (Revelation 1:19); however, he is told not to pen the details about this judgment (Revelation 10:4). From the little book in the mighty angel's hand will come an unspecified judgment. Moreover, John obeys the voice from heaven taking the book and then is told by the angel to eat it. Just like biblical prophecy, it is sweet to taste, but difficult to digest.

EMPLOYMENT POINT: *Digest God's Word and proclaim it.*

———◦◦———

December 20

Micah 4–5, with Revelation 11

But you, Bethlehem Ephrathah, though you are little among the thousands of Judah, yet out of you shall come forth to Me the One to be Ruler in Israel, whose goings forth are from of old, from everlasting (Micah 5:2).

Are you ready to meet King Jesus?

Who is like God is the meaning of Micah's name. He predicts the birth of Jesus in an obscure place: Bethlehem. (Bethlehem isn't mentioned in the list of towns in Joshua 15 or Nehemiah 11 where Judah's clans lived.) The bread of life will be born in the *house of bread*, which is the meaning of Bethlehem. Located just five miles south of Jerusalem would be the birthplace of the eternal God and King. Matthew, who writes to present Jesus as King, quotes from Micah 5:2 (Matthew 2:5–6). The fifth-century BC prophecy petrifies Herod, who perceives Jesus as a rival. Yet the wise men still pursue the newborn King!

Employment Point: *Worship and serve King Jesus today, as you await His return.*

December 21

Micah 6–7, with Revelation 12

And they overcame him by the blood of the Lamb and by the word of their testimony, and they did not love their lives to the death (Revelation 12:11).

How do you have victory over Satan?

Satan is not an insignificant foe. John lists five titles attributed to the devil that communicate his dastardly nature (Revelation 12:9). Moreover, the Book of Job informs us that he appears before God to give an account of his activity (Job 1:6; 2:1). Revelation 12 describes the point in the Tribulation when he will be expelled from heaven. After being banished from God's presence, John writes, "Woe to the inhabitants of the earth and the sea! For the devil has come down to you, having great wrath, because he knows that he has a short time" (Revelation 12:12). During the Great Tribulation, which pertains to the last half of the Tribulation, the serpent of old seeks to persecute and destroy the saints.

Employment Point: *Overcome Satan by Jesus' blood, your testimony, and by loving Jesus supremely.*

DECEMBER 22

NAHUM, WITH REVELATION 13

———◦———

Here is wisdom. Let him who has understanding calculate the number of the beast, for it is the number of a man: His number is 666 (Revelation 13:18).

ARE YOU AWARE OF THE UNHOLY TRINITY?

Revelation 12 begins the mid-point of the Tribulation with the expulsion of Satan from heaven. Next, we are introduced to the Antichrist. He possesses great power and imitates Jesus by dying and coming back to life. The world marvels at his prowess and asks, "Who is like the beast? Who is able to make war with him?" (Revelation 13:4). (Similar questions are asked about the true God in Exodus 15:11.) Then we encounter the false prophet. His mission is to point people to the Antichrist, even as the Holy Spirit directs people to Jesus. Moreover, he fashions the abomination of desolation, which comes to life and instructs the unsaved to murder the saints (Daniel 9:27; 12:11; Matthew 24:15; Revelation 13:14–15).

EMPLOYMENT POINT: *Worship God, knowing the difference between the Trinity and the unholy trinity.*

———◦———

December 23

Habakkuk, with Revelation 14

Behold the proud, his soul is not upright in him; but the just shall live by his faith (Habakkuk 2:4).

Are you walking by faith?

Habakkuk brings his problem to God. The inhabitants of Judah are wicked and seemingly getting away with their ungodliness. He pleaded, "O Lord, how long shall I cry, and You will not hear? Even cry out to You, 'Violence!' and You will not save" (Habakkuk 1:2). God's response rattles the prophet: "For indeed I am raising up the Chaldeans [Babylonians], A bitter and hasty nation" (Habakkuk 1:6). The Lord uses Babylon to chasten the southern kingdom of Judah. Indeed, Habakkuk needs to trust God in this matter. Saints through every generation must walk by faith and not sight. Three New Testament books quote Habakkuk 2:4 (Romans 1:17; Galatians 3:11; Hebrews 10:38). Four times we are reminded, "the just shall live by faith."

Employment Point: *Walk by faith, knowing that God always acts according to His perfect nature.*

December 24

Zephaniah, with Revelation 15

Who shall not fear You, O Lord, and glorify Your name? For You alone are holy. For all nations shall come and worship before You, for Your judgments have been manifested (Revelation 15:4).

Do you celebrate the matchless nature of God?

The final seven judgments of the Tribulation are about to be given (Revelation 15:1), which will culminate with the Second Coming of Jesus Christ (Revelation 19:11–21). John sees a vision reflecting the glory of God and of those who are redeemed throughout these difficult days. Moreover, the saints "sing the song of Moses, the servant of God, and the song of the Lamb" (Revelation 15:3). These two songs express praise to the perfect nature of God who gives victory to His children. Our great God enables us to triumph through the instrument of faith. John writes, "And this is the victory that has overcome the world—our faith" (1 John 5:4).

Employment Point: *Sing to the Lord, who alone gives us the victory over wickedness.*

DECEMBER 25

HAGGAI, WITH
REVELATION 16

Thus says the LORD of hosts: "Consider your ways!" (Haggai 1:7).

DO YOU HAVE HOLES IN YOUR POCKETS?

The rebuilding of the Temple had begun, but there was much to do. Sadly, God's people are more interested in renovating their houses than the Temple. Haggai queries, "Is it time for you yourselves to dwell in your paneled houses, and this temple to lie in ruins?" (Haggai 1:4). As a consequence to their wrong priorities, the prophet states, "You clothe yourselves, but no one is warm; And he who earns wages, Earns wages to put into a bag with holes" (Haggai 1:6). God would again put His blessing upon their lives if they would bring Him the glory worthy of His name and finish the construction on the Temple (Haggai 1:8). Jesus' timeless words still stand, "But seek first the kingdom of God and His righteousness, and all these things shall be added to you" (Matthew 6:33).

EMPLOYMENT POINT: *Prioritize God's work above your own, for His blessing.*

December 26

Zechariah 1–3, with
Revelation 17

And another angel followed, saying, "Babylon is fallen, is fallen, that great city, because she has made all nations drink of the wine of the wrath of her fornication" (Revelation 14:8).

How patient is God to administer justice?

Babylon is an ancient city founded by the wicked Nimrod (Genesis 10:8–12). Like father, like son, Babylon has been notoriously wicked through the ages. Jeremiah predicts the future destruction of Babylon, which was not fulfilled in 539 BC when the Medes and the Persians invaded the land. The predictions of Jeremiah speak of a total annihilation of Babylon so that it will never be inhabited again, which wasn't accomplished in 539 BC (Jeremiah 50:3, 39–40; 51:29). John dedicates two chapters to the decimation of Babylon (Revelation 17 and 18). The common linkage with both chapters is financial prosperity. Our Lord will bring down this godless system toward the end of the Tribulation, and heaven will celebrate (Revelation 19:1–6).

Employment Point: *Wait patiently upon our righteous God to enact justice.*

DECEMBER 27

ZECHARIAH 4–6, WITH REVELATION 18

This is the word of the LORD to Zerubbabel: "Not by might nor by power, but by My Spirit" (Zechariah 4:6).

WHAT SHOULD BE THE PRIME MOVER TO ACCOMPLISH PROJECTS FOR THE LORD?

The work on the Temple is not completed, so God calls Zechariah to encourage the Israelites to finish their responsibility. Joshua the high priest, who represents the nation, has been consecrated to lead the priests and minister to the people (Zechariah 3). An angel then explains a vision received by Zechariah. There is a supernatural supply of oil to the lampstand, which represents the ministry of the Holy Spirit (Zechariah 4:2). The "two olive trees" refer to Joshua the high priest and Zerubbabel the governor. God's Spirit will energize them to accomplish His work. What is impossible for men is possible with God. That is why the Lord says about the mountainous task, "Before Zerubbabel you shall become a plain!" (Zechariah 4:7).

EMPLOYMENT POINT: *Depend upon the Holy Spirit to accomplish God's work.*

DECEMBER 28

ZECHARIAH 7–9, WITH REVELATION 19

———◈———

Rejoice greatly, O daughter of Zion! Shout, O daughter of Jerusalem! Behold, your King is coming to you; He is just and having salvation, lowly and riding on a donkey, (Zechariah 9:9).

HAVE YOU CONSIDERED THE DIFFERENCE BETWEEN THE FIRST AND SECOND COMINGS OF JESUS?

Daniel predicted the exact day that Jesus would ride into Jerusalem proclaiming to be the Messiah (Daniel 9:24–27). Jesus rode His donkey with an offer of peace. Luke writes, "Now as He drew near, He saw the city and wept over it, saying, 'If you had known, even you, especially in this your day, the things that make for your peace!'" (Luke 19:41–42). The Lord's Second Coming, at the end of the Tribulation, will be to conquer His enemies and establish His kingdom. He will not ride upon a donkey offering peace but upon a white horse, and His vesture will be splattered with the blood of His enemies (Revelation 19:11–21).

EMPLOYMENT POINT: *Hasten to offer peace to the unsaved through the gospel.*

———◈———

December 29

Zechariah 10–12, with Revelation 20

And anyone not found written in the Book of Life was cast into the lake of fire (Revelation 20:15).

Are you laboring to keep people from going to the lake of fire?

Old Testament saints will reign with Jesus during the kingdom age (Daniel 12:1–3). Also, Jesus promised the apostles that they would sit upon thrones judging the twelve tribes of Israel (Matthew 19:28). Church-age saints are also rewarded with ruling and reigning with Christ during the millennial kingdom (Revelation 2:26–28; 3:21). Moreover, those who are martyred during the Tribulation will do the same (Revelation 20:4). Perhaps all of the above are the ones described as sitting upon thrones (Revelation 20:4). By way of contrast, John depicts a great white throne (Revelation 20:11). All those who stand before the seated Judge will be banished to the lake of fire.

Employment Point: *Witness as often as possible to prevent the lost going to the lake of fire, while serving the Lord—anticipating your future millennial kingdom rewards.*

DECEMBER 30

ZECHARIAH 13–14, WITH REVELATION 21

And in that day His feet will stand on the Mount of Olives (Zechariah 14:4).

ARE YOU LIVING AS IF JESUS FULFILLS ALL HIS PROMISES?

After Jesus rose from the dead He spent forty days ministering to His disciples and offering many proofs of His deity (Acts 1:3). The disciples were spellbound as they watched Jesus ascend to heaven. Two angels asked His followers, "Men of Galilee, why do you stand gazing up into heaven? This same Jesus, who was taken up from you into heaven, will so come in like manner as you saw Him go into heaven" (Acts 1:11). Jesus departed to heaven from the Mount of Olives and will similarly return. Our Lord will quickly dispatch His enemies at Armageddon during His Second Coming by slaying His foes starting at Bozrah in Edom (Isaiah 63:1–5), and will travel north until touching down on the Mount of Olives (Zechariah 14:4).

EMPLOYMENT POINT: *Honor Jesus by making disciples throughout the world, knowing that He will return.*

DECEMBER 31

MALACHI, WITH
REVELATION 22

And there shall be no more curse, but the throne of God and of the Lamb shall be in it, and His servants shall serve Him (Revelation 22:3).

ARE YOU ANTICIPATING THE REMOVAL OF GOD'S CURSE ON THE EARTH?

God tells Adam, "Because you have heeded the voice of your wife, and have eaten from the tree of which I commanded you, saying, 'You shall not eat of it': Cursed is the ground for your sake" (Genesis 3:17). Creation is personified in Romans 8 awaiting the curse to be lifted. "For the earnest expectation of the creation eagerly awaits for the revealing of the sons of God," writes Paul (Romans 8:19). Although there is a restoration of the earth during the millennial kingdom, the curse is not fully lifted. Isaiah writes about this time, "But the sinner being one hundred years old shall be accursed" (Isaiah 65:20). The glorious New Jerusalem contains no curse!

EMPLOYMENT POINT: *Worship and serve the Lord, awaiting the final removal of the curse.*
